D1528378

IN DEFENSE OF THE TEXT

Studies in American Constitutionalism
General Editors: Gary J. Jacobsohn and Richard E. Morgan

In Defense of the Text

Democracy and Constitutional Theory

Leslie Friedman Goldstein

Rowman & Littlefield Publishers, Inc.

ROWMAN & LITTLEFIELD PUBLISHERS, INC.

Published in the United States of America
by Rowman & Littlefield Publishers, Inc.
8705 Bollman Place, Savage, Maryland 20763

British Cataloging in Publication Information Available

Library of Congress Cataloging-in-Publication Data
Goldstein, Leslie Friedman, 1945-
In Defense of the Text : Democracy and Constitutional
Theory / Leslie Friedman Goldstein.
p. cm. — (Studies in American constitutionalism)
Includes bibliographical references and index.
1. United States—Constitutional law—Interpretation
and construction. 2. United States—Constitutional
law—Philosophy. 3. Judicial review—United States.
I. Title. II. Series.
KF4550.G65 1991
342.73' 02—dc20 [347.3022] 91-18613 CIP

ISBN 0-8476-7699-4 (cloth, alk. paper)
ISBN 0-8476-7704-4 (paperback, alk. paper)

Printed in the United States of America

 TM The paper used in this publication meets the minimum requirements of
American National Standard for Information Sciences—Permanence of
Paper for Printed Library Materials, ANSI Z39.48–1984.

This book is dedicated to my parents,
Shirley and Allen Friedman,
in gratitude for the many ways in which
they supported my education.

Contents

Acknowledgments

In producing a book, one accumulates many debts along the way, and it is a pleasure to be able to acknowledge some of them. Many teachers provided me with inspirational examples or influential encouragement. I am happy to acknowledge in this category Dr. Walter Kremm of Cleveland Heights High School, Rabbi Abba Hillel Silver, Rabbi Daniel Jeremy Silver, Prof. Richard Flacks, Prof. David Greenstone, Prof. Hannah Arendt, Prof. Joseph Cropsey, Prof. Leo Strauss, Prof. Walter Berns, Prof. Allan Bloom, Prof. Werner Dannhauser, and Prof. Herbert Storing. Many of these names, unfortunately, can now be prefaced with "the late"; but they still live on in my memory and in that of thousands of other students whose lives they touched, and I hope that they are somehow aware of my gratitude.

Numerous colleagues generously read parts or all of this manuscript. Their incisive comments helped me to clarify my own thoughts, even in those instances where they did not fully persuade me to their views. I know the manuscript benefited from their help, even as I know that none of them will agree with everything in it. They are H. Jefferson Powell, Suzanna Sherry, G. Edward White, Gary Jacobsohn, Richard Morgan, Ronald Kahn, Dean Alfange, Sue Davis, Jim Magee, Jim Soles, Michael Zuckert, and anonymous reviewers from the University of Wisconsin Press.

While I was working on this book I received support in a variety of forms. I received economic support from the National Endowment for the Humanities, the University of Delaware Research Fund and Supplemental Grants Fund, while I worked on parts of this book. I also benefited from the intellectual stimulation of a wonderful NEH summer seminar taught by Prof. Henry Abraham, which covered many of the themes dealt with in this book. The University of Delaware Honors Undergraduate Research Program provided me with two exceptionally able research assistants, Laurie J. Shannon and Mary Sikra. Laurie J. Shannon was the first research assistant I ever had, and she taught me many things. Mary Sikra pointed me in important directions in my explorations of the thought of Justice Black. I look forward to reading books by each of them one day. Also, while working on the book during a stay in Paris, I was encouraged by the warm collegiality and intellectual stimulation of the Centre du Théorie de Droit, at Nanterre—particularly that of Michel Troper and Françoise Michaut.

Parts of this book in altered form have already been published in the *Journal of Politics* 48, 1(1986); the *Western Political Quarterly* 40(1987–88); and *Constitutional Commentary* 4, 1(1987). I am grateful for permission to reprint portions of those articles here.

Finally, I must thank the members of my household. Phil, my husband, inspired and challenged me by his hardworking example. Ben, my son, entertained and distracted me with his juggling and piano and drum playing. The dog, Webster, and the cat, Gray Panther, were nothing but trouble, but my son wanted me to include them.

Introduction

Why Constitutional Theory?

In 1987 Ronald Reagan's nominee to the U.S. Supreme Court, Robert Bork, a federal judge with distinguished scholarly credentials, was refused confirmation by the U.S. Senate. This refusal, unlike some Senate refusals in recent decades—such as that of Nixon nominees, Clement Haynsworth and Harold Carswell—was not based on a perceived lack of qualification in the technical sense of expertise, professional ethics, judicial experience, or the like.[1] Rather, it was premised on what members of the Senate Judiciary Committee repeatedly called "constitutional philosophy." While particular results of Supreme Court decisions are often matters of national political controversy, the Bork nomination represented the first time since the New Deal that constitutional philosophy as such became a major issue of national electoral politics.

It is true that at least since the 1960s questions to judicial nominees about whether they prefer "judicial restraint" to "judicial activism" routinely surface. These, however, are not so much about particular theories of constitutional interpretation as they are a veiled version of another concern: "Do you intend to violate the Constitution? Do you intend to invent your own Constitution and impose it on us?" Just as the right answer to these bald versions of the question for judicial nominees is always "no," so the answer for the activism/restraint version is always "restraint"; and nominees are always sensible (or ambitious) enough to give that answer.

Constitutional philosophy—that is, a theory or a framework of principles to guide constitutional interpretation—is the subject of this book. (The terms "constitutional theory" and "constitutional philosophy" will be used interchangeably.) As may be apparent from this

1

definition, constitutional theory has both normative and empirical elements. Some constitutional theory (or combination of theories), as a matter of sheer fact, does underlie every judicial opinion deciding a constitutional case. A given judge may not articulate systematically or consistently or even consciously what theory or theories structure the opinion. The point of this book is not to provide a descriptive revelation of such underlying theories. Rather, the overview of contending constitutional theories provided in this book is meant to have a normative thrust. That is, this book presents an extended argument for the kind of constitutional theory that should guide American judges. Because the U.S. Supreme Court and the lower federal courts have come to exercise such enormous power in contemporary American life, such constitutional theory is of great political import. It carries such political import not in the conventional sense of fostering either liberal or conservative policies, but rather in the sense that whatever constitutional theory ends up guiding federal judges will profoundly affect the power distribution among the various branches of American government. In short, constitutional theory shapes the very nature of the polity. For that reason it comes to be of interest to political scientists as well as to citizens and U.S. senators.

A variety of constitutional theories currently contend for allegiance among the law school professoriate. Although there is no firm consensus on appropriate labels for the major contenders, a useful catalogue would have to include the following:

1. intentionalism;

2. textualism—sometimes called "interpretivism";[2]

3. extratextualism—often called "fundamental values jurisprudence" or "noninterpretivism";

4. indeterminacy;[3]

5. Dworkinism (after Ronald S. Dworkin).

Since these theories are being propounded by the educators of America's future lawyers, and, thus, of future judges, their importance for American constitutional development looms large.[4]

A brief definition of the theory that fits each of these labels can be introduced at this point, although a more nuanced description of them will come in later chapters. *Intentionalists* argue that, in the exercise of judicial review, judges may strike down only those statutes that conflict with the meaning of a constitutional clause that was intended by the original "framers" or "framers and ratifiers" of that clause. *Textualists* or *interpretivists* believe that it is inappropriate for judges to strike down statutes on the basis of anything other than a principle fairly inferable from the constitutional text (although such principle need not have been present in the conscious minds of the framers). The *extratextualists* or *noninterpretivists* believe that judges can use as the basis of judicial review not only the text of the written Constitution and its implications, but also other kinds of higher law—whether natural law or national ideals or national legal custom or simply what the judges believe to be "fundamental rights." Those jurists who believe in *indeterminacy* argue that the meaning of the Constitution is so malleable that it can be interpreted to say virtually anything and that it is thus impossible for law—particularly constitutional law—to constrain the behavior of judges. The proponents of legal indeterminacy differ among themselves as to what then should guide judges. What this book refers to as *Dworkinism* is not the entire legal philosophy of Ronald Dworkin (much of which is insightful), but rather a particular aspect of it. This aspect is his view that judges are supposed to identify vague ideas or ideals (such as "equality") in the Constitution, and then each generation of American judges is to develop new moral-legal principles (based on the judges' personal philosophy) for putting into practical law these constitutional ideals (called "concepts" by Dworkin, or called "symbols" by Dworkinian-in-this-respect Michael Perry[5]). What distinguishes the Dworkinian from the textualist in this labeling scheme is that the textualist finds legal principles (either express or implied) in the Constitution whereas the Dworkinian finds vague ideas there and then suggests that the judge should create the legal principles.

This book defends textualism against its competitors among contemporary theories of constitutional interpretation. The kind of textualism here defended will be characterized, at various points, as a "moderate version" of it. By that is meant that the judge need not expect every principle of constitutional law to be literally spelled out, word for word, in the Constitution. As John Marshall noted, and as every constitutional law professor has repeated over the years, "We must never forget that it is *a constitution* we are expounding." Constitutions must not contain the detailed "prolixity of a legal code."[6] So, this book encourages a textualism that calls upon judges to ask what general principle of law is suggested in the language of the text as considered in light of the structure of the document and in light of the structure of government set forth in the document. It is a moderate version in the further sense that the constitutional theory expects judges to adapt the constitutional principle to changes that arise in society. A principle distinguishing "unreasonable searches and seizures" by whether or not private homes are physically invaded by police must be adapted to the era of electronic surveillance. A principle forbidding invidious racial discrimination as a violation of "the equal protection of the laws" has to be adapted as a deepening occurs in the societal capacity to understand which public measures carry an invidious impact.

Beyond defending a textualist approach, this book critiques a particular reading of the constitutional text. As Chapter 4 will detail, certain sections of the Constitution can be read to assign American judges the job of deciding what are or ought to be the fundamental rights of Americans, in a way that leaves it open to judges to uphold unspecified rights—rights that the Constitution mentions neither explicitly nor by implication. This book argues that when judges announce "fundamental rights" that are nowhere implied in the constitutional text, in decisions that strike down popularly adopted laws that restricted those rights, those judges pervert the judicial function and usurp the legislative function as those roles are contemplated in the structure of government that the Constitution establishes. The foundation of this argument is the premise that the structure of government set forth in the Constitution understands the judicial role to differ in essential respects from the legislative role.

Because it is common in discussions of constitutional theory for proponents to claim that their respective approach[7] is the most legitimate heir to the jurisprudence of the "father of judicial review," Chief Justice John Marshall,[8] this book perforce begins with some debunking. Specifically, the first chapter of this book begins by demonstrating that Marshall—contrary to various scholars' claims—was not a narrow intentionalist (in the manner, for instance, of Raoul Berger); nor was he an extratextualist, in the modern sense of the term; nor was his constitutional theory—*unlike* that of some of his contemporaries—an early forerunner of Dworkinism. The constitutional theory utilized by Marshall was what is now called "textualism." An explanation and defense of the proposition that Marshall was a textualist will complete the first chapter.

Of course, the fact that John Marshall favored a certain theory does not in itself make the theory a good one. Nor does that fact make the theory the most suitable one for the late-twentieth-century United States. Later chapters will defend textualism itself. They will argue that textualism is not unsuited to our times: Indeed it was the constitutional philosophy that characterized the work of Justice Hugo Black, one of the more distinguished jurists of the second half of the twentieth century. (See Chapter 2.) Moreover, Hugo Black developed and put into practice this constitutional theory in response to a jurisprudential climate not unlike the one to which John Marshall was responding. (See Chapters 3 and 4.) Most significantly, the kind of textualism defended in this book is the constitutional theory that best fits the democratic political theory expressed in the structure and content of the Constitution of the United States. (See Chapters 4 and 5.) And finally, it will be necessary to defend textualism against the criticism—much in vogue in the 1980s—that textualism is impossible as a constitutional theory because it is impossible for any constitutional theory to provide coherent guidance in constitutional interpretation. This contemporary criticism of textualism holds that the constitutional text (like other texts of great depth, such as the Bible) is utterly indeterminate in meaning, that any number of conflicting versions of it can be equally well defended, and that thus with the institution of judicial review we are doomed to experience unconstrained raw judicial power. It is the thesis of this book that a moderate version of textualism—and one attentive to bounds of the constitutionally anticipated judicial role—offers hope of constraining such power, and this thesis is defended in the final substantive chapter. (See Chapter 6.)

The defense of textualism set forth in this book is frankly political. It is political in the sense that it derives guidance from the nature of the regime, or polity, laid out in the Constitution. Texts differ from one another. A constitutional text differs from a poetic or dramatic text. In reading a constitutional text properly, one must think in terms of the regime structure set forth therein and of the premises of political theory that underlie that regime. This book argues that Supreme Court justices as temporally far apart as John Marshall and Hugo Black shared a correct understanding of the way in which the American regime structures its judicial power. The book elaborates this understanding and defends it against its contemporary competitors.

Notes

1. Haynsworth was an eminent judge about whom some questions of professional ethics were raised. Carswell was by wide consensus a mediocre judge

with a record-high number of reversals of his decisions on appeal. Laurence Tribe, *God Save This Honorable Court*, p. 82; and Henry Abraham, *Justices and Presidents* pp. 14–17.

2. These first two versions are sometives lumped together into one. Paul Brest calls that one "originalism"; Lief Carter calls it "preservatism."

3. This school includes adherents of Critical Legal Studies (CLS) but also a group of other scholars, many of whom abjure the left-wing politics or the neo-Marxism of CLS.

4. Yet another prominent normative framework for judges is put forward by adherents of the "law and economics" school of thought, many of whom have been appointed to the federal bench by Ronald Reagan. This school has relatively little to say about constitutional law, however, and for that reason is omitted from this study.

5. Michael Perry, "The Authority of Text, Tradition, and Reason," and *Morality, Politics, and Law*.

6. *McCulloch v. Maryland*, 17 U.S. (4 Wheaton) 316 (1819).

7. E.g., Suzanna Sherry, "The Founders' Unwritten Constitution," claims that Marshall (prior to 1819) exercised extratextualist judicial review, while Gary Jacobsohn, *The Supreme Court and the Decline of Constitutional Aspiration*, ch. 5, claims Marshall as a textualist.

8. In fact the U.S. Supreme Court asserted the power of judicial review several years before Marshall joined the Court; but Marshall was the first to assert the power specifically to declare void a federal statute on the grounds of conflict with the U.S. Constitution, in *Marbury v. Madison*, 5 U.S. (1 Cranch) 137 (1803). Cf. *Calder v. Bull*, 3 U.S. (3 Dallas) 386 (1798), asserting—but not exercising—the power to declare void a state law on the basis of conflict with the U.S. Constitution; and *Ware v. Hylton*, 3 U.S. (3 Dallas) 199 (1796), declaring void a state law on the basis of conflict with a national treaty and thus with the supremacy clause of the Constitution.

1

John Marshall and Twentieth-century Jurisprudence

Three of the prominent contemporary constitutional theories—intentionalism, textualism, and extratextualism—currently contend among themselves for the mantle of heir to John Marshall's jurisprudence. In addition, certain aspects of Marshall's jurisprudence might cause it to be confused with yet another contemporary theory, that of Ronald Dworkin. This chapter will enter the fray on the side of textualism, not because proof that John Marshall favored a theory—in itself—establishes that theory as good, but because Marshall for the most part provides a useful model of the kind of textualist jurisprudence defended in this book. The textualism that he favored viewed the constitutional text as embodying certain principles of natural justice, but not all conceivable principles of justice. That combination of attributes distinguishes him both from modern positivists and from extratextualists.

A second reason for exploring Marshall's jurisprudence in this light is that decades of contention over the rightful claim to his legacy have perpetrated a certain amount of confusion as to the nature of his jurisprudence. If he is to be extolled as a model, that confusion needs to be cleared up. This chapter, then, proceeds to distinguish John Marshall's jurisprudence from (in turn) positivistic intentionalism, Dworkinism, and extratextualism.

The dilemma encountered by an honest twentieth-century defender of Marshallian jurisprudence is that Marshall's record is not without blemishes. Although himself opposed to slavery on moral grounds, and despite his insight that the Constitution embodied certain principles of

7

natural justice, he did refuse to free certain slaves in cases that came before him. Toward the end of this chapter the argument will be presented that these decisions permissive of slavery were not a necessary outcome of his jurisprudence. Indeed, a better version of what could be thought of as Marshallian jurisprudence or, at the very least, a soundly textualist jurisprudence could have produced anti-slavery decisions in those cases.

This chapter, then, has a twofold purpose. First, it aims to clarify the record by indicating where John Marshall and like-minded jurists of his day stood in relation to the jurisprudential controversies of our day. Second, and more importantly, it defends a certain kind of constitutional theory—that exemplified in the decisions of Marshall—against contemporary alternatives to it by critiquing those alternatives, specifically the narrow intentionalism of Raoul Berger, the jurisprudence of constitutional symbolism advocated by Ronald Dworkin and Michael Perry, and the extratextualism of Thomas Grey and Suzanna Sherry (among others). What makes Marshallian jurisprudence superior to these others is that it comports more closely than they do with the political theory and regime structure embodied in the U.S. Constitution. That claim is only adumbrated in this chapter, but is more fully fleshed out in Chapters 3 through 5.

John Marshall contra Intentionalism

In the twentieth century Raoul Berger has been the most prominent and most consistent defender of the constitutional theory of intentionalism.[1] That theory holds that the concrete, known, conscious intentions of prominent framers and ratifiers should govern the meaning of the Constitution for all time, unless the Constitution is explicitly amended to the contrary. Thus, for example, the First Amendment should protect speech and press no more than to prohibit governmental restraints *prior* to publication (i.e., controversial writings could be punished after publication);[2] the Bill of Rights should not be taken to restrict state (as well as federal) governments via Section 1 of the Fourteenth Amendment; the Fourteenth Amendment equal protection clause should not be read to prohibit compulsory school segregation by race; and Congress should not have power under the commerce clause (Art. I, Sec. 8, cl. 3) to regulate national industries.[3]

Berger's views have been criticized at length and in a variety of quarters,[4] and the point here is not to rehash all of the criticisms. What

Is of relevance is that, despite Berger's claims to the contrary, a persuasive case has been made in the scholarly literature that the narrow, positivist intentionalism of Raoul Berger did not characterize the jurisprudence of either John Marshall or the founding generation in general.

Although it is true that John Marshall wrote such statements as, "the *intention* is the most sacred rule of interpretation,"[5] H. Jefferson Powell has made a convincing case that the understanding of "intent" dominant among the founding generation, including Marshall, "was an attribute or concept attached primarily to the document itself. . . . The debates of framers and ratifiers, the attributed preferences of states or people, all of these were at most evidence of the Constitution's own intention."[6] Thus, the first way in which Marshall's jurisprudence differed from Berger's is that Marshall's understanding of "intent" meant essentially the *meaning* of the text, as distinguished from the conscious wishes about the text present in the minds of one or another framer.

The second difference is that Marshall carefully distinguished between the conscious, specific, concrete policy goal that may have motivated a particular constitutional clause, on the one hand, and the broader, more generalized principle, or rule of law, that the clause established, on the other hand. For Marshall, constitutional law consisted of the latter rather than the former. For Raoul Berger the choice is the reverse. For instance, Berger is convinced that the leading proponents of the Fourteenth Amendment aimed narrowly at constitutionalizing the specific provisions of the 1866 Civil Rights Act;[7] and thus Berger would read the much more broadly worded equal protection clause[8] as though it said no more than the 1866 statute, abjuring the broader principle of equal treatment by the laws irrespective of race, which the text seems to invite.[9]

Marshall explains his interpretive choice in the opposite direction in the well-known 1819 case of *Dartmouth College v. Woodward*. There, in ruling that the contracts clause (Art. I, Sec. 10, cl. 1) should be interpreted as applying to a college charter granted by George III in 1769, Marshall openly acknowledged that the protection of such charters was *not* the conscious intention of those who wrote and ratified the command "No state shall impair the obligation of contracts." Marshall wrote,

It is more than possible that the preservation of rights of this description was not particularly in the view of the framers of the clause under

consideration. . . . It is probable that interferences of more frequent
recurrence, to which the temptation was stronger, and of which mischief
was more extensive [i.e., debtor relief legislation], constituted the great
motive for imposing this restriction on the state legislatures. But although
a particular and a rare case may not . . . be of sufficient magnitude to
induce a rule, yet it must be governed by the rule . . . unless some plain
and strong reason for excluding it can be given. *It is not enough to say,
that this particular case was not in the mind of the convention, when the
article was framed, nor of the American people when it was adopted.* It
is necessary to go further [if it is to be ruled an exception], and to say
that, had this particular case been suggested, the language would have
been so varied as to exclude it. . . . The case being within the words of
the rule, must be within its operation likewise, unless there be something
in the literal construction so obviously absurd or mischievous, or repugnant to the general spirit of the instrument, as to justify those who
expound the Constitution in making it an exception.[10]

Not conscious intention of the framers but the general principle or
general rule suggested by the wording of the document, understood
within its historic context, is to be the primary guide to interpretation.
In order to know if a particular case literally covered by a constitutional clause should or should not be treated as covered by it, the judge
has to be able to discern whether such coverage produces a "mischievous" or "absurd" result; and such discernment in turn requires a
grasp of the general principle understood to be embodied in the literal
rule. Those principles, for Marshall, comprise the law of the Constitution. Thus, while Marshall could admit that protection of college
charters was probably *not* in the mind of the framers, nonetheless the
contracts clause established not just a ban on debtor relief legislation
(their conscious intention) but the general rule that the states not
unsettle the security of investments.

On this point Berger appears to misread Marshall; for he takes out
of its context a passage from Marshall's dissent in *Ogden v. Saunders*,
and in that manner shows Marshall to contradict what he wrote in
Dartmouth. From the following passage, Berger selected out just a few
words.

[T]he principles of construction which ought to be applied to the Constitution of the United States [are well known]. . . . To say that the intention
of the instrument must prevail; that this intention must be collected from
its words; that its words are to be understood in that sense in which they
are generally used by those for whom the instrument was intended; that

its provisions are neither to be restricted into insignificance, nor extended to objects not comprehended in them, nor contemplated by its framers;— is to repeat what has been already said more at large, and is all that can be necessary.[11]

This complete passage has a meaning entirely compatible with Marshall's *Dartmouth* reasoning. The "provisions" of the Constitution should not be extended to "objects" that are *neither* "comprehended in them, nor contemplated by its framers." By selective omission Berger changes this to the remark that the words of the Constitution should not be "extended to objects not . . . contemplated by its framers"—which *does* contradict the *Dartmouth* passage, but is not what Marshall said. If the words of a provision *do* "comprehend" a particular "object," this *Ogden* passage does not preclude the application of the words to that object (even if the specific object may not have occurred to the minds of the founding generation). By omitting the section about what the constitutional text "comprehended," Berger altered Marshall's apparent meaning.[12]

In addition to mistaking Marshall's textual intentionalism for a personal intentionalism and in addition to mistaking a guidance by textual principles for a guidance by narrow policy goals, Berger errs as well in reading as legal positivism what was really a natural-law-informed textualism. This rather awkward phrase "natural-law-informed textualism" is here meant as a shorthand for the belief that there are in fact principles of natural justice—or natural rights—and that these principles were incorporated into (or embodied in, or secured by) the U.S. Constitution. Thus, in contrast to the intentionalist positivism of Raoul Berger, the textualism motivating jurists of Marshall's approach is not a textualism that denies the meaningfulness or the validity of natural rights. This point has been elaborated in detail in the work of Gary Jacobsohn.[13] The essence of his argument is that jurists like John Marshall, Alexander Hamilton, and Joseph Story—the most influential progenitors of American judicial review—understood natural rights and constitutional textualism to reinforce rather than to contradict each other. Those natural rights fundamental enough to be enforced as law, in their view, had been incorporated *into* the constitutional text.

Each of these latter two correctives of Raoul Berger's misunderstanding—principle versus concrete goal and textualism versus positivism—has lent itself in the scholarly literature to a certain extremist form that produces a kind of countermisunderstanding, which in turn needs correction. Each of these alternative misunderstandings is treated in the next two sections.

John Marshall contra Ronald Dworkin

In explaining his own understanding of judicial review, Ronald Dworkin announced a distinction that sounds rather similar to the one articulated above between a concrete, specific, conscious policy goal and a broader, generalized principle. Dworkin distinguishes between a specific *conception* and a broader *concept*.[14] He has written, for instance, "[T]he difficult clauses of the Bill of Rights, like the due process and equal protection clauses, must be understood as appealing to moral concepts rather than laying down particular conceptions."[15]

Dworkin elaborated his understanding of a "concept" by explaining that it referred to "vague" ideas, such as legality, equality, and fairness. He believes these vague ideas—rather than specific conceptions of them—were what the founders constitutionalized (in phrases like "due process of law"). As he sees it, each generation of Americans, by consulting its own best understanding of moral and political philosophy, must develop conceptions for implementing the concepts embodied in the Constitution. For instance, to one generation of Americans "the equal protection of the laws" may have meant (i.e., in conception) no more than the rights listed in the 1866 Civil Rights Act—namely, equality before the law as regards the protection of life and property and the formal opportunity to acquire property. But a later generation might recognize that "equality before the law" rings hollow without equal access to jury service, and a yet later generation may conclude that the many-centuries-old practice of allowing lawyers to challenge peremptorily a certain number of jurors—even for racist reasons, if they like—violates the concept of "equality before the law."[16]

In according the Court the duty of consulting contemporary philosophy to "revise these [moral-political] principles from time to time in the light of what seems to the Court to be fresh moral insight,"[17] Dworkin was suggesting that there are not just two but, in fact, three levels of analysis. The most narrow is the applied *conception*—for example, the conception that the rights of the 1866 act embodied equal protection of the laws. The middle level of abstraction is the *principle*: One might speak, for example, of the political or moral principle that all adults of sound mind ought to be allowed to acquire, and have protection for, property, subject to any nondiscriminatory regulatory laws that aimed at the public good. (One would need a further principle or set of principles to explain the meaning of "nondiscriminatory"— but this elaboration would be tangential to the present discussion.) At the third level of abstraction, Dworkin postulated the *concept*.

A "concept," for Dworkin, in this context would simply be a vague word, like "equality." To Dworkin, as to scholars such as Michael Perry who align with him, the clauses of the Constitution[18] operate not as rule-expressible general principles (the middle level of abstraction) whose concrete applications (the level of conceptions) might change as society changes, but rather as inspirational "symbols," inspiring the judge to consult the moral philosophy of the day. The moral philosophy, then, will produce the principles that in fact guide the judge.[19]

This emphasis on Dworkin's exhortation to judges to "revise" their guiding moral-political principles from time to time perhaps needs to be qualified by the clarification that he provided in a footnote.[20] There he indicated that whatever new principle the judge arrives at must somehow *unite* his own conceptions of the constitutional concept with those conceptions held by the framers.

Dworkin has elaborated this requirement for conceptual continuity most fully in his 1986 book *Law's Empire*. In his 1977 book *Taking Rights Seriously*, Dworkin's framework seemed to be something like this: The constitutional concepts are very vague but also must be treated as unchanging (as long as the Constitution is not amended). The framers took those concepts to embody certain principles, which in turn produced certain applications (conceptions). Later judges are allowed to change the principles as they see fit, but the new principles that they produce must always cover the original conception.[21] As of 1986, Dworkin has amended the preceding "always" to something more like "whenever feasible."

Dworkin's latest set of guidelines for constitutional interpretation insists that the judge must fit his or her interpretation to constitutional history in a way that makes the constitutional history to date look the best it can look by the light of the judge's own moral-political philosophy. The judge need not find in the constitutional text those principles understood by the founding generation to be there, nor even those believed by most Americans currently to be there, so long as the interpretation the judge chooses relies on principles of justice that have at least some "purchase in American history and culture, that have played [at least some] part in the rhetoric of national self-examination and debate."[22] For Dworkin the judge must in some way account for the text,[23] but he is to read the text by espousing principles that best express his own principles of justice *and* that produce a coherent account of past precedent *and* that to some degree cohere with the contemporary and historical community's sense of justice. Obviously, no one reading can accomplish all these goals equally well, so Dworkin allows that, in any given interpretation, some past decisions of the Supreme Court or a past generation's particular conception of certain clauses may have to be viewed as "mistakes." The highest priorities in his guidelines appear to be these two: (1) coherence among the principles selected; and (2) the judge's personal political philosophy (i.e., sense of justice).

Dworkin does distinguish his own system from what he calls "crude activism" by his insistence that the judge must give as coherent an account as he can—given the two highest priorities—of precedents, the constitutional text, and the community's "political traditions and culture."[24] Still, Dworkin allows for extraordinary flexibility in treatment of both the constitutional text and what the community believes about that text. His ideal judge draws his view of the Constitution "from the most philosophical reaches of political theory."[25]

For Marshall, by contrast, it is not just the vague concept that is unchanging, but the principle or principles the textual clause embodies. The *applications* of the principle will change over time, but the principle has an identity that does not change. (This is not to deny that the principle can grow, mature, or attain a greater fullness, as society evolves. But it remains the same principle—not a new one as in Dworkin.)

In the *Dartmouth* decision (discussed above), Marshall did not just look for a vague concept—say, "obligation"—to which the Constitution somehow alluded, and concerning which the judge would then ask himself—for example—"What are my personal philosophic views on the concept of obligation, and how can I best reconcile those with existing precedents and cultural traditions?" Rather, the intrepretive process in which Marshall engaged looked much more like one that sought enduring principles of government *in* the constitutional text and structure.[26] Interestingly enough, recent research has demonstrated that this textual, rule-guided or principle-guided practice exemplified by Marshall in *Dartmouth* was in fact not the original—or one could say "founding"—version of judicial review in America. An earlier version than Marshall's actually looked much more like Dworkinian practice. Sylvia Snowiss—comparing pre-Marshallian to Marshallian practice, and even contrasting Marshall's practice to that of his contemporaries on the Supreme Court—has made a convincing case that John Marshall transformed the nature of judicial review in the United States.[27]

Professor Snowiss identifies, in fact, three stages through which American judicial review passed from 1776 to the end of Marshall's judicial tenure in 1835. First, in the 1776–87 period, judicial review tended to be based on natural law, the law of nations, or common law, and was highly controversial. Second, in 1787 with the publication of *Federalist #78*, it came to be grounded in the written, popularly ratified Constitution, and by 1803 had overcome its controversial status. And third, in the 1803–35 period of Marshall's tenure, judicial review evolved from (at first) a practice that took its bearings from the constitutional text but only in a very loose and rather Dworkinian fashion, to the rule-guided practice exemplified (by 1819) in Marshall's *Dartmouth* opinion that demanded careful, lawyer-like exegesis of the constitutional text. Chapter 3 will explore some of the political ramifications of the transition from stage one to stage two. The concern here is the transition from stage two to stage three under the leadership of John Marshall.

Prior to the transformation wrought by Marshall, judges tended indeed to use the constitutional text as something similar to what Michael Perry has called a "symbol" of the "fundamental aspirations of the political tradition"[28] or what Dworkin calls vague "concepts." That is, early U.S. judges typically alluded to "the spirit of the Constitution" or "fundamental principles of free government" assumed to be embodied in the Constitution without any careful textual analysis of the document and without even a mention of a specific clause that embodied these principles.[29] These jurists simply assumed a national consensus on fundamental principles and treated the Constitution as the evidence that Americans expected fundamental principles of natural and common law rights to operate as a check on the abuse of governmental power.[30]

As Ronald Dworkin would have judges find the content of fundamental moral-political principles in the moral philosophy prevalent in their day, so the early U.S. judges found their fundamental principles in (what they perceived to be) the consensus or shared understanding of their day. (This is not to deny that there are important differences between the jurisprudence of the 1780s–90s and that of Ronald Dworkin. The former understood fundamental principles to be more limited in number and thus permitted a far wider range of legislative discretion than would Dworkin. The argument here is simply that there are important similarities.) Like Dworkin, these early jurists took the spirit of limited government as the most salient aspect of the written constitution of the nation, rather than looking to the details of its "letter" for principled guidance. John Marshall reversed that priority.

To illustrate the contrast between the constitutional theory of John Marshall and what prevailed earlier, two representative cases will suffice. The alternative to Marshall's approach is exhibited in Justice Story's Court opinion for the 1815 case *Terrett v. Taylor*. At stake was an effort by the Virginia legislature to take back land earlier granted to the Episcopal church, so that the legislature could sell the property and use the proceeds to care for the poor. In *Terrett* the Court blocked that legislative effort. Since John Marshall five years earlier had ruled in *Fletcher v. Peck* that a grant of land by the state qualified as a contract under the contracts clause,[31] one might expect that contracts clause reasoning would figure prominently in Justice Story's opinion. Instead, his only reference to the written Constitution occurred in the following passage: "[W]e think ourselves standing on the principles of natural justice, upon the fundamental laws of every free government, upon the spirit and letter of the Constitution of the United States, and upon the decisions of the most respectable judicial tribunals."[32] The reference to the constitutional text is strikingly casual. Professor Snowiss amasses many other examples to demonstrate that Story's approach *typified* judicial review prior to John Marshall's dominance over the Supreme Court.[33]

Marshall's opinion in the *Dartmouth* case, by contrast, spends page after page discussing what the meaning of the word "contract" is, in the contracts clause; whether it does or does not properly apply to the monarchically granted, prerevolutionary corporate charter of Dartmouth College; whether his interpretation of the text does or does not comport with the framers' intent (see the preceding section of this chapter); and what might be the relevance of the latter question to constitutional interpretation.[34] For Marshall the case turned on the correct application of principles derived from what he called "the true construction of the Constitution," and he clearly meant the phrase to refer to the construing of the constitutional *text* as a legal document.

By contrast, his colleagues and predecessors viewed the text less as a Grand Statute and more as concrete evidence of a social contract; it operated as an anchor that tied American society to the fundamental principles of free government, to which principles they assumed all Americans adhered. Thus, one can read opinion after opinion by these early justices in which they do not even make clear which constitutional clause they are discussing.

Marshall, then, appears to have been acting against a Dworkin-like judicial practice that took the Constitution essentially as a symbol of an amalgam of ideas (about natural and common law rights.) Marshall's substitution of careful, textual exegesis for a kind of jurisprudence of constitutional symbolism (what I call "Dworkinism") prevailed over the years, and has had a number of important consequences.[35] For one, the shift from constitutional symbolism to constitutional textualism contributed to a mood in the United States whereby the Constitution is treated as an enforceable law that truly governs the legislative and executive branches, rather than as a vague moral exhortation to do the right thing. This mood itself is of no little moment in restraining the behavior of government officials on a day-to-day basis.[36]

Another consequence is that the textualism of Marshall tends to impart to judges the sense of being governed by the Constitution, whereas Dworkin's insistence on the continuing need for judges to revise their governing principles tends to legitimize the view that judges properly *create* the Constitution. It is true that, in the early decades of this nation, the creative aspect of looking for the fundamental unwritten principles taken to be symbolized in the Constitution was not widely recognized. But Justice James Iredell, a forerunner of Marshall in his emphasis on the constitutional text, did argue as early as 1798 that "constitutional provisions"—as distinguished from "natural justice" per se—must be the guide for judges. He warned specifically,

> The ideas of natural justice are regulated by no fixed standard; the ablest and the purest men have differed upon the subject; and all that the court could properly say, in such an event, would be, that the legislature, possessed of an equal right of opinion, had passed an act which, in the opinion of the judges, was inconsistent with the abstract principles of natural justice. [By contrast,] If any act of Congress or of the legislature of a state, violates [the] constitutional provisions, it is unquestionably void [because the people,] when they framed the federal Constitution, . . . define[d] with precision the objects of the legislative power, and . . . restrain[ed] its exercise within marked and settled boundaries.[37]

Finally, although the 1790s jurisprudence of constitutional symbolism from which Marshall broke did understand America's unwritten fundamental principles to be constant and enduring, Dworkin's (or Michael Perry's) jurisprudence of constitutional symbolism calls on the judges to provide *new* governing principles as the judges acquire fresh moral insight. This not only clashes with the social contract theory of popular sovereignty implied by the Preamble,[38] but it also clashes with the clearly stated import of Article V. Amendments to the governing principles are to be determined by "the people" as prescribed therein—not by one branch of government, whether it be legislative or judicial.

None of this discussion is meant to imply that precedents could never be overruled or constitutional doctrine never altered under a Marshallian textualism. The difference is that, under Marshallian textualism, changes in constitutional law would come at the hands of judges who believed either that they arrived at an improved understanding of principles originally contained in the constitutional text or that they needed to apply these principles in a new way because a new (social, legal, historic) context required new application.

In a Marshallian jurisprudence (as well as in the quasi-Dworkinian approach that Marshall abandoned), the governing principles would not be new; the understanding or application of them might be. Under Dworkin's concepts approach, the governing principles themselves would be new. The argument in these last few paragraphs has been that this aspect of Dworkin's jurisprudence is at odds with both the Preamble and Article V of the Constitution.

John Marshall contra Unwritten Law

Scholars disagree dramatically over what role was played by an unwritten law of natural justice or national custom in the founding period. This section attempts to shed light on that disagreement in three respects. First, it will argue that John Marshall believed that particular (written) clauses implied or contained certain basic norms of (unwritten) natural justice; his treatment of the contracts clause will be singled out to illustrate that point. Second, the argument will be presented that his colleagues on the Court whose views were close to Marshall's express similar beliefs about natural justice and parts of the written text; Justice Bushrod Washington's treatment of the Article IV privileges and immunities clause then illustrates this argument. Third and finally, this section will demonstrate that, despite the perception of Marshall and his colleagues that natural justice principles infused parts of the constitutional text, they did believe that other parts of the text might contravene natural justice. In a case of such conflict they believed it was their duty as judges to follow the positive law of the written text. It is an unfortunate fact that in a system of government based on popular sovereignty the populace may do wrong. In this part of the section, the slavery cases provide the illustrative example. They are chosen in order to demonstrate that, despite the belief of Marshall and his colleagues in natural justice principles, these men in their role clearly considered obeisance to the written legal text their primary obligation as judges.

Contract Jurisprudence

The insistence that a law against natural justice could not have the force of law had been an important rallying cry for Americans in the Revolution of 1776. This idea continued to be influential for decades in the newly independent United States, but when judges relied on it in early efforts at judicial review (dealing at this time not with laws of Britain but with measures adopted by popularly elected American legislatures), it generally landed them in trouble. The details of their *political* difficulties with natural-law-based judicial review are laid out in Chapter 3. The political fate of judicial review changed dramatically, however, once people like James Iredell, Alexander Hamilton, James Wilson,[39] and John Marshall began to defend a version of judicial review that took as its point of departure a concrete written text, an actual social compact, accepted by formal consent of the people's specially elected delegates—in other words, a version of judicial review based on a political theory of popular sovereignty as a check on legislative power.[40]

The preceding section has reviewed the Court's gradual transition from one form of text-*linked* judicial review to an even more thoroughly text-*based* version under the stewardship of John Marshall. Marshall's approach was defended above not because it was the original—or founders'—version of judicial review (although John Marshall, who played a major leadership role in the Virginia ratifying convention and who served as John Adams's secretary of state, could certainly be counted as one of the founders), but because it comported more readily with the popular-sovereignty-based political theory implicit in the text of the Constitution, particularly in the Preamble and Article V.

Because the first half-century of U.S. judicial history was a period of transition (first, from judicial review based on natural law or customary law to judicial review at least grounded in the constitutional text and, next, to judicial review consciously guided by the language of the

constitutional text), it is understandable that scholars would differ in
their reading of the cases of this period. Some have emphasized the
role of unwritten law in the founding version of judicial review,[41] while
others have emphasized the role of the text-governed judicial review
that quickly came to replace it.[42] One can read in very recent scholarship such diametrically opposed views as the following two statements—the first from law school professor Suzanna Sherry, and the
second from political science professor Christopher Wolfe.

Sherry writes,

> From 1789 until almost 1820 . . . [a]ll of the influential or significant
> Supreme Court Justices, except Iredell, wrote opinions that contained at
> least some references to extra-textual principles, *not merely as a method
> of interpreting the written constitution itself, but in order to judge the
> legality* of the challenged statute or other governmental action.[43]

Wolfe says, by contrast,

> My thesis is that . . . [nontextual, natural-justice-based] judicial review
> did exist during early American history but that it was very rare . . . and
> was usually combined with an argument from the Constitution itself or
> was sometimes simply dicta. These factors, I think justify my characteri-
> zation of it as *outside the mainstream of early U.S. constitutional his-
> tory.*[44]

A significant further clarification of this much-debated early period
has recently been produced by G. Edward White.[45] His contribution
sheds light particularly on those Marshall Court opinions often cited
or quoted for evidence that the Supreme Court justices believed, under
the supremacy clause of Article VI,[46] they had the power and the duty
to strike down state laws that conflicted with an "unwritten constitution" of natural and common law rights as well as those that violated
the written Constitution.

Those opinions, beginning with *Fletcher v. Peck* in 1810, dealt with
what were—sometimes implicitly, sometimes explicitly—contracts
clause[47] questions. White has pointed out that all of these cases arose
under the Supreme Court's diversity of state citizenship jurisdiction,
rather than under its statutory jurisdiction from the Judiciary Act of
1789 to hear challenges of state statutes that conflict with "the Constitution."[48] In other words, because in these cases the Supreme Court
was settling a dispute between citizens of two different states—a

dispute not definitively covered by either state's law or an existing federal statute—the Court was legally free to be guided by general, customary, or common law principles.

White argues convincingly that the Marshall Court did not feel free to invoke the authority of these unwritten principles for those cases arising under Section 25 of the Judiciary Act where only the Constitution could be invoked. His argument proceeds by a contrast of the pre–1820 diversity cases with the pre–1820 Section 25 contracts clause cases. In the first group, one finds "general principles" language (see *Fletcher v. Peck*, 1810; *Terrett v. Taylor*, 1815;[49] *Town of Pawlet v. Clark*, 1815[50]). In the second group, one finds only reliance on the constitutional text (see *New Jersey v. Wilson*, 1812;[51] *Dartmouth College v. Woodward*, 1819). Of particular importance in the 1819 *Dartmouth* case was Justice Story's remark, in concurrence, "The application of [fundamental principles of justice] . . . does not, from our limited authority, properly belong to the appellate jurisdiction of this Court in this case."[52]

After *Dartmouth*, White argues, the (written) contracts clause, as a matter of now-established precedent, was successfully infused with the (theretofore unwritten) fundamental principle that vested property rights are secured, and so the Court's need to rely on general unwritten principles in diversity cases had disappeared; thereafter Court simply relied on the contracts clause for diversity cases (as it had been all along *required* to do in Sec. 25 cases). The laws of state A could not be assumed in general to rule over persons residing in state B. The federal courts had needed to develop a national (civil) common law to deal with these disputes. So, to do this, they had relied on "general principles" or "fundamental principles" of law, known to them through the Anglo-American common law tradition. This generalization applies to certain oft-cited examples of unwritten-law jurisprudence, such as Story's *Terrett v. Taylor* opinion or a short section of John Marshall's *Fletcher v. Peck* opinion,[53] but Professor White notes that Marshall and Story were engaging in additional important maneuvers in these contracts clause cases.

Even as these justices acknowledged the force of unwritten fundamental principles for settling diversity cases, they—especially, at first, John Marshall—made it a point to indicate that the contracts clause and its allies, the ex post facto and bill of attainder clauses of Article I, Section 10, contained these fundamental principles of free, or republican, government. Thus, they let it be known that, by virtue of the written constitutional text, state governments *were* restrained from violating these same principles as to their own citizens. This practice fits into both of the text-related stages of judicial review identified by Snowiss, which were discussed above. In *Terrett v. Taylor*, for instance, Justice Story, exhibiting the earlier of the two approaches, alluded to the constitutional text only with that highly general phrase "the spirit and letter of the Constitution," but its context made evident that the "letter" he had in mind was that of the contracts clause.[54] His statement (see the preceding section, at note 32) made clear his view that the Constitution's letter *does* embrace these fundamental principles, even though he did not spell out in a lawyer-like fashion—in the fashion that via Marshall's opinions was to become the norm—which words produced which legal rules.

In *Fletcher v. Peck*, by contrast—an earlier case by five years, but one exhibiting the approach that would later become standard practice—Marshall decided the case by "general principles common to our free institutions," as he was quite free to do under the jurisdictional rules of the time. In doing so, however, he made a point of insisting that the contracts clause itself contained the relevant fundamental principles. In this way, Marshall was preparing for the day—which day arrived in 1819 with *Dartmouth*—when he might apply the contracts clause itself to protect the vested property rights of a citizen against that citizen's own state government.

This explanation by White has unlocked a mystery that puzzled generations of scholars: Why would John Marshall provide two alternative bases of *Fletcher v. Peck*, without choosing among them (as he did with the remark, "The State of Georgia was restrained *either* by general principles which are common to our free institutions, *or* by the particular provisions of the Constitution of the United States, from passing [this] law'"[55])?

By the time of the *Dartmouth* case, White argues, the Court was ready "to constitutionalize the takings principle [i.e., the principle that no free government may take property from A and give it to B] as a weapon against the states[56] by reading it into the Contracts Clause, and that is what Marshall, for the Court, sought to do."[57]

To sum up, then, the Marshall Court used the diversity jurisdiction cases as the occasion for articulating "principles common to our free institutions" and, having articulated the content of those principles, then planted them firmly into the text of the Constitution, particularly into the contracts clause. Once having done so, the Court then had available these fundamental vested rights principles in cases that posed

Section 25 challenges to state laws as violations of the (written) Constitution. The Constitution was not understood as having a separate unwritten component, but certain of its clauses *were* understood as containing or embodying particular principles of natural and/or common law.

Privileges of Citizenship

A striking illustration of this Marshall Court practice of reading constitutional clauses as infused with natural or common law content can be seen in the 1823 case *Corfield v. Coryell*. The opinion was delivered for the federal circuit court of eastern Pennsylvania by Supreme Court Justice Bushrod Washington. Although Bushrod Washington occasionally differed from John Marshall (for instance in the only constitutional case where Marshall wrote a dissent, *Ogden v. Saunders*, 1827), nonetheless, his views were so close to Marshall's that Justice William Johnson wrote of them that those "two judges . . . are commonly estimated as one judge."[58]

In order to settle the *Corfield v. Coryell* dispute, Justice Washington had to decide whether dredging for oysters in the oyster beds of a given state (in these circumstances, New Jersey) was a practice open to citizens from other states under the Article IV, Section 2 command "The citizens of each state shall be entitled to the privileges and immunities of citizens in the several states."

It was widely understood that "entitled to the privileges and immunities of citizens in the several states" was to be read with the qualification "upon entering states other than their own," but what was not obvious was the *content* of "the privileges and immunities of citizens in the several states." Nonetheless, Justice Washington— apparently assuming a broad consensus as to the answer—asserted that to itemize these privileges would be "more tedious than difficult." He proceeded with this description:

> We feel no hesitation in confining these expressions to those privileges and immunities which are, in their nature, fundamental; which belong, of right, to the citizens of all free governments; and which have, at all times, been enjoyed by the citizens of the several states which compose this Union, from the time of their becoming free, independent, and sovereign. . . . [T]hese fundamental principles . . . may be all comprehended under the following general heads: Protection by the government; the enjoyment of life and liberty, with the right to acquire and possess property of every

kind, and to pursue and obtain happiness and safety; subject nevertheless to such restraints as the government may justly prescribe for the general good of the whole. The right of a citizen of one state to pass through, or to reside in any other state, for purposes of trade, agriculture, professional pursuits, or otherwise; to claim the benefit of the writ of habeas corpus; to institute and maintain actions of any kind in the courts of the state; to take, hold, and dispose of property, either real or personal; and an exemption from higher taxes or impositions than are paid by the other citizens of the state; may be mentioned as some of the particular privileges and immunities of citizens, which are clearly embraced by the general description of privileges deemed to be fundamental: to which may be added, the elective franchise, as regulated and established by the laws or constitution of the state in which it is to be exercised. These, and many others which might be mentioned, are, strictly speaking, privileges and immunities [for] . . . the enjoyment . . . by the citizens of each state.[59]

Justice Washington resolved the case by concluding that the right of an outsider to make incursions into "the common property of the citizens of [a] state," such as oysters, was not one of these fundamental privileges.[60] One can discern from this list of the included privileges, however, that both natural rights (such as the right to be protected by government in the pursuit of property and the exercise of liberty) and common law rights (such as the writ of habeas corpus or the right to sue in court) were understood to be fundamental aspects of American state citizenship (more so, interestingly enough, than the elective franchise, which Justice Washington obviously understands to be restrictable by law.) Even though the Constitution said nothing explicit about protecting the writ of habeas corpus, for instance, against its potential suspension by *state* governments (regarding their own citizens), this passage makes it appear that Justice Washington (and, one presumes, his fellow Supreme Court justices) would find such an invasion to be an implicit violation of some part of the constitutional text. That appearance stems from his phrase, "which belong, *of right*, to the citizens of all free governments." If "free government" here means "republican form of government," then the Article IV, Section 4 clause guarantying such government to the states would carry the implication.[61]

It is clear that Justice Washington understood certain brief passages of the constitutional text (such as the privileges and immunities clause) to contain a relatively lengthy list of specific unwritten principles. To say that, however, is not to say that Justice Washington understood the Constitution to forbid all unjust laws. Only those laws that violated "fundamental principles" were forbidden. And (in light of the concrete rights he selected for his list) Justice Washington appears to have assumed that the truly fundamental principles had textual referents in the Constitution.

Slavery Jurisprudence

The Constitution's natural-law-infused clauses, however, had their limits. Those limits, for John Marshall, his colleague Joseph Story, and the other prominent judges of the early eighteenth century, appear to have been demarcated by clearly expressed positive law. In other words, the clauses of the Constitution were understood to reflect and be consonant with principles of natural justice *except* where the meaning of those positive clauses was widely known to contravene those principles—as, for instance, with the notorious three-fifths clause (Art. I, Sec. 2, cl. 3). As Professor White points out, the two most flagrant examples of such conflict were presented by American treatment of Indians and black slaves.[62]

An examination of early U.S. jurisprudence with regard to slavery sheds useful light on the limits of the place of unwritten law in that jurisprudence. Slavery was the legal-political practice of Americans that most violently contravened the most basic principles of natural right. This fact was widely conceded by leading statesmen and judges in the 1780–1820 period, in the era in which American judicial rhetoric emphasized most insistently the role of natural law.[63] Despite all the natural law rhetoric, however, no major American judge is known to have declared a slave free simply on the basis of natural rights. Instead, judges occasionally employed positive declarations of rights in state constitutions—with the explanation that these comported with natural justice—to free slaves;[64] or used natural justice to establish a preference for liberty in situations where two positive laws conflicted with each other; or used natural justice as an anti-slavery aid to construction in instances where positive laws were otherwise ambiguous.[65] Later, in the 1850s judges occasionally freed slaves on the basis of natural-law-infused, anti-slavery readings of the (positive) U.S. Constitution.[66] Never did a major judge facing a slavery case simply announce in the spirit of the 1770s James Otis, "A law against natural justice is no law at all."

Influential framers—even those who held slaves—understood that the slavery of American blacks violated fundamental principles of natural right. St. George Tucker of Virginia, for instance, in a 1796 essay that he reprinted as an appendix to his 1803 edition of *Black-stone's Commentaries*, quoted the statement from the Virginia constitution's Declaration of Rights that all men are by nature equally free and have inalienable rights to enjoyment of life and liberty with their means of acquiring and possessing property.[67] Tucker then wrote specifically of "the negroes," "[S]urely it is time we should admit the evidence of moral truth, and learn to regard them as our fellow men, and equals, except in those particulars where accident, or possibly nature, may have given us some advantage."[68] Moral truth made blacks the equal of whites, *even if* empirical observation might reveal whites to be advantaged in some ways. Thus, Tucker proposed a legislative plan by which Virginia would gradually free resident slaves, although the plan had little political impact.[69]

When confronted as a judge on the Virginia Court of Appeals, however, with a case involving a slave—*Hudgens v. Wright* (1806)[70]—and with a decision by Judge George Wythe that had (amid considerable natural law rhetoric) freed the slave on the basis of Virginia's Declaration of Rights, Tucker overruled Judge Wythe. Tucker explained that well-known (or, as he put it, "notoriously" known) customs had to shape one's reading of the public understanding of Virginia's Declaration of Rights. He explained that it was clear that the white public of Virginia had not understood this declaration "by a side wind to overturn the rights of [slave] property."[71]

Tucker and Wythe were not the only leading Americans to recognize the conflict between justice and slave law. Although most of the discussion of slavery at the Constitutional Convention was limited to condemnation of the slave trade, several delegates condemned slavery itself.[72] James Madison expressed sentiments that were controverted by no one when he introduced the subject of slavery at the convention with the following remark: "We have seen the mere distinction of color made in the most enlightened period of time, a ground of the most oppressive dominion ever exercised by man over man."[73]

Indeed, judges both north and south in the 1780–1830 period freely conceded the conflict between slavery and natural justice. They did this with such accord that a *pro-slavery* advocate in 1858—writing a 300-page treatise attempting to prove that the two did not conflict—had to concede that the idea that slavery is against natural law "has been almost universally adopted by courts and jurists."[74]

One more state judge example will suffice to illustrate the general pattern with which early jurists outside of the Marshall Court treated this concession. The example is that of Judge Woodward of the

Supreme Court of the Michigan Territory, who dealt with two companion slavery cases in 1807. The first—*Denison v. Tucker*—involved a conflict between the Northwest Ordinance of 1787, which forbade slavery in the territory, and the Jay–Grenville Treaty of 1794, which had explicitly protected all "property of every kind" for "all settlers and traders." Judge Woodward there announced the priority of the treaty, as positive law, over natural law. The former, he wrote, "may regulate the nature and tenure of property in a manner that contravenes the just and inalienable rights of human Nature." He then ruled for the slavemaster, explaining,

> [M]agistrates are the creatures of civilized society.
> . . . Deriving their powers and rights from this source they must necessarily be regulated by the obvious condition of the trust, an implicit obedience to the known will of the nation or society delegating it.[75]

In the companion case—*Pattinson v. Whitaker*—however, Judge Woodward ruled differently. There the conflict was not between written (treaty) and unwritten (natural) law, but rather between two forms of unwritten law: international law and natural law. The principle of international law was that one nation should return property that "strays" from another. In this case the "property" was a runaway slave. Here Judge Woodward refused to apply the international property rule to property in humans because such property "is itself unjust, and in contravention of the rights of human nature."[76]

In short, for Justice Woodward, relatively clear positive law had to be upheld even when it was unjust, but in the absence of positive law, judges were free—indeed morally obliged—to choose the more just among unwritten principles. The latter pattern is quite consistent with what the Marshall Court was doing in the early contracts-clause–diversity-of-citizenship cases.

While early U.S. jurists did differ among themselves on such questions as whether sheer text as opposed to well-known intent should determine the meaning of positive law (e.g., George Wythe as opposed to St. George Tucker), or which principle of conflicting unwritten law should govern in the absence of determinant positive law, they did not differ in the slave cases on the capacity of clear positive law to override natural justice. This range of both differences and consensus mirrors that of the views espoused by Marshall Court justices in the slave cases they decided.

The first such case was *Mina Queen v. Hepburn* (1813). It came to the Supreme Court on error from the federal Circuit Court for the District of Columbia. In order to regulate slavery in the District of Columbia, Congress had simply adopted the slave codes of Maryland and Virginia extant on December 1, 1800, for the respective portions of the District originally covered by them.[77] According to the relevant Maryland common law (i.e., unwritten law), the usual common law rule deeming hearsay evidence inadmissible was relaxed for cases involving claims of freedom by slaves, when the original speakers were deceased and thus could not testify directly. John Marshall—not himself a slaveowner, and an active Colonizationist—ruled for the Court, with all participating except Todd, that the usual common law rule rather than this Maryland exception must prevail for the District of Columbia, because to allow this evidentiary exception for slave property would unsettle the rights of property in general.[78] There was one dissent, by Justice Gabriel Duvall, who was a plantation owner but also was someone who had served for many years as a Maryland judge (including as chief justice of the Maryland general court) and for seven years as a Maryland legislator.[79] His dissent defended the Maryland common law rule exception to the general rule of Anglo-American common law, and he defended his choice on natural justice grounds:

> It will be universally admitted that the right to freedom is more important than the right of property. And people of color from their helpless condition under the uncontrolled authority of a master, are entitled to all reasonable protection.[80]

Marshall, too, referred to views on the right of freedom, but treated them as matters of moral "feelings" that did not decide legal questions:

> However the feelings of the individual may be interested on the part of a person claiming freedom, the court cannot perceive any legal distinction between the assertion of this and of any other right, which will justify the application of a rule of evidence to cases of this description which would be applicable to general cases in which a right to property may be asserted.[81]

The next two cases dealt with by Marshall Court justices were *La Jeune Eugénie* in 1822 and *The Antelope* in 1825. Between these two and the *Mina Queen* case, a slave case was decided (in 1817) by the Ohio Supreme Court with an opinion by Judge John McLean, who was to become a Marshall Court justice in 1829. In that case, *Ohio v.*

Carneal, McLean announced that a slave "in any state or country, according to the unmistakable principles of natural justice [is] . . . entitled to his freedom," but, nonetheless, "as a judge I am sworn to uphold the Constitution of the United States" (and thus cannot set free the slave in question).[82]

Despite the appearance of substantial differences between two of the Marshall Court justices—Story and Johnson—presiding on circuit in the *La Jeune Eugénie* and *Antelope* cases, respectively, both of them in fact align with McLean's view that ultimately positive law must be allowed to override natural law. Story in *La Jeune Eugénie* said a great deal about the conflict between natural justice and the international slave trade, which by that time was an illegal practice for American, British, and French nationals but was still legal for Spanish and Portuguese nationals.[83] He noted specifically that "at the present moment the traffic is vindicated by no nation, and is admitted by almost all commercial nations as incurably unjust and inhuman."[84] It also happened to be prohibited by the laws of France, and—since the ship in question was French property—justice could be done and international law honored by simply returning the property to the French government to be disposed of by French courts. This is what Justice Story did, and in a private letter to Justice Washington he described his opinion as "guarded and sober on all the ticklish points" and one that had "not meddled at all with the question of the right of slavery in general."[85]

In the *Antelope* case the facts were significantly different because the slaver ship in question (unlike *La Jeune Eugénie*) was not an empty vessel (originally it contained more than 250 purported slaves) and the cargo, the ship, and the African passengers were claimed by both the Spanish and the Portuguese governments, both of whom allowed the slave trade.[86] In the initial disposition of *The Antelope*, Justice William Johnson—unlike Justice Story—did not discuss natural justice; but like Justice Story, he disposed of the case in a manner that comported with the national laws in question. Johnson ruled, "The laws of any country on the subject of the slave trade are nothing more in the eyes of any other nation than a class of the trade laws of the nation that enacts them."[87] In this case, *some* of the purported slaves were in possession of Americans acting in violation of U.S. law. Those Africans could be set free; but the others—totalling 90 percent—had to remain in possession of their Spanish and Portuguese captors.[88]

The Johnson decision was appealed to the Supreme Court, and John Marshall settled the appeal with an opinion from which no one recorded a dissent.[89] In this opinion, Marshall portrayed the impact of national slave trade laws upon international law differently from Story by emphasizing "modern times" as opposed to the immediate moment and by focusing on silent acquiescence as opposed to overt vindication. Thus, while he acknowledged that the slave trade was "contrary to the law of nature" because "every man has a natural right to the fruits of his own labor, and no other person can rightfully deprive him of these fruits, and appropriate them against his will,"[90] nonetheless—despite its abhorrent nature—the trade had "been sanctioned in modern times by the laws of all nations who possess distant colonies" and thus "claimed all the sanction which could be derived from long usage and general acquiescence."[91] For these reasons, the slave trade "remained lawful to those whose governments [had] not forbidden it" and was thus "consistent with the law of nations."[92]

Having upheld Justice Johnson in principle, Marshall then proceeded to mitigate substantially the outcome of his decision. He ruled that there was no evidence of a valid Portuguese claim on these purported slaves and that the fraction of the Africans to be considered Spanish property was much smaller than Johnson had ruled. Instead of following Johnson in ordering 90 percent of the Africans sent to Spain and Portugal as slaves, Marshall's opinion eventually resulted in the freeing of 80 percent of the Africans as persons illegally held by Americans.[93] His opinion acknowledged that as to the unfortunate 20 percent the Court was evenly divided; three of the justices believed that since Spain could not prove the specific identity of those Africans alleged to belong to Spanish nationals, all the Africans should be freed.[94] Since the Supreme Court split evenly on this point, the effect was to uphold Johnson's circuit decision that those Africans determined to belong to Spain would be handed over as Spanish slaves. The selection process went through further appeals over a couple of years, but eventually this was done.[95]

After Marshall had left the Court, in the 1842 case of *Prigg v. Pennsylvania*,[96] his fellow justices had to face directly the conflict between natural justice and what everyone knew to be the intent of the Constitution's fugitive slave clause (Art. IV, Sec. 2, cl. 3).[97] While the justices disagreed among themselves in certain particulars, they were unanimous as to the general import and legal force of Article IV, Section 2, clause 3: Slaveowners under U.S. law had to be permitted to recapture runaway slaves. On this point even the Court's most vehemently anti-slavery justices—Joseph Story, John McLean, and William Thompson—concurred.

In sum, a careful look at the slavery cases dealt with by the Marshall Court reveals that Marshall's disposition of *The Antelope* in 1825—as determined by positive law despite a direct conflict with natural justice—was not the result of an accretion of positivism that took hold of American legal thought in the 1820s or 1830s. Rather, it reflected a relatively consistent line of American judicial treatment of slave law that dates back to the 1790s. The pattern of judicial doctrine assumed that when positive law spoke clearly, even if the message violated natural law, it was the judge's duty to follow positive law.[98]

Conclusion

One thing that this chapter should have made clear is that simple statements about "the jurisprudence of the framers" are likely to be misleading or erroneous. American jurisprudence in the last quarter of the eighteenth century and the first quarter of the nineteenth was undergoing a complex process of evolution. Moreover, what it had evolved into under John Marshall's leadership by 1815 or 1820 does not fit neatly into twentieth-century categories of jurisprudential discussion, such as "positivism" or "natural law jurisprudence." Marshall and his colleagues understood the U.S. Constitution to express (or to be "packed with," in the language of twentieth-century philosophy) certain natural law principles. Still, the political theory underlying that Constitution was one of a social contract. The people had agreed among themselves to be governed by this (positive) Constitution, and it was therefore judges' duty to enforce this Constitution even, when appropriate, against other governing officials. This understanding of the systemic role of judicial review was dominant in the United States by the 1790s,[99] and thus twentieth-century scholars like Thomas Grey who defend contemporary extratextualism on the basis of its supposed foundation in the early decades of the United States do not have a strong argument. Then, under Marshall's leadership, federal judges moved toward a more legalistic, clause-by-clause approach to interpreting or applying the Constitution, and away from the more holistic, spirit-of-the-document approach—analogous to that of Ronald Dworkin—that had prevailed for a brief period. This chapter has argued that the direction taken by Marshall away from constitutional symbolism and toward a textually rule-guided judicial practice both was more consonant with the role of judges contemplated in the constitutional text and structure, and had a salutary impact on popular and governmental attitudes toward the written Constitution.

In general, Marshallian jurisprudence took its bearings from the constitutional text and the broad principles established therein, as distinguished from the narrow, conscious intentions of the framers. On the other hand, when the slavery issue came into court, it was a rare judge who would rely on text to the exclusion of known intent to the degree requisite for freeing slaves. Still, this was not unheard of; and after a group of abolitionists in the 1840s publicized arguments to the effect that the text of the U.S. Constitution could and should be read as anti-slavery, the practice became slightly more common.[100] Moreover, no judges are known to have freed slaves on the basis *simply* of natural law, without *some* reliance on written law adopted by the people.

One could argue that those abolitionists of the 1840s and 1850s[101] who contended that, properly interpreted, the Constitution is an anti-slavery document were expressing principles of "Marshallian" jurisprudence better than John Marshall himself. In any case, they expressed textualist principles of jurisprudence with which the author of this book is comfortable. Certainly the principles of nonarbitrary government expressed by the bill of attainder, ex post facto, title of nobility, and (for the federal level) due process clauses would seem to preclude laws upholding chattel slavery. Also, slaves are everywhere in the Constitution referred to as "persons"—never as property.

Be that as it may, this chapter has established that it was characteristic of Marshall's jurisprudence to look for general principles in the constitutional text, which principles then applied as rules of law for governed and governors alike. In general, Marshall saw those textual principles as expressive of and compatible with natural justice. For the example of slavery, however, he seemed to accept that positive law could override natural law, and in such instances he believed that the judges' duty qua judge was to uphold positive law. Both of these views on slave law overwhelmingly typified American judges of the 1790–1830 period.

There were in many parts of the United States, no doubt, practical limits—whether the limits of impeachment or even of lynching—on how much judges could accomplish in an anti-slavery direction. These sorts of limits are embedded in the American commitment to popular government. In any event, it is not his willingness to leave slavery in place that caused Marshall's jurisprudence to be singled out as a model in this chapter. Rather it was his understanding of the centrality of the constitutional text as the shaper of constitutional law and his perspi cuity in grasping that the Constitution must be viewed as a statement of broad, generalizable principle rather than narrow, conscious intent. Moreover, to some degree—albeit not so great a degree as some of his more thoroughly anti-slavery contemporaries—he did grasp that those principles whenever possible are to be read as expressive of and compatible with natural rights. To the degree that he did this, his jurisprudence provides an enduring model for contemporary American constitutional theory.

Notes

1. Others who claim to espouse intentionalism—most prominently ex-Judge Robert Bork—tend to waiver when their favorite clauses are at stake. See, e.g., Robert Bork,"Neutral Principle and Some First Amendment Problems." This flexibility on their part makes their version of intentionalism more defensible than Raoul Berger's, but his is singled out for criticism here precisely because his lack of flexibility makes his intentionalism the most consistent and thoroughgoing version of it available in the literature.

2. That this narrow version represents the dominant legal understanding of the framers' generation is documented in Leonard Levy, *The Emergence of a Free Press*, although Levy does not endorse Berger's jurisprudence of original intention.

3. Raoul Berger, *Government by Judiciary*, chs. 7–8; Berger, *Federalism*.

4. E.g., "Symposium"; Dean Alfange, "On Judicial Policymaking and Constitutional Change"; Walter Murphy, "Book Review, Constitutional Interpretation"; H. Jefferson Powell, "The Modern Misunderstanding of Original Intent," and "The Original Understanding of Original Intent."

5. Powell, "Modern Misunderstanding," p. 1533, provides this quote of John Marshall, "A Friend of the Constitution," *Alexandria Gazette* (July 2, 1819), as cited in G. Gunther, ed. *John Marshall's Defense of* McCulloch v. Maryland, pp. 155, 167.

6. Powell, "Modern Misunderstanding," p. 1534.

7. The Civil Rights Act of 1866 (Act of April 9, 1866, ch. 31, 14 Stat. 27) provided that citizens of the United States

> of every race and color, without regard to any previous condition of slavery . . . , shall have the same right . . . to make and enforce contracts, to sue, be parties, and give evidence, to inherit, purchase, lease, sell, hold, and convey real and personal property, and to full and equal benefit of all laws and proceedings for the security of person and property, as is enjoyed by white citizens, and shall be subject to like punishments, pains, and penalties, and to none other, any law, statute, ordinance, regulation, or custom, to the contrary notwithstanding.

8. "[N]or [shall any state] deny to any person within its jurisdiction the equal protection of the laws." Fourteenth Amendment, Sec. 1.

9. Cf. Justice John Marshall Harlan's dissent in *Plessy v. Ferguson*, 163 U.S. 537 (1896), at 552.

10. *Dartmouth College v. Woodward*, 17 U.S. (4 Wheaton) 518 (1819), at 644. Emphasis added.

11. *Ogden v. Saunders*, 25 U.S. (12 Wheaton) 213 (1827), at 332.

12. Berger, *Government by Judiciary*, p. 378.

13. Gary Jacobsohn, *The Supreme Court and the Decline of Constitutional Aspiration*, chs. 4 and 5.

14. Ronald Dworkin, *Taking Rights Seriously*, pp. 134–37.

15. Dworkin, *Taking Rights Seriously*, p. 147.

16. The U.S. Supreme Court prohibited racially based peremptory challenges of jurors in *Batson v. Kentucky*, 106 S.Ct. 1712 (1986).

17. Dworkin, *Taking Rights Seriously*, p. 137.

18. Dworkin exempts from this discussion the essentially housekeeping clauses of the Constitution, such as those specifying the length of terms of office of government officials—i.e., those clauses that are not matters of principle and on the stability of which the government must rely in order to function effectively. Ronald Dworkin, *Law's Empire*, pp. 367–68.

19. Michael Perry, "The Authority of Text, Tradition, and Reason," pp. 564–66; Perry, *Morality, Politics, and Law* (hereinafter MPL), ch. 6. This is not the place for an extensive account of all the particulars of the ways in which Perry's jurisprudence does or does not match that of Dworkin. The point here is that Perry, like Dworkin, looks to the constitutional text simply for anchors, or word symbols, of vague, "highly indeterminate" (Perry, MPL, p. 149) "values or ideals" (MPL, p. 163), "purposes and projects" (MPL, p. 165). While Perry sometimes does refer to these ideals with words like "aspirations" or "principles," he considers them to be so vague that judges who share a given aspiration "*may disagree radically*" (his emphasis) as to its practical content (MPL, p. 155). The degree of generality that characterizes his understanding of constitutional ideals is apparent in the examples of them that he itemizes: "social justice, brotherhood and human dignity" (MPL, p. 139), "self-critical rationality" (MPL, p. 160), and "liberty and justice for all" (MPL, p. 165). These terms obviously convey a far greater degree of generality than would a "principle" in the sense that I am using the word, viz., a broad (but still determinate) rule of law.

20. Dworkin, *Taking Rights Seriously*, pp. 137 and 136n.

21. Pursuing the example elaborated in the text, one could say that the opposition to the Southern Black Codes that motivated both the Civil Rights Act of 1866 and the Fourteenth Amendment is the conception that has to be included in whatever new principles get developed to implement "equality before the law."

22. Dworkin, *Law's Empire* (hereinafter LE), pp. 364–65, 376, 377.

23. Dworkin, LE, p. 380.

24. LE, p. 378.

25. LE, p. 380.

26. For an illuminating account by a contemporary jurist who endorses Marshallian textualism, see Ralph Winter, "The Growth of Judicial Power."

27. Sylvia Snowiss, "From Fundamental Law to Supreme Law of the Land: A Reinterpretation of the Origin of Judicial Review" (hereinafter FLSL), and *Judicial Review and the Law of the Constitution*. Cf. Suzanna Sherry, "The Founders' Unwritten Constitution."

28. Perry, "Authority of Text, Tradition, and Reason," p. 564.

29. For examples, see Justice Chase's opinion in *Calder v. Bull*, 3 U.S. (3 Dallas) 386 (1798), and Justice Story's in *Terrett v. Taylor*, 13 U.S. (9 Cranch) 43 (1815).

30. Snowiss, FLSL, pp. 27–52.

31. *Fletcher v. Peck*, 10 U.S. (6 Cranch) 87 (1810), at 135–39.

32. *Terrett*, at 52.

33. Cf. Sherry, "Founders' Unwritten Constitution," for further discussion of these examples—but discussion that treats them as extratextualism rather than Dworkinism.

34. *Dartmouth*, at 640–45.

35. In addition to the consequences I discuss in the text below, Snowiss argues that one consequence of Marshall's "subordination of constitutional spirit and first principle to constitutional text" was to make judicial review much closer to the routine judicial practice of statutory interpretation and thus a less "delicate and awful" exercise than it had earlier been. She also sees it as (unlike the two earlier phases of judicial review) the beginning of judicial supremacy. See Snowiss, FLSL, pp. 51–52. I am not here endorsing these two arguments.

36. Madison, upon introducing the Bill of Rights for the consideration of the First Congress, noted that a written bill of rights might have this kind of restraining effect both on the general public and on the branches of government. Regarding the public at large, he said,

> As [written bills of rights] have a tendency to impress some degree of respect for them, to establish the public opinion in their favor, and to rouse the attention of the whole community, [a written bill of rights] may be one means to control the majority from those acts to which they might be otherwise inclined.
>
> *Debates and Proceedings in the Congress of the United States* (hereinafter cited as *Annals*), vol. 1, p. 455.

Regarding government power, Madison said:

> If [these amendments] are incorporated into the constitution, independent tribunals of justice will consider themselves in a peculiar manner the guardian of those rights; they will be an impenetrable bulwark against every assumption of power in the

legislative or executive; they will be naturally led to resist every encroachment upon rights expressly stipulated for in the constitution by the declaration of rights. *Annals*, vol. 1, p. 457.

37. *Calder*, at 399. This excerpt has rearranged the original order of Iredell's sentences. Each of the two bracketed phrases indicates the break between passages that have been reordered.

38. "We the people . . . do ordain and establish this Constitution." Preamble.

39. In his lectures on law during 1790–91, James Wilson defended both natural-law-based judicial review and text-based judicial review. James Wilson, *Works*, vol. 1, pp. 326–31. As the latter became more accepted by the American public, the frequency of the former waned in practice. See Chapter 3 for details.

40. This discussion, too, is elaborated in Chapter 3.

41. Sherry, "Founders' Unwritten Constitution"; Murphy, "The Art of Constitutional Interpretation"; Thomas Grey, "Do We Have an Unwritten Constitution?" and "Origins of the Unwritten Constitution," and "The Original Understanding and the Unwritten Constitution."

42. Jacobsohn, *Decline of Constitutional Aspiration*, ch. 5; Christopher Wolfe, *The Rise of Modern Judicial Review*.

43. Sherry, "Founders' Unwritten Constitution," p. 1175. Emphasis added to stress the distinction from the text-based-but-natural-justice-infused version that took root around 1790.

44. Wolfe, *The Rise of Modern Judicial Review*, p. 108. Emphasis added.

45. G. Edward White, *History of the Supreme Court of the United States: The Marshall Court and Cultural Change*.

46. "This Constitution, and the laws of the United States which shall be made in pursuance thereof, and all treaties made, or which shall be made, under the authority of the United States, shall be the supreme law of the land, and the judges in every state shall be bound thereby, anything in the constitution or laws of any state to the contrary notwithstanding." Art. VI.

47. No state shall . . . pass any . . . law impairing the obligation of contracts." Art. I, Sec. 10.

48. Material in this paragraph and the next nine paragraphs relies on G. E. White, *Marshall Court*, ch. 9, and pp. 173–81 and 674–75.

49. *Fletcher* and *Terrett* cited above in notes 31 and 29, respectively.

50. *Town of Pawlet v. Clark*, 13 U.S. (9 Cranch) 292 (1815).

51. *New Jersey v. Wilson*, 11 U.S. (7 Cranch) 164 (1812).

52. *Dartmouth*, at 708.

53. *Fletcher*, at 135–36 and 139.

54. G. E. White, *Marshall Court*, pp. 608–12.

55. *Fletcher*, at 139. Emphasis added.

56. This principle was protected against the federal government with the Fifth Amendment command, "nor shall private property be taken for public

use without just compensation''; but the Constitution contained no such command for the state governments.

57. G. E. White, *Marshall Court*, pp. 612–28 and 173–81.

58. G. E. White, *Marshall Court*, p. 344.

59. *Corfield v. Coryell*, 6 Fed. Cases 546, no. 3230 (1823), at 551–52.

60. Ibid., at 552.

61. "The United States shall guarantee to every state in this union a republican form of government." Art. IV, Sec. 4.

62. G. E. White, *Marshall Court*, ch. 10. See also Murphy, "Art of Constitutional Interpretation," pp. 142–43; William Wiecek, *The Sources of Antislavery Constitutionalism in America 1760–1848*; and Robert Cover, *Justice Accused*. For a contrasting analysis of the slavery cases of Virginia, which reads them as based on perceived conflicts between two natural rights—liberty and property—see Sherry, "The Early Virginia Tradition of Extra-textual Interpretation."

63. Sherry, "Founders' Unwritten Constitution," ends the period at 1820. Some other scholars put the shift toward positivism around 1830.

64. This was the procedure used by Judge George Wythe in *Hudgens v. Wright*, 1 Hen. & M. 133 (Va., 1806), later to be overruled by St. George Tucker. See G. E. White, *Marshall Court*, pp. 685–87; Cover, *Justice Accused*, pp. 50–55. It was also the procedure of Chief Justice William Cushing of the Massachusetts Supreme Court in the *Commonwealth v. Jennison* case in 1783. See Cover, *Justice Accused*, pp. 43–50.

65. Cover, *Justice Accused*, chs. 5 and 4.

66. Cover, *Justice Accused*, pp. 183–93.

67. G. E. White, *Marshall Court*, p. 683, quoting Tucker, *Blackstone's Commentaries*.

68. Tucker, *Commentaries*, vol. 2, app. H, pp. 54–55.

69. G. E. White, *Marshall Court*, pp. 684–85.

70. *Hudgens*, cited in note 64.

71. Cover, *Justice Accused*, pp. 51–55; G. E. White, *Marshall Court*, pp. 685–88.

72. See James Madison, *Notes of Debates in the Federal Convention of 1787*. The following delegates made remarks condemning slavery: Gouverneur Morris on July 11 (p. 276); Randolph on July 12 (p. 279); King on August 8 (p. 409); Gouverneur Morris on August 8 (p. 411); L. Martin on August 21 (p. 502); Sherman on August 22 (p. 503); Colonel Mason on August 22 (p. 503–4); Ellsworth on August 22 (p. 504); Gerry on August 22 (p. 506); Sherman on August 22 (p. 507); Williamson on August 21 (p. 531); Madison on August 25 (p. 532); unidentified speaker said to be expressing consensus view on September 15 (p. 648).

73. Madison, *Notes*, p. 77 (June 6).

74. Cover, *Justice Accused*, pp. 8 and 98, citing T. R. R. Cobb, *The Law of Negro Slavery*.

75. Cover, *Justice Accused*, pp. 89–90, citing William Blume, ed., *Transactions of the Supreme Court of Michigan*, vol. 1, pp. 385 ff., quote from 387–88.

76. Cover, *Justice Accused*, p. 90, citing Blume, *Transactions*, at vol. 1, pp. 414–17.

77. Wiecek, *Sources*, pp. 100–101.

78. *Mina Queen v. Hepburn*, 11 U.S. (7 Cranch) 290 (1813), at 295.

79. G. E. White, *Marshall Court*, pp. 690 and 322.

80. *Mina Queen*, at 299.

81. Ibid., at 295. Although this chapter is a defense of John Marshall's general jurisprudence, I certainly do not believe that he decided every case correctly, nor do I believe that he did a particularly impressive job with the slave cases. On those cases my personal views are closer to those of the abolitionists who argued that the Constitution could and should be read as an anti-slavery document—people like Lysander Spooner, Alvan Stewart, Gerrit Smith, Salmon P. Chase, William Goodell, and the mature Frederick Douglass. See Wiecek, *Sources*, ch. 11; Frederick Douglass, *The Life and Writings of Frederick Douglass*, vol. 2; Cover, *Justice Accused*, pp. 150–58; Foner, *Free Soil, Free Labor, Free Men*, ch. 3. This group was not even publishing its arguments prior to 1837. They were most vocal in the 1840s and 1850s. According to Robert Cover, these abolitionists' view "that slavery was unconstitutional was so extreme as to appear trivial." Cover, *Justice Accused*, p. 156. I would argue that appearing extreme or trivial is not the same as being mistaken.

Despite my disagreements with Marshall's holding, I include this lengthy discussion of the slave cases in order to demonstrate that, even in the very early years of the American judiciary, natural law per se was not viewed as adequate grounds to invalidate clear positive law.

82. G. E. White, *Marshall Court*, p. 690; see also Cover, *Justice Accused*, p. 244.

83. G. E. White, *Marshall Court*, pp. 691–96.

84. *La Jeune Eugénie Case*, 26 Fed. Cases 832 (1822), at 847, cited in G. E. White, *Marshall Court*, p. 693.

85. G. E. White, *Marshall Court*, p. 696.

86. G. E. White, *Marshall Court*, pp. 693–703.

87. G. E. White, *Marshall Court*, p. 694.

88. G. E. White, *Marshall Court*, pp. 694–95.

89. Justice Story 17 years later wrote in a private letter that Marshall's opinion "overruled" Story's *La Jeune Eugénie* decision, but that Story continued to believe he was right and the *Antelope* majority wrong (evidently on the question of how to determine the extant rule of international law). G. E. White, *Marshall Court*, pp. 699–700, citing Joseph Story, *Life and Letters*, vol. 2, p. 43.

90. *The Antelope Case*, 10 Wheaton 66 (1825), at 120.

91. Ibid., at 115.
92. Ibid., at 122.
93. G. E. White, *Marshall Court*, pp. 699–703.
94. Justice Todd was not participating. White speculates, following John Noonan, *The Antelope*, that the three anti-slavery voters were Story, Thompson, and Duvall. G. E. White, *Marshall Court*, pp. 669n–700n.
95. G. E. White, *Marshall Court*, pp. 700–701.
96. *Prigg v. Pennsylvania*, 41 U.S. (16 Peters) 539 (1842).
97. "No person held to service or labor in one state, under the laws thereof, escaping into another, shall, in consequence of any law or regulation therein, be discharged from such service or labor, but shall be delivered up on claim of the party to whom such service or labor may be due." Art. IV, Sec. 2, cl. 3.
98. Another case handled by the Supreme Court shortly after Marshall left it was *United States v. Amistad*, 40 U.S. (15 Peters) 518 (1841). It is described in Cover, *Justice Accused*, pp. 109–12, and is consistent with the pattern of judicial thinking elaborated in this chapter.
99. This claim is defended in detail in Chapter 3.
100. See Cover, *Justice Accused*, pp. 183–93.
101. See note 81 above.

2

Paradoxes of Justice Hugo Black: Text, History, and Structure

Even if John Marshall did have a sound grasp of the principles animating the American regime and of how those principles shaped an appropriately text-constrained judicial role, a late-twentieth-century reader might nonetheless wonder whether a text constructed to guide government 200 years ago can still prove a viable guide to judicial decisionmaking. This chapter addresses that question by suggesting that the example of Justice Hugo Black demonstrates the feasibility of a jurisprudence that does guide itself by principles contained in the constitutional text and yet is not hopelessly anachronistic (as a narrowly intentionalist jurisprudence would be, at least if combined with the arduous amending process of the Constitution). As in the discussion of John Marshall, the point here is not to show that Justice Black was the perfect jurist, nor that he never handed down a wrong decision. It is rather to show that he successfully, and with relative consistency, utilized a moderately textualist jurisprudence. This jurisprudence was guided primarily by the wording of the constitutional text and its structure—both the structure of it as a text and the political structure of government set forth in the text.

The Paradoxical Justice Black

Justice Black's jurisprudence presents a number of paradoxes. For instance, he is sometimes dismissed out of hand by constitutional scholars because of his supposed reliance on "literal" readings of the constitutional text. The assumption that he was a literalist stems primarily from his frequent insistence after 1951, with regard to freedoms protected by the First Amendment, that "No law means no law."[1] The depiction of Justice Black as a mechanistic literalist, however, is incompatible with a good deal of the evidence.

His sensitivity to the elusiveness of language, even of boiler-plate legal terms, is illustrated in a dissent concerning the right of Americans (under the full faith and credit clause, Art. IV, Sec. 1) to have divorces treated as binding when obtained out of state: Black argued that citizens' rights should not be put at risk on the basis of their ability to "guess" accurately how a judge or jury will reach a "legal and factual conclusion resulting from a consideration of the two most uncertain word symbols in all the judicial lexicon, 'jurisdiction,' and 'domicile.' "[2]

Moreover, when he examined parts of the Constitution other than the First Amendment, he did not routinely conclude that "no law means no law." In a 1941 case, *Wood v. Lovett*, where he was called on to interpret the clause "No state shall . . . pass any . . . law impairing the obligation of contracts" (Art. I, Sec. 10, cl. 1), he produced a strikingly permissive reading. He quoted at length and with approval a number of passages from *Home Building and Loan v. Blaisdell* (1934),[3] including these: "[T]he prohibition is not an absolute one and is not to be read with literal exactness like a mathematical formula"; "The question is . . . whether the legislation is addressed to a legitimate end and the measures taken are reasonable and appropriate to that end"; and "In all such cases the question becomes . . . one of reasonableness, and of that the legislature is primarily the judge."[4] These are hardly the thoughts of someone who believes always that "no law means no law."

In addition to his supposed literalism, another attribute of his jurisprudence that has incurred opprobrium in certain quarters is Justice Black's supposed insistence on rigidly maintaining the narrow, centuries-old, original meaning of constitutional terms, no matter how dated that meaning may have become. Some of the language of his opinions does fuel this characterization—for example, his objection to the Court's application of the phrase "unreasonable search and seizure" to electronic eavesdropping and wiretapping: "I do not believe that it is the proper role of this Court to rewrite the Amendment in order 'to bring it into harmony with the times' and thus reach a result that many people believe to be desirable."[5] On the other hand, this accusation of a rigid originalism, like the accusation of sheer literalism, founders on a more complete look at the evidence. For instance, Justice Black wrote in the *Wood v. Lovett* case quoted above, "The *Blaisdell* decision represented a realistic appreciation of the fact that ours is an evolving society and that the general words of the contract clause were not intended to reduce the legislative branch . . . to helpless impotency."[6] In another case, involving loud sound trucks, Black insisted that the First Amendment phrase "freedom of speech" ought to be interpreted to mean that "all present instruments of communication, as well as others that inventive genius may bring into being, shall be free from government censorship or prohibition."[7] Again, these are not the thoughts of a jurist who refuses to adapt the Constitution to changing societal conditions.

From this brief introduction to the opinions of Justice Black, one can conclude that it is probably mistaken to describe his jurisprudence as "simply" anything. There are a number of puzzling aspects in his constitutional theory, and it is the purpose of this chapter to unravel three of them in particular. The first concerns the interrelationship and relative priorities among textual language; the specific historic, "original" intent behind—or understanding of—that language; and broader purposes that might be inferred from the combination of text and history in order to adapt the Constitution's clauses to new societal conditions. The second puzzle involves the dilemma of what to do when the most sensible contemporary reading of the constitutional text appears to conflict with its historic, original meaning. The third concerns the relation between the literal text of the Constitution and the overall structure or spirit of that document.

Text, Purpose, and Judicial Outcome

Justice Black, in his 1947 dissent to *Adamson v. California*,[8] presented a succinct summary of his understanding of the mutual relations among the constitutional text, the specific intentions of its historic authors, broader purposes underlying their intentions, and later historical developments. He wrote,

> I cannot consider the Bill of Rights to be an outworn 18th century "strait jacket." . . . Its provisions may be thought outdated abstractions by some. And it is true that they were designed to meet ancient evils. But they are *the same kind of human evils* that have emerged from century to century wherever excessive power is sought by the few at the expense of

the many. In my judgment the people of no nation can lose their liberty so long as a Bill of Rights like ours survives and its *basic purposes are conscientiously interpreted, enforced and respected so as to afford continuous protection against old, as well as new, devices and practices which might thwart those purposes.*[9]

Unlike specific-intent theorists like Raoul Berger or former Attorney General Edwin Meese, Hugo Black understood that limiting the Constitution's reach to the specific "human evils" that affected our eighteenth-century forebears would be an error. Rather than look only to the *same* human evils, Black says one should apply a constitutional clause to the same *kind of* evils that the framers opposed. Black's language suggests the need to construct principles of law broader than the specific intentions of the eighteenth century—principles of law that might articulate the "basic purposes" of the provisions of the document.

It is worth noting that he speaks of the "basic purposes" of a set of definite provisions in the text. Unlike Ronald Dworkin and jurists of a similar mind (see Chapter 1), Justice Black was not content to extrapolate from the document concepts at such a high level of abstraction that they provide little definite guidance to the judge—such concepts as, for instance, freedom from "excessive power" in the hands of a powerful few. This passage shows that Justice Black is perfectly capable of drawing abstractions at that level and at comprehending their relation to the constitutional document, but he does not rely on those abstractions for his constitutional theory. Instead he urges judges to seek out the basic purposes suggested by particular evils and then treat the Constitution as banning all "devices and practices" that represent modern-day equivalents of the specific items that were the target of those basic purposes.

This jurisprudence shares the two basic attributes of the constitutional theory of John Marshall outlined in Chapter 1. It looks to the text for broad principles rather than narrow intentions, but insists on principles specific enough to provide real guidance rather than just casting about for inspirational word symbols. It should be acknowledged, however, that following the right constitutional theory does not guarantee that a justice will always arrive at the right or perfect result, nor does it guarantee that two different justices will arrive at the same result.

For instance, in the *Schmerber v. California* case (1966), where the Court by 5–4 upheld the involuntary extraction of blood from a drunk-driving suspect, both the majority opinion by Justice Brennan and the dissent by Justice Black utilized the constitutional theory endorsed by John Marshall and Hugo Black. Both looked for a guiding principle in the language of the Constitution and in the precedents that had over the years interpreted that language. The Court by the time of *Schmerber* had established that the Fourteenth Amendment due process clause made applicable to the states the Fifth Amendment stricture that "no person shall be compelled in any criminal case to be a witness against himself."[10] Interpreting that clause in *Schmerber*, Justice Brennan (for the majority) found the guiding principle to be that government may not compel or forcibly seize from a suspect "testimony" (written or oral) or "communicative" acts like a nod of the head, as distinguished from physical evidence like fingerprints, appearances in a line-up, and so forth—which the state may compel. Having elaborated the principle, Brennan fairly easily concluded that a blood sample was on the permitted side of the line.[11] Justice Black, by contrast, found the core principle or basic purpose of the clause to forbid the forcible *extraction from within the accused* of evidence then used to convict— whether the extraction be of words, oral or written, or of physical evidence.[12] For Black too, once the principle was elaborated, the rule was not hard to apply.

As *Schmerber* exemplifies, some cases present genuinely difficult choices, and the governing principle does not simply shine forth from the text with beaconlike clarity. But to acknowledge this difficulty and the reality of judicial discretion is not to characterize textualist judges as drifting in uncharted waters. In explaining the guiding principles in *Schmerber*, for instance, Justice Brennan acknowledged that there is a very broad "complex of values" that are the "constitutional foundation underlying" the specific self-incrimination privilege. At that foundation are such values as the "respect a government . . . must accord to the dignity and integrity of its citizens . . . respect [for] the inviolability of the human personality." These values, however, are not themselves the rule or the principle. That rule is more narrow and concrete: "The privilege has never been given the full scope which the values it helps to protect suggest."[13]

Making a parallel argument, Justice Black in dissent in 1965 in *Griswold v. Connecticut* against the establishment of a general "right to privacy," wrote, "I like my privacy as well as the next one but I . . . admit that government has a right to invade it unless prohibited by some specific constitutional provision." He noted that there was not any textual passage forbidding government to abridge individual privacy per se; rather there were "guarantees in . . . specific constitutional provisions . . . designed in part to protect privacy at certain times and places with respect to certain activities" such as the guarantee against "unreasonable searches and seizures."[14]

Thus, a justice employing a genuinely textualist jurisprudence does not just infer inspirational word symbols such as "human dignity" or "privacy" and claim that these, rather than rules of law, are what guide her or him. The text and the precedents that have interpreted it often will permit a range of choice in the selection of guiding principles, but this will be a far more constrained choice than would be produced by the Dworkinian jurisprudence of constitutional symbolism elaborated in Chapter 1.

Other cases might be listed where not only Justice Black in dissent but also his opponents in the majority (or vice versa) were both utilizing a textualist, rule-guided jurisprudence. For instance, in the 1967 cases where the Court ruled, over Black's dissent, that electronic eavesdropping involved a "seizure" of private conversations and thus was governed by the Fourth Amendment rules for search warrants and the like, both sides looked for principled guidance in the text.[15] Justice Black focused on the fact that the text itemized only *tangible* items—persons, houses, papers, and effects—and the fact that eavesdropping per se had a long history as an accepted police technique. He thus concluded that the text reached only physical trespass and seizure of tangible things—not mere conversations. The majority in each case focused on the fact that the clause attempts to ensure that people will be "secure" against "arbitrary invasions by government officials" in places traditionally deemed private.[16] One can disagree with either side and still recognize that both sides presented a reasonable, textualist defense for their principle.

In sum, constitutional theories do not decide cases; judges do. And constitutional theories can neither render judges perfect nor make their decisions mathematically predictable. A textualist jurisprudence does constrain judicial discretion but never can eliminate it.

Text and History

Up to this point, the argument has explored Justice Black's understanding of the relation between specific textual clauses and broader purposes aimed at by those clauses and has acknowledged that judges who share Justice Black's (or John Marshall's) understanding of this relation would not necessarily agree with one another as to the outcome in a given case. Not yet discussed has been Justice Black's understanding of the respective roles of textual language and historic context as aids to discerning the "basic purpose," or core principle, of a given clause. Nor has the discussion yet dealt with the problem of potential conflict between text and history. How did Justice Black react when the most plausible or sensible reading of the text in *his* day, as he saw it, happened to conflict with what had *originally* been viewed as the most plausible reading of the text?

One can give a short answer and a long answer to this question. The short answer is that Justice Black, who often claimed to be guided by "original intent" or "original understanding," never admitted that what he viewed as the most sensible reading of the text differed from its original understanding. What this short answer means about Black's approach to the Constitution requires a longer answer.

From his earliest days on the Court up through the months just before his death,[17] Justice Black claimed that textual language and the historic context that gave rise to that language were the two polestars of his interpretive approach.[18] The claim that Justice Black took his guidance from text and history, however, does not reveal how he weighed the relative priorities of each or how he understood them to inform each other. To pursue those questions, one must examine particular arguments that Black presented. Those arguments concerning text and history can usefully be divided into two categories.

The *first category* contains a number of fairly well-known constitutional doctrines defended by Justice Black:

1. the idea that the First Amendment "absolutely" protects from government punishment the peaceful discussion of public affairs;[19]

2. the idea that the Fourteenth Amendment "incorporates" the first eight amendments of the Bill of Rights, applying them to state governments;[20]

3. the arguments concerning the Fourth and Fifth Amendments that have already been discussed in this chapter;

4. the claim that the "by the people" phrase in Article I, Section 4 of the Constitution meant that House of Representative districts

within a given state must be equal to each other in terms of population;[21] and

5. the view that Congress could regulate the age of voters in both congressional and presidential elections but not in state elections.[22]

Justice Black's historical arguments for all of these doctrines can be categorized as legitimately controversial, in the sense that for each doctrine there are some historic documents, events, or precedents that support Justice Black's reading of the text, even though there may be other documents that support an alternative reading.

If this category were the whole picture, it would appear that Black's approach was to discover that reading of the text which seemed to him most sensible from the use of language in, and from the structure of government created by, the document, and then to see if he could discover some historical evidence in support of his view. When he could, he used it. Nonetheless, language and structure of government appear to take priority over history for him. This last conclusion seems correct because no matter how much historical evidence was ever marshalled against any of Justice Black's own constitutional doctrines, whether by dissenting justices or by legal scholars, one never reads Black saying, "Now that I have seen more historical evidence, I have altered my reading of the text." The point is not that he was unwilling to admit a change of conclusion as to what the text meant; it is that he systematically refrained from attributing his changes to new historical evidence about original intent.[23]

This interpretation essentially says that for Justice Black—despite his frequent references to "original intent"—the text is primary, and history is secondary. While this reading fits the material in the category just described (that of legitimate controversy), it cannot be stretched to cover certain other things Justice Black said about constitutional history. Those statements comprise the *second category* of Black's treatment of the text versus history question. Within this category fit claims Justice Black made about the historic understanding of the constitutional text that can fairly be described as not just controversial but startling or even shocking—or, to speak more bluntly, claims by Justice Black that appear to be patent distortions of history.[24] The standout doctrine in this category is Justice Black's claim that "the *understanding from the beginning of the country*" was "that the whole Bill of Rights, including the Due Process Clause of the Fifth Amendment, was a guarantee that all persons would receive equal treatment under the law."[25] Justice Black is making this remark with specific reference to *Bolling v. Sharpe* (1954),[26] the decision that used the Fifth Amendment due process clause to desegregate Washington, D.C., public schools. The District of Columbia had theretofore never operated schools that were anything but racially segregated. *Bolling v. Sharpe* in effect inserted into the Fifth Amendment due process clause (restraining the federal government) the ban on invidious racial discrimination always understood to apply to states from the equal protection clause of the Fourteenth Amendment. *Bolling* relied in part, and with good reason, on Black's *Korematsu v. United States* (1944) opinion.[27] In *Korematsu*, Black had ruled that legal restrictions imposed by the federal government on the rights of a single racial group were "immediately suspect" and subject to "the most rigid scrutiny," and were permitted only if justified by "pressing public necessity" or "circumstances of direst emergency and peril." This language requiring imminent public danger before rights could be restricted is strongly reminiscent of the "clear and present danger" test that Black and the Court majority were using during the 1940s to protect First Amendment rights. And, as Justice Black frequently pointed out, there is no stronger language in the Constitution than the "Congress shall make no law . . ." of the First Amendment. Thus, despite the lamentable outcome of that case for Japanese-Americans, *Korematsu* established the rule that the Fifth Amendment forbids—as forcefully as any part of the Constitution forbids anything—that the federal government discriminate against any single racial group.[28]

In *Korematsu* Justice Black did not bother with original intent discussions. But 20 years later, in a footnote to a case utterly unrelated to race (*Griswold v. Connecticut*),[29] he goes out of his way to claim that this prohibition on racial discrimination was the *original* understanding of the due process clause of the Fifth Amendment. This is a startling, not to say bizarre, claim. There is ample evidence that in the earliest days of the republic the federal government *did* discriminate on the basis of race.[30] There is not any evidence of due-process-clause-based protests against this discriminatory legislation on the part of any of the leading framers.[31] Moreover, Black himself is on record as aware of the long history of racially discriminatory congressional legislation. In his opinion for *Takahashi v. Fish and Game Commission* (1948), he itemized a long list of historic racial restrictions by the federal government,[32] which regulations there he characterized frankly as drawn "on the basis of race and color classifications."[33]

Why would Justice Black designate a principle as "the understanding [of the Fifth Amendment] from the beginning of the country" when he knew Congress flouted it repeatedly both before and after the Fifth Amendment was adopted? One possibility is that Justice Black meant by his phrase "the understanding" to connote the idea of the *correct* understanding of the text—that is, the most sensible reading of the text—whether people at the time knew it or not. This is a somewhat strange usage for the word "understanding,"[34] but it also fits another of Justice Black's odd category-two assertions.

Before the discussion of that second problematic passage, it is worth emphasizing the interpretation of Justice Black being offered here. The argument is that Justice Black occasionally seems to have claimed the mantle of history for understandings of the text that by no stretch of the imagination can be believed to have been consciously intended by the authors or ratifiers of the text. He seems to label "original understanding" what he takes to be the true, correct understanding of the text (whether people at the time knew it was correct or not), perhaps out of a belief that the meaning (or understanding or intent) of a text does not change over time, even if people's view of it does. What this amounts to, of course, is an elevation of text *over* history. It looks to the words and overall document and draws a conclusion *despite* original intention. What is remarkable is that Justice Black then *calls* this "original understanding."

The second example of a strange claim that seems to meet this description of Justice Black's thought—that is, his transformation of history to make it fit the correct understanding of text—occurred in a discussion by him of the Court's own precedents. In 1964 in *Jackson v. Denno*,[35] Black made a number of assertions about recently decided cases that seem to be contrary to the facts. First, he claims, "this Court held in *Chambers v. Florida*, 309 U.S. 227, 235–38 (1939)," that "due process of law" as applied to trials means "a trial according to the 'law of the land,' including all constitutional guarantees, both explicit and necessarily implied from explicit language, and all valid laws enacted pursuant to constitutionally granted powers."[36]

In fact, there is no phrase in Black's opinion for the Court in *Chambers* that closely approximates this supposed holding. This passage describes what Black had *wanted* the Court to rule in *Chambers*— that is, what Black believed "due process of law" *should* be taken to mean. Instead, Black had ruled in *Chambers* that

the due process provision of the Fourteenth Amendment . . . was intended
to guarantee procedural standards adequate and appropriate, then and

thereafter, to protect . . . people charged with, or suspected of, crime by those holding positions of power and authority. . . . [It expressed] the fundamental idea that no man's life, liberty or property be forfeited as criminal punishment for violation of that law until there had been *a charge fairly made and fairly tried in a public tribunal* free of prejudice, passion, excitement, and tyrannical power. . . . [T]he forfeiture of the lives, liberties, or property of people accused of crime can only follow if procedural safeguards of due process have been obeyed.[37]

Here Black inserted a footnote where he cryptically listed the habeas corpus provision, the bill of attainder and ex post facto clauses, the treason procedure clauses and "The Bill of Rights (Amend. I–VIII)." He follows this with a "Cf." and then a list of fundamental British bills of rights starting with the Magna Carta. While this footnote might be taken as subtly conveying to the *Chambers* holding the meaning he imputed to it years later, whatever force this footnote might have had was sharply undercut by his statement two footnotes earlier in *Chambers* to the effect that "this court has declined to adopt in many previous cases" the "current of opinion . . . that the Fourteenth Amendment was intended to make secure against state invasion all the rights, privileges and immunities protected from federal violation by the Bill of Rights (Amendments I to VIII)."[38] Nowhere does Black say in *Chambers* that the Court has decided to undo this "declining." Yet in *Jackson v. Denno* 24 years later, he characterized himself as having done so. What he did do in *Chambers* was to reaffirm the approach of precedents with which he personally disagreed. He wrote in *Chambers* that the Fourteenth Amendment requires states to conform to "fundamental standards of procedure in criminal trials" (i.e., traditional standards such as notice of the charge and a fair hearing). He ruled specifically that compelling a confession by techniques of police "terror" violated those "fundamental standards." Contrary to the later *Denno* characterization, the *Chambers* opinion referred to no specific constitutional clause either explicit or "necessarily implied from explicit language" for the conclusion that this police terror violated fundamental standards.

In *Jackson v. Denno* Black further rewrote history with the following passage:

The Fifth Amendment provides that no person shall in any criminal case be compelled to be a witness against himself. We have held in *Malloy v. Hogan*, 378 U.S. 1 [decided one week earlier] that the Fourteenth Amendment makes this provision applicable to the States. And we have held that this provision means that coerced confessions cannot be used as evidence to convict a defendant charged with a crime. See e.g., *Haynes v. Washington*, 373 U.S. 503; *Chambers v. Florida*, 309 U.S. 227; *Brown v. Mississippi*, 297 U.S. 278.[39]

An examination of the *Haynes*, *Chambers*, and *Brown* cases reveals that nowhere in them, contrary to Black's suggestion, does one find a discussion of "this provision" of the Fifth Amendment. Black believed that the Court *should* have relied on the idea that the Fourteenth Amendment imposed the first eight amendments on the states. But what the Court did rely on in these cases was not a Fifth Amendment argument; rather it was that a confession obtained in an "unfair and inherently coercive context . . . cannot be said to be the voluntary product of a free and unconstrained will, as required by the Fourteenth Amendment." In short, "coercive" police techniques used to "extort confessions" surpass the "bounds of due process."[40] *Haynes* rules that such police coercion violates the due process clause of the Fourteenth Amendment itself. The Court does *not* rule there that such coercion violates the self-incrimination provision of the Fifth and for *that* reason transgresses due process, despite Black's claim of the opposite in retrospect. Textual passages in *Chambers* and *Brown* similarly defy Black's later characterization of those cases.

Why would Black so blatantly misdescribe such recent cases?[41] He could not have hoped to fool his brethren about their own very fresh history. The answer seems to lie, again, in his rather persistent effort to claim that history means what it should mean. Black believes the Court *should* have used the text of the Fifth Amendment to reach its conclusion that the Fourteenth Amendment forbids coerced confessions. The Court (prior to 1964) did not do so, although Black evidently (privately) did. Black somehow leapt to the conclusion that since the constitutional text *should* have guided this recent history of the Court's due process decisionmaking, it had in fact done so. This is another way of saying that Justice Black ignored actual judicial history when it did not support the priority he gave to the constitutional text.

This lengthy excursus into Justice Black's occasional distortions of history has been included not by way of endorsing this aspect of his approach. It has been included, rather, because his frequent use of phrases like "original intent" or "original understanding" may obscure more than it clarifies. Those phrases overemphasized the dominance of history in Justice Black's jurisprudence. In fact, while Black gave some consideration to historical context and to early precedents (as any responsible judge must), his real commitments in terms of a guiding constitutional theory were to the textual language, the constitutional document as a whole, and to the political structure the text seemed to create. Thus, it is appropriate to turn next to Black's understanding of the relationship between specific pieces of the text and the overall structure of the Constitution.

Text and Structure: Parts and the Whole

As noted above, Justice Black's self-description typically mentioned text and history as the guiding lights of his jurisprudence. The argument so far has been that text was a more decisive consideration for him than history. At this point there needs to be added a third element, one to which Justice Black rarely alluded but that often seems to have guided his reading of the text. This third element of his jurisprudence is constitutional structure—sometimes the overall structure of the constitutional document; sometimes the structure of government established by the document. Constitutional structure operated in Justice Black's jurisprudence in three ways:

1. It informed his reading of specific clauses, guiding his interpretation of the language.

2. His belief that the Constitution established a governmental structure of separated and checked powers motivated him to strive to find textual guidance where other justices were comfortable with ambiguity.

3. Black used the structure of the constitutional text to supplement textual silence, filling in gaps that would be left if text were the only guide.

The argument here is not that Justice Black is unique in these respects. John Marshall's deservedly famous opinions in *McCulloch v. Maryland*[42] and *Barron v. Baltimore*[43]—to take just two examples— manifestly use constitutional structure to inform the text. The point is, rather, that a well-grounded textualism must take structure into account,[44] and that Hugo Black provides one example of a modern Supreme Court justice whose jurisprudence does that (even though his self-descriptions tended to omit mention of structural principles per se).

Structure Informs Text

Even Justice Black's supposed First Amendment literalism—his "no law means no law," which often put him in dissent in favor of greater freedom of expression than his colleagues believed was required—was informed and buttressed by structural argument concerning the nature and purpose of representative government (representative government being the basic political structure established by the constitutional text).

> [I]mperative is the need to preserve inviolate the constitutional rights of free speech, free press and free assembly in order to maintain the opportunity for free political discussion, to the end that government may be responsive to the will of the people and that changes, if desired, may be obtained by peaceful means. Therein lies the security of the Republic, the very foundation of constitutional government.[45]

Some of Justice Black's most important interpretive arguments, in fact, would make little sense without the insight that they were informed by concerns about political structure. For instance, Justice Black's opinion for the Court in *Wesberry v. Sanders* (1964), purported (as usual) to be based on language and history. "We hold that, construed *in its historical context, the command* of Art. I, Sec. 2, that Representatives be chosen 'by the people of the several states' means that as nearly as practicable one man's vote in a congressional election is to be worth as much as another's."[46] While there is some historical and textual support for Justice Black's view that representatives in the House were expected to come from districts of equal population size within a state,[47] there is also plenty of historical support and some textual support marshalled in the dissenting argument of Justice Harlan that district size was a matter deliberately left to the states, subject only to the exclusive supervisory power of Congress.[48] If text and historic practice alone were the only guidelines, Justice Harlan's view might prevail. But Justice Black does in *Wesberry* identify a core element of the structure of the national government: the differing principles of representation of the legislative branch created in Article I. This is the key to his argument.

> It would defeat the principle solemnly embodied in the Great Compromise—equal representation in the House for equal numbers of people—

for us to hold that, within the States, legislatures may draw the lines in such a way as to give some voters a greater voice in choosing a Congressman than others. The House of Representatives . . . was to represent the people as individuals.[49]

And, one could add, the Senate was to represent the states as states. Black is correct in noting that the House was constructed to represent voters in proportion to their numbers—that is, to be the branch exhibiting the purest version of representative democracy. That Justice Harlan can score minor points on the imperfections with which this principle was actualized—imperfections relating to the three-fifths clause, or the practical need to structure elections along state lines, or the political need to assure each state at least one representative— does not substantially refute Justice Black's main point. Population-based representation for the House was a fundamental principle embedded in the structure of the national government. This principle guides Black's reading of text and history, and makes sense of the outcome of the case.

Apart from the substantive issue of proper representation, the *Wesberry* case posed a difficult procedural question. Article I, Section 4, clause 1 and Article I, Section 5, clause 1 clearly designated the state governments as the regulators of congressional elections in the first instance, and gave Congress a higher supervisory power over the "time, place, and manner" of the elections.[50] Since the Constitution utterly omits mention of judicial supervision of this process, Justice Harlan dissents to the effect that Congress was meant to have *exclusive* supervisory power over this matter. While Justice Black was not one to intervene readily in a subject matter textually designated as within the purview of Congress,[51] he also understood the judicial role—in the American tripartite, separation-of-powers scheme—to include the duty of checking abuses of power in the other branches.[52] As he saw it, it was no less an abuse of constitutionally demarcated power for Congress to allow voting districts to approximate the old British "rotten boroughs"—a well-known bête noire of the American revolutionaries—than it would be for Congress, say, to punish a state for fraudulent voting by depriving the voters in one-third of the states from having representation in the House. Either behavior would violate the Article I, Section 4 command that representatives be chosen "by the people" and would—like any other violation of the law of the Constitution, require judicial condemnation—if presented in an appropriate case.

Structure Directs Judge to the Text

That Black believed the judicial role calls for checking abuses of power by the other branches is not exceptional; it is, in fact, axiomatic for a member of the U.S. judiciary. Black's understanding of this role, however, implicated the text and structure of the Constitution in a way that is somewhat unusual for an American judge. All judges will acknowledge in principle that some questions require policy determinations that are left by the Constitution to the legislative branch. Justice Black, however—more than most—insisted that the Constitution's tripartite division of powers calls upon judges to look for textual guidance to their decisions and to avoid making decisions when the Constitution fails to provide a discernible rule of guidance. Justice Black was notorious for protesting that phrases like "fundamental fairness" or "not arbitrary" or "shocking to the conscience" provide no real limits for judges and instead serve as open invitations to judges to behave as legislators. As will be detailed at greater length in Chapter 4, these protests concerning the due process clauses were at base arguments about the structure of government set forth in the text of the Constitution. This point about Justice Black's jurisprudence can be fleshed out here by attention to a less well-known example.

The example concerns an apparent flip-flop by Justice Black in a pair of cases arising under the contracts clause. In the first of the pair, *Wood v. Lovett* (1941), the majority ruled that a state law restricting certain property rights the state had granted in a law two years earlier[53] was void, since the restriction impaired the obligation of contracts. Here Black dissented, arguing—first—that, due to technicalities of the specific contract in the facts of this case (involving a quitclaim deed), the contract had not been in any way impaired[54] and—second and more broadly—the contracts clause did not forbid "a rational compromise between individual rights and public welfare" when the state is "regulating its exercise of the taxing power or [passing a law] relating to a State's disposition of its public lands."[55] In this case, he maintained, the state was doing both.

Where Justice Black looks, at first blush, like he is reversing this position is in the 1965 case *El Paso v. Simmons*. There it looks like the Court majority has moved over to align itself with Black's earlier *Wood v. Lovett* dissent, for it favorably quotes the same passages from *Home Building and Loan Association v. Blaisdell* that Black favorably quoted in *Wood*.[56] Black nonetheless dissents again, accusing the Court of "balancing away" individual rights under the contracts clause, and appears to have exchanged places with the majority, now aligning himself with the very *Wood v. Lovett* majority whom he had opposed 24 years earlier.

El Paso, like *Wood*, involved "a State's disposition of its public lands." Texas in 1910 had passed a law allowing sales of land at low down payment and low interest rates, and this law specified that if the land were forfeited for failure to make payments it could be reclaimed later (without time limit) as long as a third-party sale had not intervened. In 1941 Texas tightened this law, imposing a five-year time limit on the reclaiming option. The Court majority reasoned that this limit did not impair the substance of the land purchase contract: It was "hardly burdensome" to the original purchasers[57] and thus did not "destroy the limitation" on states that the contracts clause imposed.[58] Black disagreed and insisted that, even if his *Wood v. Lovett* dissent had prevailed, it "would not have supported the Court's holding" here.[59]

If one looks at the most extravagant language from Black's lengthy *Wood v. Lovett* quotations of the *Blaisdell* majority (some of which appears in the text at note 4 above), the *El Paso* dissent does look like a complete about-face. But that extravagant language—permitting the states in effect to adjust contracts in ways that the states find reasonable, which language *would* pretty much "read the Contracts Clause out of the Constitution"[60]—was not the whole picture of Black's *Wood v. Lovett* dissent. He had established an explicit caveat there to the effect that he was reserving judgment on some implications of the *Blaisdell* language: "[W]hether I believe that the language quoted from the *Blaisdell* opinion constitutes the ultimate criteria upon which legislation should be measured I need not now discuss."[61] He also put into the record in *Wood* his concern that some criteria be developed, for otherwise the contracts clause would leave judges too much at large to impute their own notions of policy into the Constitution (i.e., to behave as legislators).

> There is not, perhaps, in the Constitution any article of more ambiguous import, or which has occasioned, and will continue to occasion, more discussion and disagreement, . . . or the application of which to the cases . . . will be attended with more perplexity and embarrassment . . . and it will not be surprising if, in the discharge of it, great diversity of opinion should arise.[62]

In other words, Justice Black feared that, if the Court's criterion for deciding contracts clause cases was as amorphous as the reasonableness test enunciated in *Blaisdell*, the clause would continue to retain its "ambiguous import." That ambiguity would pose the twin dangers of abuse of judicial power (in the form of illegitimate intrusion into the legislative sphere of policymaking) and abuse of legislative power (over the rights of the individual singled out for protection by the Constitution).[63] Both the abuses would violate the constitutional structure of separated and limited powers.

In his *El Paso* dissent, Black finally elaborated the criteria he believed should guide the Court's reading of the otherwise dangerously ambiguous contracts clause. In characteristic fashion he turned for help to other parts of the *text* of the Constitution—in this instance, to the just compensation clause of the Fifth Amendment. The question of whether "compensation" was provided turns out to be the unifying thread tying together Black's approval of *Blaisdell*, his dissent in *Wood*, and his dissent in *El Paso*. In the statute upheld in *Blaisdell*, the state "provided for compensation to the mortgagee for the resulting delay in enforcement."[64] In the statute that Black wished to uphold in *Wood*:

> Arkansas law protected the [third party] purchaser *by providing that he should be reimbursed and made whole* in case his tax purchase was set aside for irregularity. . . . [T]he entire plan of the state . . . shows a *scrupulous desire to provide compensation* for the purchaser.[65]

By contrast, the law that Black would strike down in *El Paso* did not honor this text-affirmed principle of just compensation, which Black took to be the informing principle of the contracts clause: "[A] State may not pass a law repudiating contractual obligations *without compensating the injured parties.*"[66] Thus, as was characteristic of his overall jurisprudence, Justice Black combed the text for evidence as to basic purposes of the document. He then utilized these purposes to provide guiding rules that would hem in judicial as well as legislative power, so as to maintain the constitutional structure of government.

Structure Supplements Text

Finally, Justice Black's self-description as one whose jurisprudence hews to textual language and history denigrates the importance that he in fact accorded to constitutional structure as a supplement in instances of textual silence. Evidence of this kind of influence from constitutional structure shows up both in Justice Black's votes and in his opinions.

In 1941 Justice Black cast a concurring vote with the plurality opinion of Justice William O. Douglas for the case *Edwards v. California*.[67] This opinion reasoned that the right to travel freely among the states was a "privilege or immunity" of national citizenship under the Fourteenth Amendment, inferred not merely from the commerce clause, as maintained by the majority, but by "the nature and essential character of the national government."[68] Despite the text's silence about a right to travel freely from one state to another, the text clearly established a national structure of government, and this national structure was the foundation of the right, which the Fourteenth Amendment privileges or immunities clause (fortified by the supremacy clause of Art. VI, Sec. 2) then protected against state abridgment. Justice Black's supposed literalism did not keep him from embracing this unwritten right.[69]

Inferences strictly from voting behavior, even from alignment with separate concurring or dissenting opinions, are perhaps unreliable because the individual justice has refrained from articulating his or her own rationale for the vote, but on the role of structure as a supplement to text Justice Black's voting pattern is confirmed by an important opinion that he did author. This opinion set forth the Court's judgment in the 1970 case of *Oregon v. Mitchell* (four justices concurring with half of it and the other four justices concurring with the other half), and the decision precipitated a constitutional amendment (the Twenty-sixth). In *Oregon v. Mitchell*, Justice Black voted with four justices to uphold Congress's authority to give 18-year-olds the vote for congressional and presidential elections, but with the other half of the Court to strike down that portion of the law which attempted to give 18-year-olds the vote for state and local government elections.

Scholars familiar with Justice Black's textualism must not have been surprised to read him in *Oregon v. Mitchell* relying for Congress's power to let 18-year-olds vote in congressional elections on the passage in Article I, Section 4 that empowered Congress to "alter such regulations" as the state may adopt concerning "the time, place, and manner of holding" congressional elections. On the other hand, concerning presidential elections the Constitution says (in Art. II, Sec. 1),

Each State shall appoint in such manner as the legislature thereof may direct, a number of electors equal to [its] number of Senators and Representatives [to choose the president]. . . .

. . . The Congress may determine the time of choosing the Electors, and the day on which they shall give their votes; which day shall be the same throughout the United States.

Article II seems to contrast rather pointedly with Article I in omitting any mention of a congressional power to supervise the "manner" of holding presidential elections. Justice Black responded to this lacuna by concluding that it is accidental rather than deliberate, and therefore not portentous. He wrote in *Oregon v. Mitchell,*

> It cannot be seriously contended that Congress has less power over the conduct of presidential elections than it has over congressional elections. . . .
>
> [I]nherent in the very concept of a supreme national government with national officers is a residual power in Congress to insure that those officers represent their national constituency as responsively as possible. This power arises from the nature of our constitutional system of government and from the Necessary and Proper Clause.[70]

> Acting under its broad authority to create and maintain a national government, Congress unquestionably has power under the Constitution to regulate federal elections.[71] The Framers of our Constitution were vitally concerned with setting up a national government that could survive. Essential to the survival and to the growth of our national government is its power to fill its elective offices and to insure that the officials who fill those offices are as responsive as possible to the will of the people they represent.[72]

The second of these passages is written specifically in support of an ostensibly second issue—namely, endorsing Congress's power to regulate the residency requirements and absentee ballot rules for participation in presidential elections.[73] The two specific questions of the power to set age requirements and the power to set residency requirements are, however, merely two branches of the same root issue (as Justice Black himself indicated): Does Congress have the power, despite constitutional silence and despite explicit delegation of the power to the state legislatures, to regulate the qualifications of voters for presidential elections?

Black's *Oregon v. Mitchell* opinion in answer to this root question has been quoted virtually in its entirety here[74] in order to underline the extent to which he was willing to rely on constitutional structure to supplement a textual silence. Black does so forthrightly and without any show of embarrassment. To the contrary, he treats the legitimacy of his endeavor as obvious. Black makes it plain that he believes a judge would be remiss in his or her duty if he or she attempted to interpret the text simply by literal reliance on words without the guiding light of the overall constitutional structure.

Conclusion

The conclusions for this chapter can be succinctly put. Justice Hugo Black endorsed and utilized with relative consistency a moderately textualist jurisprudence that followed the guidelines and examples for such a jurisprudence established by John Marshall in such cases as *Marbury v. Madison* (1803), *Dartmouth College v. Woodward* (1819), and *McCulloch v. Maryland* (1819). Justice Black was singled out here not because he is the sole exemplar of this approach but rather because, as modern justices go, he embraced this constitutional theory more fully and with more consistency than most.

The argument presented here has acknowledged that two justices may both use the same constitutional theory, including textualism, and still arrive at differing conclusions both as to what is the guiding legal principle and as to what is the specific case outcome. This chapter has also argued that original intent and history in general seem to have shaped Justice Black's views to a considerably lesser degree than his self-descriptions claimed, although he certainly sometimes took historical context into account. Instead, textual language and governmental structure seemed to be the most important considerations—the ones that operated with the most weighty force—in Black's constitutional theory. In fact, when he spoke of "original intent," he sometimes appears to have meant the "true intent" of the language or the document itself, apart from the conscious beliefs of its authors.

This tendency by Justice Black to elevate text over original intention is compatible with Justice Marshall's insistence (elaborated more fully in Chapter 1) in the *Dartmouth* decision that the serious question should not be, "Is this case what the framers had in mind?" Rather, it should be, "What general principle of law is suggested in the language of the text, and does this case fall under that general principle?" This moderate textualism of both Hugo Black and John Marshall expressed an understanding of the judicial role that derives from, and is thus eminently suitable for, the tripartite separation of powers in the American constitutional structure.

Notes

1. See. e.g., Edmund Cahn, "Mr. Justice Black and the First Amendment 'Absolutes': A Public Interview."
2. *Williams v. North Carolina*, 325 U.S. 226 (1945), Black dissenting, at 277.
3. *Home Building and Loan v. Blaisdell*, 290 U.S. 398 (1934).
4. *Wood v. Lovett*, 313 U.S. 362 (1941), Black dissenting, at 382–83.
5. *Katz v. United States*, 389 U.S. 347 (1967), Black dissenting, at 364.
6. *Wood*, at 383.
7. *Kovacs v. Cooper*, 336 U.S. 77 (1949), Black dissenting, at 102.
8. *Adamson v. California*, 332 U.S. 46 (1947), Black dissenting, at 68.
9. Ibid., at 89. Emphasis added.
10. *Malloy v. Hogan*, 378 U.S. 1 (1964). See also *Mapp v. Ohio*, 367 U.S. 643 (1961).
11. *Schmerber v. California*, 384 U.S. 757 (1966), at 760–65.
12. Ibid., at 773–78.
13. Ibid., at 762.
14. *Griswold v. Connecticut*, 381 U.S. 479 (1965), Black dissenting, at 508–10.
15. *Berger v. New York*, 388 U.S. 41 (1967), and *Katz v. United States*, 389 U.S. 347 (1957).
16. *Berger*, at 53.
17. Justice Black died in September 1971, one week after resigning from the Supreme Court.
18. See, e.g., *McNair v. Knott*, 302 U.S. 369 (1937), at 371; *United States v. Raynor*, 302 U.S. 540 (1938), at 543; *Connecticut General Life Insurance v. Johnson*, 303 U.S. 77 (1938), Black dissenting, at 85; *Oregon v. Mitchell*, 400 U.S. 112 (1970); *New York Times v. United States*, 403 U.S. 713 (1971), Black concurring, at 714.
19. See, e.g., *Beauharnais v. Illinois*, 343 U.S. 250 (1952), Black dissenting, at 275; and *New York Times v. Sullivan*, 376 U.S. 254 (1964), Black concurring, at 293. Cf. Leonard Levy, *The Emergence of a Free Press*.
20. See discussion in Chapters 4 and 6; and also Michael Kent Curtis, *No State Shall Abridge*, and literature cited therein.
21. *Wesberry v. Sanders*, 376 U.S. 1 (1964), cf. dissent by Justice John Marshall Harlan, at 20.
22. *Oregon v. Mitchell*, 400 U.S. 112 (1970), cf. the various plurality, concurring, and dissenting opinions there.
23. See, e.g., *West Virginia Board of Education v. Barnette*, 319 U.S. 624 (1943), Black concurring, at 643; and *Morgan v. Virginia*, 328 U.S. 373 (1946), Black dissenting, at 387.
24. There might be added yet a third category for the text versus history problem, in which would fit opinions by Justice Black that put forth doctrine

contrary to original meanings of the text but where, rather than distort history or make controversial claims about it, Black is simply silent about the problem of history. See, e.g. *Johnson v. Zerbst*, 304 U.S. 458 (1938), and discussion of it in Anthony Lewis, *Gideon's Trumpet*, pp. 112–15.

25. *Griswold* (cited in note 14), Black dissenting, at 517 n. 10. Emphasis added.

26. *Bolling v. Sharpe*, 347 U.S. 497 (1954).

27. *Korematsu v. United States*, 323 U.S. 214 (1944).

28. By contrast with Justice Black's *Korematsu* opinion, earlier precedents had pointedly noted, "The Fifth Amendment contains no equal protection clause," *Hirabayashi v. United States*, 320 U.S. 81 (1943), at 100, "and it provides no guaranty against discriminatory legislation," *Detroit Bank v. United States*, 317 U.S. 329 (1943), at 337–38. See also *Currin v. Wallace*, 306 U.S. 1 (1939), at 14; *LaBelle Iron Works v. United States*, 256 U.S. 377 (1921), at 392. Still, the *Hirabayashi* opinion had started to edge toward Justice Black's *Korematsu* reasoning by acknowledging that "in most circumstances" legislative classifications by race are "irrelevant" and therefore would constitute "such discriminatory legislation . . . as amounts to a denial of due process." *Hirabayashi*, at 100–101. In contrast to Justice Black, however, Chief Justice Stone did not go so far as to claim that his *Hirabayashi* interpretation matched the original understanding of the Fifth Amendment.

29. See note 25.

30. In 1790 Congress limited naturalization to white aliens; in 1792 it restricted enrollment in the national militia to able-bodied white, male citizens; in 1810 it excluded Negroes from carrying U.S. mails; and in 1820 it authorized citizens of the District of Columbia to elect white city officials and to adopt a special code of laws regulating free Negroes and slaves. See Leon Litwack, *North of Slavery*, p. 31.

31. Beginning in the 1840s, radical abolitionists did construct the argument that, properly understood, the due process clause prohibited slavery and required for blacks equal protection of the laws, but even they did not assert the more audacious claim that this was the original intent of its framers. See William Wiecek, *The Sources of Antislavery Constitutionalism in America 1760–1848*. These "radical" views on the Fifth Amendment eventually were imposed on the states in the Fourteenth Amendment equal protection clause. See Curtis, *No State Shall Abridge*, pp. 8, 42–45; W. W. Crosskey, "Charles Fairman, 'Legislative History,' and the Constitutional Limits on State Authority"; and *Adamson* (cited in note 8), Black dissenting, at 93, 95, 97, 101–7.

32. *Takahashi v. Fish and Game Commission*, 334 U.S. 410 (1948), at 412 n. 1.

33. Ibid., at 418.

34. However, it is not terribly far from the framers' approach as described by H. Jefferson Powell, "The Original Understanding of Original Intent."

35. *Jackson v. Denno*, 378 U.S. 368 (1964), Black dissenting and concurring in part, at 401.

36. Ibid., at 407.

37. *Chambers v. Florida*, 309 U.S. 227 (1939), at 236–37. Emphasis added.

38. Ibid., at 235–36 n. 8.

39. *Denno*, at 408.

40. *Haynes v. Washington*, 373 U.S. 503 (1963), at 514–15.

41. Black was fully capable, on the other hand, of accurately describing these same cases. See, e.g., *Adamson*, Black dissenting, at 86–87.

42. *McCulloch v. Maryland*, 17 U.S. (4 Wheaton) 316 (1819).

43. *Barron v. Baltimore*, 32 U.S. (7 Peters) 243 (1833).

44. This argument is fully developed in Charles Black, *Structure and Relationship in Constitutional Law*.

45. *American Communications Association v. Douds*, 339 U.S. 382 (1950), Black dissenting, at 453 (quoting Chief Justice Hughes).

46. *Wesberry*, at 7–8. Emphasis added.

47. Thus, this ruling would fit into category one described above: the legitimately controversial.

48. *Wesberry*, Harlan dissenting, at 20.

49. *Wesberry*, at 14.

50. Art. I, Sec. 4, cl. 1 reads:

> The times, places, and manner of holding elections for senators and representatives, shall be prescribed in each state by the legislature thereof; but the Congress may at any time by law make or alter such regulations, except as to the places of chusing [sic] senators.

Art. I, Sec. 5, cl. 1 reads:

> Each House shall be the judge of the elections, returns, and qualifications of its own members.

51. Black frequently dissented to argue that the Court should leave it to Congress, under the commerce clause, to decide whether state legislation imposed an "undue burden" on the free flow of commerce among the states. See e.g., *Adams Manufacturing v. Storen*, 304 U.S. 307 (1938), Black dissenting, at 316; *Gwin, White, and Prince v. Henneford et al.*, 305 U.S. 434 (1939); *Northwest Airlines v. Minnesota*, 322 U.S. 292 (1944), Black concurring, at 301; *South Pacific v. Arizona*, 324 U.S. 761 (1945), Black dissenting, at 784; *Hood & Sons v. Dumond*, 336 U.S. 525 (1949), Black dissenting, at 550; *Dean Milk v. Madison*, 340 U.S. 349 (1951), Black dissenting, at 357. But cf. *Morgan v. Virginia*, 328 U.S. 373 (1946), Black concurring, at 386, agreeing to strike down a state law on grounds that it burdened interstate commerce in the context of a state law mandating racial separation of railroad passengers. As Justice Black makes clear in this group of dissents and concurrences, his concern was much influenced by his memory of the judicial abuse of power in

economic cases that had precipitated the Court-packing effort of Franklin Roosevelt.

He was also loathe to interfere with the congressional–executive war power in the notorious *Korematsu* decision (cited in note 27). See also *Z&F Assets v. Hull*, 311 U.S. 470 (1941), Black concurring, at 490, urging the Court to leave decisions under the War Claims Act to the legislative and executive branches.

52. Black specifically documents that this role was enunciated in the ratification debates. *Wesberry*, at 16, text for n. 45.

53. The earlier law had removed from persons who had forfeited property due to failure to pay taxes their erstwhile legal right to reclaim the property from third-party purchasers upon payment of the back taxes, the purchase price of the property, and interest, if the reclaiming party could later prove some technical irregularity (which was apparently common) in the third-party purchase. The two-years-later law (now being voided by the Court majority over Black's protest) reinstated this earlier right to reclaim the property, and thus operated as a restriction on what for two years had been the enhanced property rights of third-party purchasers.

54. I am indebted to H. Jefferson Powell for an explanation of this point.

55. *Wood*, Black dissenting, at 386.

56. See quotes discussed above in text at note 4; cf. *El Paso v. Simmons*, 379 U.S. 497 (1965), at 508–9.

57. *El Paso*, at 517.

58. Ibid., at 509.

59. Ibid., at 527 n. 17.

60. Ibid., Black dissenting, at 523.

61. *Wood*, Black dissenting, at 383.

62. Ibid., at 381, quoting Judge Livingston from an 1817 case.

63. *El Paso*, Black dissenting, at 533.

64. Ibid., Black dissenting, at 524.

65. *Wood*, Black dissenting, at 384–85. Emphasis added.

66. *El Paso*, Black dissenting, at 527. Emphasis added.

67. *Edwards v. California*, 314 U.S. 160 (1941), at 177–81.

68. Ibid., at 178, quoting Justice Moody.

69. Black understood interstate travel as a right specifically of *national* citizenship and thus protected by the American scheme of government against *state* abridgment. He did believe that, under its (textually-based) commerce power, Congress could legitimately regulate the interstate movement of persons, as he indicated by his vote with Chief Justice Warren's dissent in *Shapiro v. Thompson*, 394 U.S. 618 (1969), at 644–55.

70. *Oregon* (cited in note 22), at 124, text and note.

71. Black used the word "unquestionably" despite his knowledge that on this point of setting voter qualifications Justice Harlan not only questioned the assertion but disagreed vehemently and at great length. Ibid., at 152–229.

72. Ibid., at 134.

73. On this issue seven justices concurred with Justice Black, offering alternative rationales; and only Justice Harlan dissented.

74. The only omission was Black's citation of a single 1934 precedent—. *Burroughs v. United States*, 290 U.S. 534—to buttress his argument.

3

Popular Sovereignty, the Origins of Judicial Review, and the Revival of Unwritten Law

The preceding two chapters explicated the textualist jurisprudence that this book is defending by showing how it operated in the opinions of John Marshall and Hugo Black. This chapter presents the historical, political, and theoretical origins of that jurisprudence, with special attention to how it displaced its early competitor: a jurisprudence of natural or unwritten law. The argument here draws together research from a variety of sources to argue that American constitutional theory in the 1776–1803 period underwent a profound transformation. Central to that transformation were changes concerning the meaning and importance of the concept of government by consent of the governed. As the significance of popular sovereignty within American constitutional theory increased, the place of unwritten law in judicial review commensurately shrank. Moreover, this judicial move away from reliance on unwritten law appears to have contributed to a rapid increase in the popularity of the institution of judicial review. These very dramatic changes point to the need for public law scholars to reconsider currently influential arguments about the unwritten-law origins of judicial review.

Although the modern Supreme Court has not dared to say it aloud, a good deal of the current scholarship on the Court—the scholarship of "extratextualists" or "noninterpretivists"[1]—maintains that unwritten law is a perfectly legitimate basis on which the Court may declare statutes void. The contribution of the natural law tradition to the initial development of the judicial review element of American constitutional history is an old story.[2] What has been revived is the view that, even after the United States adopted a written Constitution ratified by popularly elected conventions, many of its framers and ratifiers continued to believe that judges should enforce unwritten rights—rights neither mentioned nor implied in that document—against laws enacted by popularly elected legislatures.

Unwritten-law theories of judicial review experienced a heyday during the first few decades of the twentieth century,[3] but fell into disfavor with the decline of economic substantive due process. After the Supreme Court accepted the New Deal, public law orthodoxy in the United States returned to the outlook that took its bearings, first, from the well-known defenses of judicial review in Hamilton's *Federalist #78* and John Marshall's opinion in *Marbury v. Madison*, both of which ground the judges' power to strike down statute law firmly in the higher power of the sovereign people who adopted the supreme legal rules of the constitutional text, and, second, from the well-known discussion at the Constitutional Convention, exhibiting a consensus that foresaw judicial review as a safeguard of the written Constitution that was about to be ratified by the people.[4] According to this position, after tentative experiments with an unwritten natural law or common law approach to judicial review (e.g., *Fletcher v. Peck* in 1810), the Supreme Court abandoned its reliance on unwritten rights in favor of reliance on the constitutional text, since the latter had a firmer grounding in American constitutional theory.[5]

In the 1970s—apparently stimulated by the *Griswold–Eisenstadt–Roe* series of right-to-privacy decisions, as the earlier generation had been inspired by the economic substantive due process decisions[6]—a group of prominent judicial scholars once again took up the cause of unwritten-law judicial review. Both Thomas Grey and Walter Murphy[7] argued that it was the conscious intent of the framers and the widespread understanding of the ratifying generation that written constitutions could not completely codify the higher law, and they claim textual support for this view in the Ninth Amendment. Their arguments, along with a variety of other factors including the policy preferences of scholars, appear to have been influential; the 1980s spawned many new defenses of unwritten-law judicial review.[8] Thomas Grey's original argument covered the period up to and including the Revolution of 1776;[9] he later extended it through 1810.[10] Suzanna Sherry has extended it further, through 1819.[11] Walter Murphy's argument sweeps more broadly, covering Supreme Court history from 1789 to the present.[12] This chapter focuses more narrowly on the critical period between 1776 and 1789 and assesses the impact that the new American political institutions had on the idea—popular in the 1760s and 1770s—that judges could and should strike down statutes that conflicted with the unwritten fundamental law of reason and custom.

In 1787 the American people institutionalized popular sovereignty at the national level with a set of practices not in effect in 1776: They established a written constitution, drawn up by a specially elected set of representatives, and ratified by the people via another set of specially elected delegates. These practices emerged gradually and unevenly among the 13 states after the Revolution, and their emergence was accompanied by an evolution in American constitutional theory. This chapter analyzes both the transition in American constitutional theory that took place between 1776 and the writing of the Constitution in 1787, and the effect on judicial review of the new practices concerning constitution writing and ratification in the period from 1787 until 1803—the date of the landmark *Marbury v. Madison* decision. My thesis is that American constitutional theory underwent a rapid and profound evolution during that quarter-century. In particular, the significance attached to the concept of "government by consent of the governed" rose dramatically, even as that concept itself took on a transformed meaning. This process was accompanied by a notable decline in the outlook that it was appropriate for judges to strike down statutes on the basis of unwritten law, and by a dramatic increase in the acceptance of judicial review.[13]

The evidence for this thesis appears in a variety of disparate sources that have never before been all drawn together. These strands of evidence include the work of historians such as Bernard Bailyn[14] and Gordon Wood[15] on early American political ideology; the work on early state constitutions by Donald Lutz,[16] Willi Paul Adams,[17] and others; and opinions by early state supreme courts and the eighteenth-century federal courts, as analyzed relatively often by traditional public law scholars and more recently in a prize-winning essay by Sylvia Snowiss.[18]

Once woven together, these strands create a convincing pattern of argument that challenges the assumption that extratextual judicial review was understood to be the norm in 1791, much less that it was the prevailing norm by 1803. My argument points to profound changes during 1776–1803 in the American understanding of four concerns:

1. the meaning of "government by consent of the governed";

2. the relationship between that concept and the practice of writing and ratifying constitutions;

3. the relationship between that concept and the age-old debate over legislative versus judicial supremacy; and

4. the relationship between that concept and the debate (reintensified by Grey's and Murphy's scholarship) over textual versus extratextual judicial review.

These changes produce the conclusion that the correlation by the early 1800s between the increased popularity of judicial review and the increased reliance on government-by-consent-of-the-governed to justify that review was not mere coincidence. Rather, the new combination is best understood as a reflection of the new constitutional theory and practice prevalent in the United States by that time.

1776–1786: The First Decade of Free Republicanism

No one seriously doubts that some conception of a higher law of natural justice influenced the colonists during the heated decade of the 1760s and in the years leading immediately to the Revolution. James Otis's protestation against the Writs of Assistance to the effect that "an Act against the Constitution is void: an Act against natural Equity is void" was characterized by John Adams as politically galvanizing. Adams remarked that all who heard Otis left the meeting "ready to take arms . . . [and] then and there the child Independence was born."[19] After the break from England, however, as popular sovereignty took on an increasingly dominant role both in the legislative process and in the constitution-making process, the public understanding of the restraining role to be played by a higher law of nature or of ancient custom seems to have shifted accordingly.

Government by Consent of the Governed re: Legislation

Although "government by consent of the governed" has been a political shibboleth in America at least since the seventeenth century,[20] its meaning has undergone some twists and turns over the past 300 years. Since the early colonies were settled by groups organized as stockholder companies, their company/colonial charters generally granted voting rights to the adult males[21] who belonged. These voters selected local governing bodies that were generally left alone by the British authorities.[22]

What began as virtually universal manhood suffrage accompanying virtual home rule in the early 1600s became radically transformed by the early 1700s, as more and more people immigrated who belonged neither to the local company nor the local church. By the early eighteenth century, property and religious requirements for suffrage were fairly stringent, resulting in an essentially oligarchical system; yet Americans still spoke and wrote of living under government by consent of the governed. During this period, the assumption of a homogeneous community that shared a single common good prevailed. This view supported the notion—which was to fall into disfavor during the break with England but later to be reasserted for domestic circumstances—that the nonvoters could be virtually represented as the voters were actually represented.[23]

By the 1770s, popular consent in the sense of suffrage rights for adult males had yet again transformed itself. Religious exclusion had become quite lax, and the ready availability of property had caused the electorate—at least of the northern colonies—to include substantial majorities of the adult male population. Despite mild property qualifications, voter turnout rates for adult males in the North in the 1770s compare favorably with those in the contemporary United States.[24]

The dispute with England over virtual representation did not really destroy the concept in America, although it put the idea under enough of a shadow that suffrage restrictions were somewhat loosened in the early post-Revolution constitutions. Vermont instituted universal manhood suffrage; and New Hampshire, Delaware, Georgia, and North Carolina lifted restrictions to the point that one scholar describes them as having "virtually guaranteed" universal manhood suffrage (in the cases of the latter three, for nonslaves). Moreover, Pennsylvania changed its rules to the point that 90 percent of adult males qualified. Kentucky entered the union with universal adult white male suffrage in the 1790s.[25] Also, significantly, after the Revolution the size of state legislative bodies was greatly expanded, sometimes doubled or tripled. The logic here was to put the people in closer touch with their representative, and the expansion apparently had the effect—fostered also by changes in popular attitudes brought about by the Revolution—of bringing a much larger portion of the socially "common" element into state legislatures.[26]

By the late 1770s, then, the colonial maxim of "government by consent of the governed" was already referring to a rather dramatically new reality produced by America's peculiar history and revolutionary experience. In the British theory the House of Commons was thought to "re-present" the people and to act in their behalf, as distinguished from by their instructions. The people being re-presented were thought of as having a homogeneous interest and as sending the most virtuous and honorable of their number off to Commons to speak for them. The manner of selection (who participated, what size election districts, etc.) was not particularly important, except that all who participated in the selection needed to have an independent will and a stake in the community (read: property). The sense in which "the people" were thought to give consent to public policy was that they shared in the lawmaking process: Commons had to consent in the name of the people as did Lords in the name of the nobility or landed property and the monarch in the name of the whole nation.

The American colonies, of course, had no house of aristocrats, and until the crisis of the 1760s the king had left them pretty much to be ruled by their own assemblies. These assemblies did generally have an upper house appointed by the crown, and also had to work with a governor appointed by the crown, but these colonial upper houses were not really second legislative chambers in the full sense. Although they had some legislative responsibilities, they functioned largely as advisers to the governor.[27] Thus, the legislative houses elected by the people in the American colonies had a much more dominant role over policy than did Commons in England.[28] Moreover, property requirements that were essentially the same for voters in the colonies as in England produced a colonial electorate that was a much greater proportion of the population because land was so much more readily available in the New World.[29]

The Revolution intensified these already large differences from the British pattern by bringing about the deliberate expansion of the electorate and of the size of the legislatures. Also, the legislatures themselves were radically democratized by making even the upper chamber elective, and by generally allowing the same people to vote for its members who voted for the lower house members.[30]

One additional change greatly enhanced the role of popular consent in the legislative process. Accustomed to thinking of the crown as peculiarly the ruler and the judges as royal lackeys (for judges had been less politically independent in the colonies than in England), the early post-Revolution state constitutions radically weakened both the executive and judicial branches, and tended to place them under the thumb of the legislatures.[31] With an independent executive veto out of the picture, legislation really could be viewed as the will of the people (at least if one considers "people" in the sense of the majority of males).

Consent of the Governed to the Constitution of Government

The Pilgrim Code of 1636 stated, "We . . . freeborn subjects of the state of England . . . do ordain constitute and enact that no act imposition law or ordinance be . . . imposed upon us . . . but such as shall be imposed by consent of the body of associates or their representatives legally assembled."[32] This is an assertion of a right of popular consent to legislation, or to government policy, not of a right in the people to determine the structure of government and the limits of its power. The notion of the latter evolved more slowly in America. It was stimulated by a variety of historical circumstances, by the social contract theories of Hobbes, Pufendorf, Vattel, and Locke, and by the tradition of corporate charters—originally granted by the crown, but later written by the colonists, often for their own consumption.[33] But it was also impeded by the higher law tradition of natural and common law exemplified by Sir Edward Coke and by the eighteenth-century theory that viewed the legislature as embodying the people.

The sixteenth- and early-seventeenth-century colonial charters gradually evolved from authorizations for commercial (and religious) enterprises into frames for local government.[34] Also, the distance from England and the absence of a professional American bar in the seventeenth century made it useful to compile in writing the basic legal rights and privileges of Englishmen, which were in turn understood to be derived from the principles of human nature and/or from the Judaeo-Christian moral code.[35] Thus, the seventeenth century had familiarized Americans with the practice of having their elected representatives draw up charters of the people's liberties; these were understood to be declarations of the common understanding, rather than grants of rights as such.

The Lockean principles embodied in the Declaration of Independence put forth as self-evident truth the idea that individuals by nature are equally free and freely choose to empower government to secure their natural rights. Moreover, they retain an indefeasible right to "alter or abolish" their "form" of government if they decide that it has become destructive of their rights. With this pronouncement, it became the acknowledged birthright of all Americans to live under a form of government to which they had given consent. A paraphrase of this conception of popular sovereignty can be found in eight of the 14 (counting Vermont) state constitutions adopted between 1776 and 1780.[36] It may thus come as a surprise to the untutored reader that the first six constitutions adopted by the American states were adopted not by any extraordinary act of the people, but rather by the state legislatures.[37] Even after Delaware (1776), North Carolina (1776), and New York (1777) innovated by having constitutions drawn up by conventions specially elected for the purpose, four additional states continued the pattern of having the legislative body write the constitution. Not until 1780 did the technique of specially elected constitutional drafting conventions become de rigueur in every state.[38] And not until the Massachusetts Constitution of 1780 was the additional step of ratification directly by the people tacked onto the process. This new technique was employed for only five of the constitutions adopted between 1780 and 1800 (Massachusetts, Pennsylvania, two New Hampshire constitutions, and the U.S. Constitution with the imperfect mechanism of elected ratifying conventions).[39] During the late 1770s and early 1780s, state legislatures amended constitutions, claimed power authoritatively to interpret them, and in a substantial number of cases flagrantly violated them.[40]

Apart from the legislature's power over the writing of the constitution, the very meaning of a constitution as a restraint on government was quite different in the late 1770s from what it became in the nineteenth century. While scholars can debate the question whether more Americans sided with Coke or with Blackstone as to the issue of Parliament's supremacy against the courts as final interpreter of the British "constitution,"[41] the way that American state constitutions were worded before 1787 makes it difficult to read them as placing any effective restraints on legislatures. The constitutions of those years contained bills of rights that were often worded in the form of moral admonitions; some of their clauses called upon government to adhere firmly "to justice, moderation, temperance, frugality, and virtue" (e.g., Virginia, 1776). Where the 1787 U.S. Constitution has the imperative commands "shall" or "shall not," these earlier state documents would have "ought" or "recommend" (as in "freedom of the press ought not to be restrained"—Pennsylvania, 1776). Probably most telling, almost all the early state constitutions suggested circumstances where the legislature would be permitted to violate what were being declared to be "rights": "But no part of a man's property shall be taken from him . . . without his own consent, *or that of the legislative body of the people"* (New Hampshire, 1784, Art. XII, emphasis added).[42] Finally, it is at least suggestive that, while executives' oaths of office in these early constitutions included the duty to uphold the document, the oaths of legislators and judges did not.[43]

This legislative power over constitutions stemmed from the prevailing assumption in 1776 that the legislature re-presented the people. That "ruler" whose arbitrary power the revolutionaries wanted to hem in had been eliminated from the picture. It would take time for the idea to dawn on Americans that they might have a use for constitutions as a check on themselves qua rulers. It seemed in 1776 that constitutions could be used instead for expressing the public consensus on how government would be arranged and what it should be doing.

The old idea of a higher law that limited government had not disappeared; in fact, writing down this law was one way that Americans believed they were improving on the British system. Although some— like James Otis in 1765,[44] and Ellsworth and James Wilson opposing the ex post facto clauses at the Constitutional Convention[45]—argued that it would be a mistake to try to codify the basic privileges available to all Anglo-Americans as a matter of "right reason," most were persuaded that explicit confirmation of those rights in a visible, concrete document would be beneficial.[46] Nonetheless, the prevailing idea in 1776 was that people in the states had these rights not because the written constitutions embodied them, but rather because right reason—as applied to human nature and as evolved through the Anglo-American tradition—revealed their truth. The state constitutions' declarations of rights were just that: They were announcements of rights that would exist with or without the announcement; they were not viewed as withholdings of powers from the government, because powers over those rights were not viewed as transferable or alienable.[47]

As one of the more striking examples of this outlook one can cite arguments from the 1786 Rhode Island Supreme Court case of *Trevett v. Weeden.* Trial by jury had been denied to certain defendants; and the state constitution, adapted from the colonial charter virtually unchanged by the legislature,[48] had no explicit guarantee of trial by jury but did guarantee "all liberties and immunities of free and natural subjects . . . [of] England."[49] The attorney James Varnum, in a pamphlet that was widely publicized and was being sold in Philadelphia during the Constitutional Convention,[50] used this clause to argue that the right was "a fundamental, a constitutional right," and one the courts must enforce; but, in the fashion of the times, he buttressed his argument with allusions to natural rights. He traced the right to a jury trial back to the Magna Carta and to custom even older than that, and argued it was an institution for providing practical security to people's natural right to equal liberty. His argument explicitly assumes that the rule that judges must enforce natural rights is even more obvious than the rule that they must enforce constitutional ones.[51] The court tried to duck a direct clash with the legislature and resolved the case by denying their own jurisdiction, but the case nonetheless aroused much controversy.

Changes in the 1780s

That the mid–1780s were years of genuine political crisis in the United States is by now well documented. Abuses of legislative power were legion: paper-money schemes, tender laws, suspension of debt collection, legislative interferences with trial by jury, bills of attainder, grants of exemption from the standing laws, and so on.[52] One scholar documents reported instances of legislative interference with ongoing trials in at least three states and cites Jefferson as his authority in claiming that this also went on in a fourth.[53] In the course of this crisis, the dominant American political ideology underwent a profound shift.

The earliest and crucial change was that the people developed a sense of themselves as separate from the legislative body. This gradually led to a number of important shifts after 1780. First, drafters of state constitutions, realizing that the legislature did have the power of rulers and that such power could usefully be checked, moved toward strengthening the executive and judicial branches.[54] Second, beginning with the Massachusetts Constitution of 1780, states moved (albeit haltingly) toward combining the writing of constitutions by specially elected bodies with the ratification of them by the people.[55] Once constitutions really were emerging out of popular consent, the institutional groundwork was laid for a popular-sovereignty-based theory of higher law and of judicial review. Just such a theory came forth in the mid–1780s. In addition, popular sovereignty was working its way into the authoritative structuring of constitutions and into legislative activities; the American tradition of petitioning legislators evolved into a custom of delivering insistent and binding "instructions." The power to give such instructions was enshrined in constitutions, and the legislators took these instructions quite seriously.[56] Thus, in a paradoxical development, the 1780s was a period of an increase in the direct power of the people to legislate through instructions and an increase in the power of the people to check legislation through their role as authors of binding constitutions. The first full-blown American theory of popular control over government through a written constitution appears to have been developed in the pamphlet *Conciliatory Hints* by Thomas Tudor Tucker in 1784.[57] In calling for a constitutional convention in South Carolina to replace the legislatively adopted charter with one that would have more legitimacy, Tucker reasoned, "In a true commonwealth . . . all authority is derived from the people at large, held only during their pleasure. . . . No man has any privilege above his fellow-citizens, except . . . what they have thought proper to vest in him." Thus, a constitution should be based "on the firm and proper foundation of the *express consent of the people, unalterable by the legislature*, or any other authority but that by which it is to be framed . . . [and] it should be declared to be paramount to all acts of the legislature."[58] Within a year, Gouverneur Morris similarly expressed the sentiment that if a constitution can be changed by the legislature, it is no constitution.[59] Once this outlook became widespread, the legislature could be viewed as neither the rulers nor the people but as the deputies of the people. This idea had been implicit in Locke and in the Declaration of Independence and explicit in the writings of Samuel Pufendorf and Emmerich Vattel, with which educated, politically active Americans were familiar.[60] However, not until the 1780s did the idea begin to find institutional expression in the United States via constitutional conventions and extralegislative ratification.

The earliest experiments with judicial review also occurred in the 1780s in state supreme court cases; and as with the theory of consent to the constitution, a role for popular sovereignty emerged only gradually.[61] It was not unusual for arguments and court opinions for these cases to rely on unwritten "constitutional" rights, as well as on written texts. For instance, in 1784 attorney Alexander Hamilton argued in *Rutgers v. Waddington* that the New York law at issue was void on the ground that it conflicted with the Articles of Confederation, the Treaty of Peace, and the unwritten law of nations.[62]

During this period and continuing into the decade of the 1790s, judicial review was extremely controversial. Opposition to it ranged from denials of its legitimacy made by opposing counsel (in *Rutgers v. Waddington* and *Commonwealth of Virginia v. Caton*, 1782),[63] to the questioning of it by judges on the bench (also in *Commonwealth v. Caton*[64] and in *Rutgers v. Waddington*[65]). There were also the more extreme reactions of popular mass protest meetings (surrounding *Rut-*

gers v. Waddington)[66] and popular petitions to state legislatures against it (concerning *Holmes v. Walton*, N.J., 1780).[67] Legislatures, too, opposed judicial review by holding votes that censured its exercise or perceived exercise (in the cases of *Rutgers v. Waddington*;[68] and *Trevett v. Weeden*, R.I., 1786[69]), and through attempts to outlaw it (in reaction to *Bayard v. Singleton*, N.C., 1786–87;[70] and *Holmes v. Walton*[71]). In some instances, legislatures insisted that judges accused of engaging in judicial review present themselves at the legislature to account for their (mis)behavior (as happened with respect to *Bayard v. Singleton*[72] and *Trevett v. Weeden*[73]), and there were even serious efforts to impeach and remove from office such judges (in response to *Trevett v. Weeden*[74] and *The New Hampshire Ten Pound Act Case*, 1786–87[75]).

In sum, the first decade of independence was a period of extreme commitment to popular sovereignty. Judges and attorneys, however, sometimes argued for a judicial power to reject popularly supported statues that conflicted with an unwritten higher law. And judicial review during this period—a period in which it was not understood to be limited to the enforcement of a popularly adopted written text—was highly controversial.

1787–1803: The Merger of Majority Will and Wisdom

Popular sovereignty was very much in the air in 1787, but whether it could be saved from itself was an open question. Leading statesmen were in despair over the lack of republican virtue that the state republics had produced; what had been thought a contradiction in terms in 1776—"democratic despotism"—seemed to be at the door-step.[76]

The ingenious Federalist solution to the problem (to make a very long story short) was to turn the people against themselves. The people qua nation could be used to limit the people qua states. Within the nation, majority rule would prevail; but the majority would be sliced three ways; once for the House, once for the Senate, and once for the president. Similarly, for ascertaining the voice of "the people" to amend the Constitution, extraordinary majorities would be sliced three ways: two-thirds in the House, two-thirds in the Senate, and three-fourths for the state legislatures.

Any of these three embodiments of the people would be given the power to block action by the parallel other version of the people. Thus, by making the sense of the community very deliberate indeed, the Federalists hoped to make it more likely that majority will would approximate civic wisdom, thereby bringing about at the level of public policy (if not in the individual soul) at least an analogue for republican virtue. True to the essence of this solution, the Federalist scheme for adoption of the Constitution utilized popular approval through ratifying conventions. This enhanced the potential acceptability of popular-sovereignty-based theories of judicial review to be applied at the national level.

As was the case with the argument that only a written constitution could properly allow for popular control over legislatures, the germ of the idea that judicial review should be viewed as an instrument of popular sovereignty seems to have been first published in America in Thomas Tudor Tucker's *Conciliatory Hints*[77] (mentioned in the previous section). In that 1784 pamphlet, Tucker rehearsed the familiar Lockean arguments on reasons for entry into the social compact, on the delegating of power from the people to the government, and on the idea that, if legislatures "should exceed the powers vested in them, their act is no longer the act of the constituents."[78]

But Tucker added certain suggestions that pointed toward an American improvement on the Lockean theory that had justified the American Revolution. He criticized the British "constitution" as lacking a peaceful remedy for oppression: Parliament's "privileges are undefinable, because it is impossible to say, how far they may be extended without rousing the people to a tumultuous opposition or civil war; for with them there is no other remedy against tyranny and oppression."[79] Americans now had the heaven-sent opportunity for an express statement from the people as to the limits of legislative power. Moreover, the people would be well advised to contrive "the terms of the compact or constitution . . . to provide a remedy . . . without outrage, noise or tumult" for all cases where the rulers resort to a "traitorous abuse of trust."[80] Although Tucker does not detail this remedy for avoiding appeal to the sword, he does in the same pamphlet suggest that a problem of recent importance in a sister state—inadvertent transgression of the constitution by the legislature—could have been avoided had only that constitution "expressly declare[d] that no act of the legislature contravening it should be of force" in the courts of law.[81] Tucker thus suggests that judicial review might serve as the peaceful alternative to revolution and also as the institutional guardian of the people's sovereignty.

In 1786 in preparation for a state supreme court case, *Bayard v.*

Singleton, the attorney James Iredell elaborated a more complete theory along those lines in a North Carolina newspaper; moreover, he outlined the same arguments in a letter in August 1787 to Richard Spaight, a delegate then attending the Constitutional Convention. Sylvia Snowiss has made a convincing case that Iredell's arguments provided the inspirations both for Hamilton's explanation of judicial review in *Federalist #78* and for James Wilson's explanation of it in his lectures on law, delivered in 1790–91 but published in 1793.[82] Both Hamilton and Wilson were enormously influential in shaping the American understanding of judicial review and its relation to popular sovereignty. Iredell's newspaper argument was as follows:

> The power of the Assembly is limited and defined by the Constitution. It is a creature of the Constitution. . . . The *people* have chosen to be governed under such and such principles. They have not chosen to be governed, not promised to submit upon any other; and the Assembly have no . . . right to obedience on other terms. . . .
>
> The [judicial] duty . . . I conceive, in all cases is to decide according to the *laws of the State*. It will not be denied, I suppose, that the constitution is a *law of the State*, as well as an act of Assembly, with this difference only, that it is the *fundamental* law, and unalterable by the legislature, which derives all its power from it. One act of Assembly may repeal another act of Assembly. For this reason the latter act is to be obeyed and not the former. An act of Assembly cannot repeal the constitution, or any part of it. For that reason, an act of Assembly, inconsistent with the constitution, is *void*, and cannot be obeyed, without disobeying the superior law to which we were previously and irrevocably bound. The judges, therefore, must take care at their peril, that every act of Assembly they presume to enforce is warranted by the constitution, since if it is not, they act without lawful authority. This is not a usurped or a discretionary power, but one inevitably resulting from the constitution of their office, they being judges for the benefit *of the whole people, not mere servants of the Assembly.*[83]

This argument echoes that of Varnum in 1786, but it significantly omits the Locke-based natural rights argument and the divine law argument, standing instead squarely on the Vattel-based constitutional theory of popular consent as a source of limits on legislative power. It fleshes out Thomas Tudor Tucker's skeletal suggestion that the people's written constitutional limits on legislatures can be enforced by courts of law.

Although Iredell indicated his awareness of, and seemed at this time to endorse, the natural-justice-based version of judicial review as well (a version he was later explicitly to disavow[84]), he made a point of noting the singular advantage of a judicial review power grounded squarely in a written constitution:

> Without an expressed constitution the powers of the legislature would undoubtedly have been absolute (as the Parliament of Great Britain is said to be) and any act passed, *not inconsistent with natural justice* (for that curb is avowed by the judges even in England) would have been binding on the people. The experience of the evils . . . attending an absolute power in a legislative body suggested the propriety of a real original contract between the people and their future government. . . .
>
> It really appears to me, the exercise of the [judicial] power is unavoidable, the Constitution *not being a mere imaginary thing, about which ten thousand different opinions may be formed, but a written document* to which all may have recourse.[85]

It was this kind of judicial review that the principle of popular sovereignty now supported.

Iredell's description of judicial review required that judges "take notice of" any direct clash between a statute and a constitution and consider the constitution as a law of superior obligation, because it comes from "the whole people."[86] Hamilton's famous version of the argument from *Federalist #78*, reads thus:

> [E]very act of a delegated authority, contrary to the tenor of the commission under which it is exercised, is void. No legislative act, therefore, contrary to the Constitution, can be valid. To deny this would be to affirm that the deputy is greater than his principal; that the servant is above his master; that the representatives of the people are superior to the people themselves. . . . If there should happen to be an irreconcilable variance between [a statute and the constitution], that which has the superior obligation and validity ought, of course, to be preferred.[87]

And James Wilson put it this way:

> From the constitution, the legislative department, as well as every other part of government derives its power: by the constitution, the legislative, as every other department, must be directed: of the constitution, no alteration by the legislature can be made or authorized. . . . The constitution is the supreme law of the land: to that supreme law every other power must be inferior and subordinate.
>
> Now, let us suppose, that the legislature should pass an act manifestly

repugnant to some part of the constitution; and that the operation and validity of both should come regularly in question before a court, forming a part of the judicial department. In that department, the "judicial power of the United States is vested" by the "people," who "ordained and established" the constitution. . . . Two contradictory rules . . . cannot possibly be administered. . . . The supreme power of the United States has given one rule: a subordinate power . . . , a contradictory rule: the former is the law of the land: as a necessary consequence, the latter is void. . . . In this manner . . . it is the duty of a court of justice, under the constitution of the United States, to decide.[88]

Subsequent to the development and propagation of these popular-sovereignty-based rationales for judicial review, a rather dramatic transformation of its legitimacy can be observed. Judicial review lost its controversial status during the 1790s and gained acceptance not only among the judiciary but also in state and federal legislatures as well as, presumably, in the popular mind. Legislative attacks on the principle of judicial review died out.[89] In contrast to mass protests and impeachment attempts, one reads of instances where legislatures amended statutes in order to comply with judicial objections (for example, *Kamper v. Hawkins*, 1793).[90] During the early years of the U.S. Congress, repeated allusions were made to the propriety of judicial examination of the constitutionality of federal statutes.[91] In 1799, when several state legislatures announced replies to the Virginia and Kentucky Resolutions' interposition doctrine, they pointedly spoke of the U.S. Supreme Court as the final interpreter of the U.S. Constitution.[92]

By 1802, high courts in eight of the states had endorsed judicial review,[93] and federal courts had followed suit, endorsing the concept in a number of instances prior to 1803.[94] In the judicial decisions where judicial review was discussed at any length, the prominence of the Iredell–Hamilton–Wilson popular consent theory is unmistakable.[95] In the 15 state supreme court cases between 1789 and 1802 where judicial review was arguably at issue,[96] nine contained judicial defenses of the power. Of those, seven either quoted or paraphrased the Iredell–Hamilton–Wilson rationale. The two that presented an alternative argument, quoting Sir Edward Coke and relying on the Magna Carta and "common right and reason," were both South Carolina cases: *Ham v. M'Claws*, 1789; and *Bowman v. Middleton*, 1792.[97] It is instructive that in two subsequent South Carolina cases—*Lindsay v. Commissioners*, 1796; and *White v. Kendrick*, 1805—the Coke approach is dropped and replaced by the will-of-the-people-as-higher-law argument.[98] During the 1790s judicial review not only gained a mighty ally in the Iredell–Hamilton–Wilson argument concerning popular consent to the rules of the Constitution, it also gained renewed strength from tougher wording in the state constitutions. Copying the example of the U.S. Constitution, the six post–1790 eighteenth-century constitutions adopted "shall" in bills of rights in place of the formerly preferred "ought." In sum, the 1790s in the United States witnessed a change in the very concept of written constitutions. Now they were written in a language meant to be binding, and they were viewed as binding at least in part because they expressed "the consent of the governed." To a nation that took its bearings from the Declaration of Independence, this was no small addition to the argument.

1803 and the Future

According to Snowiss, when John Marshall established judicial review over congressional statutes in *Marbury v. Madison*—although he restricted judicial power to the enforcement of written rules—he transformed the Court's power from one limited to Iredell's concept of "a clear and urgent case" of clashing provisions (see Iredell, concurring, in *Calder v. Bull*, 1798)[99] to a power to expound the various doubtful meanings of the Constitution. In Marshall's hands it became a judicial power to choose one interpretation against other reasonable, conflicting ones that the legislature may have chosen. Paradoxically, Snowiss[100] sees this as clearly an expansion of judicial power over the earlier version of judicial review, which, although based on unwritten-law concepts, was limited to a narrow range of fundamental natural/ common law rights.[101] By contrast, the versions of unwritten higher law of contemporary scholars like Thomas Grey and Walter Murphy would take judicial power altitudes beyond Marshall's plateau of judicial exposition of the written constitutional text. Grey would have us learn from the Supreme Court the content of our "basic national ideals of individual liberty and fair treatment,"[102] and Murphy would allow the Court to strike down any law that conflicted with the justices' notion of the "dignity of the individual."[103]

The higher-unwritten-law background of judicial review, which Grey traces up until 1776, did not disappear in 1787 after the Constitution was drafted. It appears influential in judges' decisions well into the nineteenth century. The opinion of Justice Salmon Chase for *Calder v. Bull* (1798) and the opinion of Chief Justice John Marshall in *Fletcher v. Peck* (1810) exhibit the transitional trait of acknowledging natural law/common law support for their position and also grounding it in exposition of the constitutional text. Justice Chase explains that the ex post facto clauses of the Constitution do not apply to the statute at hand, and he explains why; but he also says that "the genius, nature, and the spirit of our state governments, amount to a prohibition of [fundamentally unjust] laws: and the great principles of law and reason forbid them."[104] These unwritten principles would make such acts of our legislatures void even "if they had not been expressly restrained."[105] But the clear implication is that the Constitution does expressly forbid violations of fundamental justice. Marshall, too, covered his bets both ways, declaring in *Fletcher* that "either by general principles which are common to our free institutions, or by the particular provisions of the Constitution of the United States," the law in question was void.[106]

As American society became less homogeneous, and presumably less consensual, and as scholars became more positivistic in their outlook during the nineteenth century, these unwritten-law justifications gradually disappeared, although they later resurfaced in the form of extremely controversial "noninterpretive" readings of the constitutional text, most notoriously in the doctrine of substantive due process.[107] Perhaps that disappearance is related to the fact that Americans were starting to view natural justice as that which Iredell had described as "a mere imaginary thing, about which ten thousand different opinions may be formed."[108] But the *political* success of a judicial review anchored firmly in the theory of popular consent to the constitutional text was very likely also a factor in the judges' shift.

This chapter has been essentially an account of the relative weakness of judicial review in the first decade of the Confederation, when it was based primarily on unwritten natural rights, and an account of its rapid flourishing starting in the mid–1780s once it was grounded in a constitutional theory that stressed popular consent to government as articulated in a written, boundary-setting document. There is currently a boom in noninterpretivist (or extratextualist) scholarly commentary, which views judicial review as a more or less unbounded charter to judges to fill in for Americans the content of their unwritten "national ideals."[109] Perhaps this account of the early days of judicial review will prove a cautionary tale for such scholars.

Notes

1. E.g., Thomas Grey, "Do We Have an Unwritten Constitution?" and "Origins of the Unwritten Constitution: Fundamental Law in American Revolutionary Thought"; Arthur S. Miller, *Toward Increased Judicial Activism*; Michael Perry, *The Constitution, the Courts, and Human Rights*; Philip Bobbitt, *Constitutional Fate*; Suzanna Sherry, "The Founders' Unwritten Constitution."

2. E.g., Andrew McLaughlin, *The Court, the Constitution, and Parties* (hereinafter CCP); Edward S. Corwin, "The Higher Law Background of American Constitutional Law," *Court over Constitution*, and *The Doctrine of Judicial Review*; Benjamin F. Wright, *American Interpretations of Natural Law*; Charles H. Haines, *The American Doctrine of Judicial Supremacy*; Clinton Rossiter, *Seedtime of the Republic*; Bernard Bailyn, *Ideological Origins of the American Revolution*, pp. 189–90.

The recent criticism of this tradition by Walter Berns in "Judicial Review and the Rights and the Laws of Nature," on the grounds that none of these scholars understood the true meaning of "the doctrine of modern natural rights and natural law from which . . . we derive . . . our constitutionalism," is somewhat beside the point (however powerful Berns's elucidation of Locke, Hobbes, Vattel, and Pufendorf may be). The question is not the true import of Locke's theories, but rather what those theories meant to our revolutionary framers. When a man as well read and as serious in his scholarship as John Adams could assert that Locke, Cicero, and Aristotle all taught the same thing about natural law—not to mention the dozens of lesser figures who exhibit the same confusion—it does not really matter that Berns is correct in realizing Locke intended to reject rather than endorse the tradition of Cicero and Aquinas.

Rossiter, *Seedtime*, p. 353—for instance—quotes Adams:

Natural law and right are . . . revolution principles. They are the principles of Aristotle and Plato, of Livy and Cicero, and Sidney, Harrington, and Locke: the principles of nature and eternal reason; the principles on which the whole government over us now stands.

3. McLaughlin, CCP; Edward S. Corwin, "A Basic Doctrine of American Law"; Haines, *Judicial Supremacy*.

4. Max Farrand, ed., *The Records of the Federal Convention of 1787*, vol. 1, pp. 97, 109, vol. 2, pp. 28, 73, 76, 78, 93, 248, 299, 376, 428, and vol. 3, p. 220. Also, Haines, *Judicial Supremacy*, pp. 126–35; Corwin, *Doctrine of Judicial Review*, pp. 10–13; but cf. Leonard Levy, "Judicial Review, History, and Democracy: An Introduction."

5. See, e.g., Gerald Gunther, *Cases and Materials in Constitutional Law*, p. 506.

6. In neither *Griswold v. Connecticut*, 381 U.S. 479 (1965), *Eisenstadt v. Baird*, 405 U.S. 438 (1972), nor *Roe v. Wade*, 410 U.S. 113 (1973), did any justice ever say in so many words, "It is our job to discover the unwritten natural rights of Americans and enforce them as fundamental law." Instead (with the exceptions of Justices Douglas and Clark, who struggled valiantly and unpersuasively in *Griswold* to demonstrate that the right of married couples to use contraceptive devices was implied in the words of the First, Third, Fourth, Fifth, Ninth, and Fourteenth Amendments), the justices adopted or returned to the theory that the due process clauses (Fifth and Fourteenth Amendments) require them to identify the most important liberties for Americans and to guard these against undue legislative invasion. Although they did not spell it out, this "identifying" process amounts to an invocation of unwritten law.

7. Walter Murphy, "The Art of Constitutional Interpretation."

8. For a review and critique of this literature, see Chapter 4.

9. Grey, "Origins."

10. Thomas Grey, "The Original Understanding and the Unwritten Constitution."

11. Sherry, "Founders' Unwritten Constitution."

12. Murphy, "Art."

13. My thesis thus drastically curtails the import of the work of Thomas Grey as a useful guide for current Supreme Court practice. To curtail similarly the import of Walter Murphy's essay, "Art," would be beyond the scope of this chapter; for that discussion, see Chapter 5.

14. Bailyn, *Ideological Origins.*

15. Gordon Wood, *The Creation of the American Republic 1776–1787*, and *Representation in the American Revolution.*

16. Donald Lutz, *Popular Consent and Popular Control* (hereinafter PCPC).

17. Willi Paul Adams, *The First American Constitutions.*

18. Sylvia Snowiss, "From Fundamental Law to Supreme Law of the Land: A Reinterpretation of the Origin of Judicial Review in the U.S." This essay was originally presented at the American Political Science Association meeting of 1981, and was then revised and published in 1987 as "From Fundamental Law to Supreme Law of the Land: A Reinterpretation of the Origin of Judicial Review." Snowiss then expanded the arguments into a book-length treatise, *Judicial Review and the Law of the Constitution.* All page references in this chapter will be to her original essay (which hereinafter will be cited as FLSL1).

19. John Adams, *The Works of John Adams*, vol. 2, p. 521, and vol. 10, pp. 247–48.

20. Lutz, PCPC, pp. 24–31.

21. The exclusion of females from the body politic was rarely discussed. For a few exceptions during the founding era, see J. Adams, *Works*, vol. 9, pp.

375–78 (commenting in 1776); James Wilson, *The Works of James Wilson*, vol. 1, pp. 83–89 (commenting in 1790–91); and Thomas Jefferson, *The Writings of Thomas Jefferson*, vol. 7, p. 36 (commenting in 1816).

22. Lutz, PCPC, pp. 24–26 and 100–101; Julius Goebel, *History of the Supreme Court of the U.S.: Antecedents and Beginnings to 1801*, pp. 3–4, 85; W. P. Adams, *First*, pp. 230–33.

23. Lutz, PCPC, pp. 100–105; Bailyn, *Ideological Origins*, pp. 61–175; Wood, *Creation*, pp. 167–85.

24. Lutz, PCPC, pp. 24–26, 100–105. Cf. George Lee Haskins, *History of the Supreme Court of the U.S.: Foundations of Power—John Marshall, 1801–1815*, p. 41; Chilton Williamson, *American Suffrage from Property to Democracy*; J. R. Pole, *Political Representation*; and Charles S. Hyneman, "Republican Government in America: The Idea and Its Realization," pp. 15–16.

25. Lutz, PCPC, pp. 105–8.

26. Elisha Douglass, *Rebels and Democrats*; Jackson T. Main, "Government by the People: The American Revolution and the Democratization of the Legislature"; Lutz, PCPC, pp. 106–10; Wood, *Creation*, pp. 167–68.

27. Lutz, PCPC, p. 102.

28. W. P. Adams, *First*, p. 231.

29. Lutz, PCPC, pp. 87–88.

30. W. P. Adams, *First*, pp. 293–307. Gestures were made in the direction of having an upper house that would represent "Property" in accordance with traditional Anglo-American Whig theories of balanced government (i.e., balanced between the principles of human numbers and property), by imposing much stiffer property requirements on candidates for the upper house than on candidates for the lower house. These gestures proved futile because the groups of voters were the same, and the resulting state senates proved indistinguishable in behavior from the state assemblies. See Lutz, PCPC, pp. 88–89, 108–9, 207–8; Wood, *Creation*, pp. 206–14; Main, "Government by the People."

31. Wood, *Creation*, pp. 135–50, 160–73; Lutz, PCPC, p. 44.

32. Ward, *Statism in Plymouth Colony*, p. 17.

33. Lutz, PCPC, pp. 27–29, presents a list of these charters.

34. Bailyn, *Ideological Origins*, pp. 189–93; Goebel, *History*, pp. 3–4; McLaughlin, CCP, pp. 249–65.

35. Bailyn, *Ideological Origins*, pp. 193–98 and 187–89.

36. Hyneman, "Republican Government in America," pp. 15–16; Ronald Peters, "The Written Constitution," p. 174; W. P. Adams, *First*, pp. 63–65, 138.

37. Lutz, PCPC, p. 45; Peters, "Written Constitution," pp. 171–72.

38. Lutz, PCPC, p. 83.

39. Lutz, PCPC, pp. 45, 65–69, 71–75, 81–84. Cf. Peters, "Written Constitution," p. 172. Charles Warren suggests that "The States" in 1776 introduced the idea that only extralegislative bodies have proper authority to write or

amend constitutions. Charles Warren, *Congress, the Constitution, and the Supreme Court* (hereinafter cited as CCSC), pp. 16–17. In fact, the popular acceptance of this idea, as measured by its institutionalization into constitutions, took much longer than Warren indicates. Gerald Stourzh, by contrast, acknowledges the gradualism of the transition (1776–88) but provides none of the evidence in support of his correct insight. Gerald Stourzh, "The American Revolution, Modern Constitutionalism, and the Protection of Human Rights," p. 166.

40. Lutz, PCPC, pp. 62–65, 121; Wood, *Creation*, pp. 274–75, 279; Snowiss, FLSL1, pp. 13–14; Goebel, *History*, pp. 101, 142; Edward S. Corwin, "The Progress of Constitutional Theory between the Declaration of Independence and the Meeting of the Philadelphia Convention," pp. 511–20.

41. Compare Grey, "Origins," with Bailyn, *Ideological Origins*, ch. 5; see also Herbert Storing, "The Constitution and the Bill of Rights," p. 37.

42. Lutz, PCPC, pp. 61–68, 49, 35; Wood, *Creation* pp. 271–73; Peters, "Written Constitution," pp. 176–77; cf. Stourzh, "American Revolution," pp. 168–69.

43. Goebel, *History*, p. 108.

44. Bailyn, *Ideological Origins*, p. 189; Wood, *Creation*, p. 277.

45. Farrand, *Records*, vol. 2, p. 376.

46. Bailyn, *Ideological Origins*, pp. 189–90, 192; Wood, *Creation*, pp. 266–68; Snowiss, FLSL1, p. 16; Gary Jacobsohn, "E.T."; and the frequently cited opinion of Judge Tucker in *Kamper v. Hawkins*, 1 Virginia Cases 20 (1793).

47. Grey, "Origins " and also "Original Understanding," produced the most recent treatment, but much evidence of this is in the older work cited in note 2 above. See also Wood, *Creation*, pp. 456–57; and Storing, "Constitution and the Bill of Rights," p. 37.

48. Goebel, *History*, p. 139 n. 147.

49. F. N. Thorpe, *The Federal and State Constitutions, Colonial Charters, and Other Organic Laws of the States, Territories, and Colonies*, vol. 6, p. 3220.

50. McLaughlin, CCP, pp. 44–45; William W. Crosskey, *Politics and the Constitution in the History of the United States*, vol. 2, pp. 962–65.

51. James Varnum, *The Case* Trevett against Weeden, p. 29. Varnum's pamphlet provides further evidence of the confusion about natural law philosophy in the minds of the eighteenth-century statesmen that underlies the disagreement between Walter Berns and Thomas Grey (see note 2). In order to establish judicial duty to declare the statute void, Varnum first invoked Locke's *Second Treatise* for the principle that government may not violate the inalienable natural right of the people to life, liberty, and the security of property. Varnum, *Case*, pp. 20–22. He then paraphrased and quoted at some length E. Vattel's *The Law of Nations or Principles of the Law of Nature* (1758) to make the point that the people through a social compact establish the fundamental law, or constitution, which then operates as a limit on the

legislators, who are only the deputies of the people and who derive their commission through the constitution. Thus, their power is limited thereby. Varnum, *Case*, pp. 23–25. Varnum was applying this argument to a constitution adopted by the legislature! Probably aware that the argument's applicability to Rhode Island was—to state it mildly—questionable, Varnum tried to buttress his case with the argument that, obviously, judges could not or should not enforce statutes that violate natural law or divine law. He gave as a hypothetical instance of the former an order that a man vacate his home for six months, and as an instance of the latter an order that a man kill his own child. He then tried to tie these assertions to Vattel's theory by an argument that says, essentially, higher authority is higher authority; whether it is God or the people qua sovereign, judges must obey it:

> But the judges, and all others, are bound by the laws of nature in preference to any human laws, because they were ordained by God himself anterior to any civil or political institutions. They are bound, in like manner, by the principles of the constitution in preference to any acts of the General Assembly, because they were ordained by the people[!] anterior to and created the powers of the General Assembly.
>
> Varnum, *Case*, p. 29.

52. Corwin, "Progress of Constitutional Theory," pp. 511–20; Wood, *Creation*, pp. 403–25; Lutz, PCPC, pp. 116–22. See also James Madison's essay of 1787 in *The Writings of James Madison*, vol. 2, pp. 361 ff.

53. Goebel, *History*, pp. 98–99.

54. Lutz, PCPC, p. 45; Wood, *Creation*, pp. 161, 447–63.

55. Lutz, PCPC, pp. 62–65, 71–75, 81–83; Stourzh, "American Revolution," p. 166. See Wood, *Creation*, ch. 8, for a brilliant discussion of how the American extralegislative and sublegislative tradition of political activities by the people "out-of-doors" became transubstantiated in the 1780s into supralegislative authority.

56. Lutz, PCPC, pp. 115–18; Wood, *Creation*, pp. 363–89; W. P. Adams, *First*, pp. 246–49.

57. Thomas Tudor Tucker, *Conciliatory Hints Attempting . . . to Remove Party Prejudice*. Originality attributed in Wood, *Creation*, pp. 280–82.

58. Tucker, *Conciliatory Hints*, cited in Wood, *Creation*, p. 281. Emphasis added.

59. Haines, *Judicial Supremacy*, p. 95.

60. Berns, "Judicial Review," pp. 66–74; Wood, *Creation*, p. 284; McLaughlin, CCP, pp. 68–74.

61. These court decisions were generally not published. They are reviewed in Haines, *Judicial Supremacy*, chs. 4–7; Snowiss, FLSL1, pp. 10–16; Edward S. Corwin, "The Establishment of Judicial Review," pp. 110–20; Goebel, *History*, pp. 124–41; McLaughlin, CCP, pp. 41–50; Crosskey, *Politics and the Constitution*, vol. 2, pp. 944–75; and Warren, CCSC, pp. 43–48. The most thorough are Haines, Goebel, and Crosskey.

62. Julius Goebel, *The Law Practice of Alexander Hamilton*, pp. 282–315, 393–419.

63. Haines, *Judicial Supremacy*, pp. 98–104; Corwin, "Establishment of Judicial Review," pp. 110–20.

64. Haines, *Judicial Supremacy*, pp. 95–98; Crosskey, *Politics and the Constitution*, pp. 952–61; Goebel, *History*, pp. 126–28.

65. Haines, *Judicial Supremacy*, pp. 98–104; Crosskey, *Politics and the Constitution*, pp. 962–65.

66. Same sources as note 65.

67. Haines, *Judicial Supremacy*, pp. 92–95; Crosskey, *Politics and the Constitution*, pp. 948–52.

68. Haines, *Judicial Supremacy*, p. 104; Crosskey, pp. 962–65.

69. Haines, *Judicial Supremacy*, pp. 105–12; Goebel, *History*, pp. 137–41.

70. Haines, *Judicial Supremacy*, pp. 112–20; Crosskey, *Politics and the Constitution*, pp. 971–75.

71. Haines, *Judicial Supremacy*, pp. 92–95.

72. Haines, *Judicial Supremacy*, pp. 112–20; Crosskey, *Politics and the Constitution*, pp. 971–75.

73. Haines, *Judicial Supremacy*, pp. 105–12; Goebel, *History*, pp. 137–41.

74. Same sources as note 73.

75. Crosskey, *Politics and the Constitution*, pp. 968–71.

76. Wood, *Creation*, p. 404 (paraphrasing John Adams).

77. Tucker, *Conciliatory Hints*; although Wood, *Creation*, pp. 280–82, originally drew my attention to this Tucker essay, he does not note its formative contribution to an American theory of judicial review.

78. Tucker, *Conciliatory Hints*, pp. 612–14, 622–23.

79. Tucker, *Conciliatory Hints*, p. 612.

80. Tucker, *Conciliatory Hints*, p. 614.

81. Tucker, *Conciliatory Hints*, p. 627.

82. Snowiss, FLSL1, p. 16, and *Judicial Review and the Law of the Constitution*. See related speculations in Wood, *Creation*, pp. 460–61; Goebel, *History*, p. 130; Haines, *Judicial Supremacy*, pp. 116–20; McLaughlin, CCP, pp. 74–75 n. 1; and Stourzh, "American Revolution," pp. 169–72.

83. Griffith McRee, ed., *Life and Correspondence of James Iredell*, vol. 2, pp. 145–49. Emphasis in original.

84. In *Calder v. Bull*, 3 U.S. (3 Dallas) 386 (1798), at 398, Iredell wrote,

If a government . . . were established by a Constitution which imposed no limits on the legislative power, the consequence would inevitably be, that whatever the legislative power chose to enact, would be lawfully enacted, and the judicial power could never interpose to pronounce it void. It is true that some speculative jurists have held, that a legislative act against natural justice must, in itself, be void, but I cannot think that, under such a government, any court of Justice would possess a power to declare it so.

85. McRee, *Life*, vol. 2, pp. 148, 173–74. All emphasis added.
86. Letter to Spaight, 1787, in McRee, *Life*, p. 173.
87. *Federalist Papers*, #78, p. 467.
88. Wilson, *Works*, vol. 1, pp. 329–31. Like the early Iredell, Wilson acknowledged the additional invalidity of laws violating natural justice; see his *Works*, vol. 1, pp. 326–29.
89. State supreme court cases exercising judicial review on the basis of state constitutions after 1789 are canvassed in Haines, *Judicial Supremacy*, ch. 7, and McLaughlin, CCP, pp. 19–30.
90. Haines, *Judicial Supremacy*, pp. 152–57.
91. Warren, CCSC, ch. 4; cf. Crosskey, *Politics and the Constitution*, pp. 1028–46.
92. McLaughlin, CCP, pp. 16–17; Haines, *Judicial Supremacy*, pp. 189–91. Under interposition doctrine, each individual state had the final say over the meaning of the federal Constitution, and could "interpose" itself as a shield between federal government power and its own citizens.
93. Corwin, *Doctrine of Judicial Review*.
94. Charles Warren, *The Supreme Court in U.S. History*, ch. 1; McLaughlin, CCP, pp. 10–16; Haines, *Judicial Supremacy*, ch. 8; Goebel, *History*, pp. 778–84.
The Supreme Court cases were *Cooper v. Telfair*, 1800; *Calder v. Bull*, 1798; *Hollingsworth v. Virginia*, 1798; *Hylton v. United States*, 1796; *Van Horne's Lessee v. Dorrance*, 1795. The lower federal court cases were *The First Hayburn Case*, 1792; *Ogden v. Witherspoon*, 1802; *Minge v. Gilmour*, 1798; and *United States v. Callender*, 1800.
95. This point is also made by Snowiss, FLSL1, pp. 18–19, but she presents none of the evidence there.
96. See Haines, *Judicial Supremacy*, ch. 7; McLaughlin, CCP, pp. 19–30.
97. *Ham v. M'Claws*, 1 Bay 93 (S.C., 1789); *Bowman v. Middleton*, 1 Bay 252 (S.C., 1792).
98. *Lindsay v. Commissioners*, 2 Bay 61 (S.C., 1796); *White v. Kendrick*, 1 Brevard 469 (S.C.,1805).
99. *Calder*, at 399.
100. Snowiss, FLSL1, pp. 2, 4–5.
101. See also Jacobsohn, "E.T.," pp. 25–27; Berns, "Judicial Review."
102. Grey, "Do We Have?" p. 706.
103. Murphy, "Art," pp. 155–59.
104. *Calder*, at 388.
105. Ibid.
106. *Fletcher v. Peck*, 10 U.S. 87 (1810), at 139.
107. But cf. Murphy, "Art."
108. McRee, *Life*, vol. 2, pp. 173–74.
109. The next chapter discusses several examples of this trend.

4

Judicial Review and Modern Judicial Scholarship: A Question of Power

As indicated in Chapter 3, much of the recent literature about constitutional law is dominated by the debate over extratextualism, or noninterpretivism. Chapter 4, however, will stress a somewhat different division: that between scholars who wish to minimize judicial discretion and those who would maximize it. This division provides a richer analytical breakdown, making possible a refinement of the textualist versus extratextualist debate. Textualism, or interpretivism, per se does not answer the question as to *which* interpretation of the constitutional text to select. Thus, for instance, the justice often described as the quintessential interpretivist—Justice Hugo Black—was no more an interpretivist than his frequent foil, Justice Felix Frankfurter. What really divided them was a difference of opinion over the degree to which judicial discretion ought to be constrained by some expression of will from a popularly responsive branch of government. This difference guided their respective choices of textual interpretation, most notably in procedural due process cases.

This chapter locates *in* the constitutional text support for a certain kind of political constraint on the Court but implicit rejection of other political constraints (such as those advocated recently by John Agresto). It also identifies, particularly in the overall structure of government based on a tripartite separation of powers, textual grounds for constraining the Court in terms reminiscent of the old political question doctrine—terms frequently defended by Justice Black. In short, it argues that the American conception of judicial power as separated from legislative power—a conception the Constitution establishes as law—calls upon the justices to interpret the Constitution in such a way that decisions are textually guided rather than unguided. Judges must fill the open-ended clauses of the Constitution with principles that are traceable not to a justice's own vision of national ideals, but to some expression of the will of the sovereign people (i.e., some statute or some aspect of the constitutional text).

The Nature of Judicial Power

A specter is haunting contemporary Supreme Court criticism. It is the specter of the political question doctrine. The doctrine is as old as the Supreme Court's assertion of the power to declare void federal laws. "Questions in their nature political," opined Chief Justice Marshall— that is, questions that are matters of sheer policy discretion—will be decided by those departments of government whose officers are each "accountable only to his country in his political character and to his own conscience." Courts, by contrast, will settle questions of law; in fact it was "emphatically the province and duty of the judicial department to say what the law is."[1] The written Constitution indicates by its own words, which prohibit various sorts of legislative or executive acts, that it is intended to be a law above laws. Thus it too, Marshall argued, is appropriately subject to the judicial expounding power. Still, that power is a power to expound law, not to make it up wholesale.

This principle, distinguishing the power to interpret law—law adopted by the people or their agents—from the power to make policy over matters of political discretion, has been re-endorsed throughout Supreme Court history.[2] In the Court's earliest post-*Marbury* effort to explain this distinction,[3] Justice Henry Baldwin wrote that "the true boundary line between political and judicial power and questions" is delimited by the following distinctions:

> A sovereign decides by his own will which is the supreme law within his own boundary; A court, or judge, decides according to the law prescribed by the sovereign power, and that law is the rule for judgment. . . . [A court is always] bound to act by known and settled principles of national or municipal jurisprudence as the case requires.[4]

Of course, if this doctrine were an obviously accurate description of reality, judicial review would pose no problem for democracy. Invalidation of unconstitutional law would be an exertion in aid of, rather than in conflict with, "the will of the people" who adopted the high law of the Constitution for themselves and as a beneficent legacy to their posterity.[5] Every time the framers' posterity vote and elect officials who have to swear to uphold the Constitution (Art. VI, Sec. 3), these voters would be renewing the acknowledgment that they do indeed consent to its rules.[6] And the judicial restraining of unconstitutional actions by government officials appointed to follow the rules of the Constitution would simply be the application of the will of the sovereign people to the people's agents, who agree in advance to follow that will.

Well, this—more or less[7]—is the tale told by *Marbury v. Madison*.[8] But nobody buys it anymore. As should have been clear since at least the time of *Marbury* (where Marshall declared unconstitutional part of a statute written and adopted by a legislature consisting largely of framers and ratifiers), constitutions, statutes, and treaties do not interpret themselves. And reasonable persons may differ as to which interpretation really expresses the will of the people. That in itself is not the problem, though, because that, after all, is why we have judges—to provide authoritative applications of generalized rules to specific instances where there is a dispute as to their proper application.[9] The problem with *Marbury* credibility seems to occur, and periodically recur, whenever the Supreme Court pronounces "textual interpretations" that stray so far from the constitutional text that judicial scholars have trouble convincing themselves that the Court is really expounding law "as the courts know law" (i.e., applying preexisting, known principles), rather than simply making up rules as would a political body. Thus, certain decisions by the Court set off crises of judicial legitimacy. The first of these was produced by the *Dred Scott* case in 1857;[10] another was triggered by the economic substantive due process decisions of the early twentieth century.[11] For our generation, *Brown v. Board of Education of Topeka* (1954)[12] seems to have set off another crisis—if not of judicial legitimacy, then of judicial identity. This crisis of judicial identity has constitutional scholars in a flurry over a very back-to-basics question: What is the proper role of the Supreme Court in the American political system?[13]

Phase One of the Modern Crisis: *Brown* and Its Aftermath

In response to the *Brown* decision, Alexander Bickel (of Yale Law School) wrote a much-cited article in the 1955 *Harvard Law Review*[14] in which he demonstrated, by thorough historical research, that "section 1 of the Fourteenth Amendment . . . carried out . . . relatively narrow objectives and hence, *as originally understood*, was meant to apply neither to jury service,[15] nor suffrage, nor anti-miscegenation statutes, nor segregation."[16] Bickel went on to argue, however, that the Warren Court was quite justified in refusing to follow the "original understanding" of the sovereign people who had written and adopted the Fourteenth Amendment, because those people knew the Constitution to be a "broadly worded organic law not [to be] frequently or lightly amended." And, operating with this knowledge, the framers of the Fourteenth Amendment had deliberately rejected proposed language of a narrow and concrete focus in favor of wording "more receptive to 'latitudinarian' construction," in order to put into the supreme law of the United States a language "sufficiently elastic to permit reasonable future advances"—"a line of growth" in the direction of a higher societal morality than that for which the citizens of 1868 were ready.[17]

Bickel was suggesting that in many of its parts—the "open-textured" ones—the Constitution as an organic law is a constitution of aspiration, containing moral principles meant to endure but also meant to evolve along with the moral level of the people themselves.[18] He urged justices to take this hope for growth into account when they interpret the document, even to the degree of contravening the known purposes of the congressional authors of a constitutional amendment.[19] Admitting that the known intentions of the Constitution's authors should sometimes be violated, however, opened up a veritable Pandora's box of judicial-power possibilities. If the conscious and announced intent of the law's author could be transgressed by a court purporting to interpret *that law*, what, if anything, remained of the political question doctrine? In other words, what remained of the idea that courts interpret and apply the will of the sovereign rather than ruling as sovereign themselves?

Bickel's next three books attempted to answer this question,[20] as did two influential articles from the 1959[21] *Harvard Law Review*—one by Henry M. Hart[22] and one by Herbert Wechsler.[23] Today these responses to the dilemma posed by *Brown* are misread in certain quarters, by anachronistically applying to them terminology developed in the heady constitutional climate of the 1980s—terms like "extratextualist" or "noninterpretivist." In fact, all three scholars were attempting to develop criteria to be followed by the courts in their job as interpreters of the constitutional text.

As guides for "constitutional interpretation," Herbert Wechsler suggested following "the text of the Constitution when its words may be decisive," and giving weight to "history" and "precedent" as well. He argued at length that the assessing of the relative role of these three elements in the interpretive task is to be done by means of reasoned principles. To deny, he insisted, that there are proper criteria to guide the Court in its interpretive task would be to render the Court "a naked power organ" rather than a "court of law."[24]

Hart cited Wechsler approvingly.[25] And when he described the Supreme Court as "destined to be the voice of reason, charged with the creative function of discerning afresh and of articulating and developing impersonal and durable principles . . . ," Hart made clear that he was talking about principles for interpreting the law. The rest of his sentence reads thus: ". . . principles of constitutional law, and impersonal and durable principles for the interpretation of statutes and the resolution of difficult issues of decisional law."[26]

And Bickel wrote of the Court that, in acting on "its power *to construe and apply the Constitution*," it must ever be mindful of constitutional text, history, and precedent as "sources of inspiration"—if not the "wellspring" of judgment—but that the Court must also find its reasoned principles in "the evolving morality of our tradition" and must prudently refrain from taking cases when the application of firm, reasoned principles to them would be politically unwise.[27]

Another leading work of this period, by Charles L. Black—while not denying any of the guidelines of text, precedent, history, societal moral tradition, or reasoned principle—added an argument for the wisdom and propriety of finding guidance in the plan embedded in the overall structure of government. But, again, he proffered this suggestion in order to guide the courts in interpreting "the great vague words of the Constitution."[28]

Thus, the battle among critics of the Court in the post-*Brown* decade[29] took place over the terrain of whether the Court was following the proper guidelines in doing its job of interpreting the more malleable phrases of the Constitution—those phrases like "due process" and "equal protection" that had been, as it were, *intended* by the framers to take on *unintended* meaning as society evolved. Those parts of the constitutional text were intended by the framers to evolve and grow in meaning as society developed, and to grow in ways that simply could not be foreseen, or in any literal sense planned on, in advance.

(The open and approving acknowledgment by constitutional scholars

that the Supreme Court sometimes defies the conscious, specific intent
of the authors of the law that the Court purports to be interpreting
stimulated, as well, a wave of secondary skirmishes over the question
of how active the Court ought to be in affecting public policy. This
issue—the "activism" versus "restraint" controversy—although important, is secondary in the sense that it addresses not what the Court
ought to be doing but when, or how often, the Court ought to do it. It
is, for that reason, not a concern of this book.)[30]

Phase Two of the Crisis: *Griswold* and Its Aftermath

The Court itself removed the main battlefield to a new plateau in 1965.
In *Griswold v. Connecticut*[31] the Supreme Court reasserted the long-
discredited doctrine of "substantive due process" in order to protect
a right nowhere mentioned in the Constitution—one the justices called
"marital privacy," which meant at the time a right for married people
to be free of governmental interference into their decision whether to
use birth control devices. In the opinions for *Griswold*, no member of
the majority except Justice John M. Harlan openly admitted that the
doctrine of substantive due process was being resurrected;[32] but concurrences by Justices Byron White and Arthur Goldberg can be read
as implicitly saying as much, and the dissents so characterized the
decision.[33] Later, in 1973, Justice Potter Stewart—who had switched
from dissent to concurrence[34]—as well as most of the original *Griswold*
majority[35] acknowledged that the doctrine of substantive due process
to support unmentioned constitutional rights had been readmitted to
U.S. constitutional law.

This doctrine had been discredited on a variety of grounds, but the
criticism of interest here would go as follows: Substantive due process
reads the due process clause of the Fourteenth and Fifth Amendments
as licensing U.S. judges to decide (for and by themselves) what rights
are fundamental in the United States. If *they* believe certain rights to
be of fundamental importance in American society (i.e., in the good
society), then—even if the Constitution neither mentions them nor
alludes to them—the courts may so announce.[36]

Once they have pronounced a particular right "fundamental"—such
as the right to use contraception,[37] or the right to be free from
government interference in "decisions so fundamentally affecting the
person as the decision whether to bear or beget a child"[38]—the
electorally responsive branches of government may not, absent very

compelling exigency, abridge it. So-called substantive due process turns the justices from interpreters of a legal text (albeit an opaque, amorphous, plastic one) into Grand Prohibitors of legislation[39] who may prohibit any law that strikes them as a very bad one on the grounds that the particular freedom invaded by this law is fundamental in American society. Once so prohibited, the law will continue to stay prohibited (short of a judicial overruling) as long as at least one-third plus one of the membership of either house of Congress also dislikes the law, or at least one legislative house in each of 13 of the 50 states does. In other words, it is highly impracticable for the people of the United States, if they disagree with the Court on the fundamentalness of any particular aspect of freedom, to override the Court through constitutional amendment. Through substantive due process the Court can directly legislate rights. The justices do not have to derive them from any expression of the sovereign will. So the distinction put forth in the original political question doctrine disappears; and Americans wind up, on various topics, ruled by nine persons appointed for life who are more or less immune to the influence of majority sentiment.

This reclaiming of judicial power via the resurrection of substantive due process thus radicalized the tension that had always existed between judicial review and democracy. Constitutionalism itself expresses a desire by the people (embodied in the hypermajority needed for constitutional ratification and amendment) to restrain themselves (in the form of future legislative majorities) by basic principles deemed worthy of enduring until a new hypermajority wills a change.[40] Constitutionalism could, in theory, be maintained by having popularly elected officials enforce on themselves the enduring principles (and such a system would be more democratic, in the sense of majoritarian), but the principles are more likely to operate as effective restraints on popularly responsive officials if they are enforced by an aloof, disinterested body. To the extent that there are a range of legitimate interpretations of those enduring principles and to the extent that there may be a distance between the defensible interpretation by the elected branches and the defensible interpretation superimposed by the judiciary, there exists an inevitable tension between judicial review and democracy. But still, that degree of tension is arguably a worthy price for an effectively constitutional democracy.

What the doctrine of substantive due process does is to lift the judges out of this picture—where they act as agents within a process of self-restraint by the people—and put them into the new role of independent restrainers of the people. In place of the people's appointing the justices to enforce rules adopted by the people, the due process clause is turned into a license from the people that says to the justices: "Restrain us when you deem it necessary."

These implications were apparent in 1965, but not very many Americans cared to oppose the idea that persons who wanted to use contraceptive devices should be allowed to; so *Griswold v. Connecticut* went more or less unnoticed.[41] After 1973, however, when *Roe v. Wade*[42] extended the Court's logic about a right to contraception and struck down the criminal abortion statutes of all but a handful of the states, a kind of pandemonium broke loose in judicial scholarship. No longer was the Court legislating at the margins against curious, outdated, and nationally unpopular state laws; now it was legislating in bold and broad strokes, dramatically shaping the life of the nation. And it was doing so in its Grand Prohibitor mode, with no apparent embarrassment at the idea that it needed no referent in the constitutional text for its assertion that there is a fundamental right to choose to have an abortion.[43] The justices were obviously doing something other than interpreting law, and they were doing it in ways that had tremendous societal impact. Scholars began to line up on either side of this new development; a searching reexamination of the role of judicial review in American society is in progress.

Current Divisions in Judicial Scholarship

A number of scholars, as might have been expected, reacted against this new development. John Ely produced the most impressive of the criticisms along traditional lines—that is, the judges were stepping outside the role of judges and this was inappropriate.[44] Raoul Berger took up the outpost at the furthest extreme opposing the new trend— insisting that the only legitimate role for judges is to follow the exact and specific intent of the framers where such intent is discoverable, so that even *Brown* for him was an illegitimate use of judicial power.[45]

But a surprisingly large number of scholars lined up in support of the new power of the Court to create unwritten rights. Thomas Grey argued that the defense of "extratextual" rights by judges has a respectable and lengthy (but relatively neglected) history in the United States, and that it is therefore thoroughly appropriate for justices to announce and enforce as law their perception of national ideals.[46]

Walter Murphy essentially seconded this argument, documenting a natural rights tradition in Supreme Court jurisprudence and defending the idea that the Court behaves appropriately when it strikes down laws that conflict with the overriding spirit (albeit not the letter or even, as it were, implied letter) of the Constitution—a spirit whose essential underlying message is "the inviolability of the human personality."[47] Suzanna Sherry, too, built on Grey's foundation, documenting judicial extratextualism in America's early decades.[48]

Michael Perry wrote a book defending the judicial enforcement of values "not constitutionalized by the framers" in cases dealing with human rights, on the grounds that such exercise of "noninterpretive" judicial review will benefit our polity and is not dangerous because it is limitable by the jurisdiction-denying power of our electorally accountable Congress.[49]

Laurence Tribe[50] and Philip Bobbitt[51] have defended the creation of unwritten rights by the Court on these three grounds: (1) that the Constitution's spirit and structure assume and imply a society under limited government; (2) that the latter concept itself is freighted with the notion that certain intimate aspects of the human personality are off limits to the government; and (3) that it is appropriate for the judges to elucidate those limits when legislators fail to acknowledge them.

And Arthur S. Miller has argued for open abandonment of the supposed pretense that the Constitution operates or has operated in any meaningful way as written law. Rather, it has been from the start a merely "empty vessel" into which judges poured their own values. Miller has urged that we drop the charade, avoid appointing lawyers to the Supreme Court (for they are victims of the "legalized brain damage" of a law school education), and appoint instead persons renowned for ethical wisdom who would act as our "Council of Elders" throwing out any laws that conflict with "the Good."[52]

These scholars are in no sense at an extremist fringe of judicial studies; they are among its most respected figures—professors at leading law schools, producers of books for Harvard, Yale, and Oxford Press. The bandwagon of noninterpretive, or extratextual, judicial review seems to be displaying unstoppable momentum.[53]

Indeed, even as he wrote a masterful book (*Democracy and Distrust*) attempting to constrain it, John Ely provided (or acknowledged) very important ammunition for the noninterpretivist argument. According to Ely, the text of the Constitution itself undercuts the argument that judges ought to stick to interpreting the text of the legal document and abjure the noninterpretive activity of creating unwritten rights. For the text itself, Ely argued, mandates extratextual discovery (or creation) of rights. The textual passages that do this—that acknowledge an unspecified body of substantive rights all government officials, including judges, are expected to honor—are, according to Ely, the Ninth Amendment and the privileges or immunities clause of the Fourteenth Amendment.

> *Ninth Amendment.* The enumeration in the Constitution, of certain rights, shall not be construed to deny or disparage others retained by the people.
> *Fourteenth Amendment (in Sec. 1).* No state shall make or enforce any law which shall abridge the privileges or immunities of citizens of the United States.

I find Ely's discussion of the Ninth Amendment quite unconvincing, since the most direct reading of the language and history of the amendment seem to support the traditional view that it functions merely as a warning—supplemental to the Tenth Amendment—not to read the existence of a Bill of Rights as a derogation of the idea that the federal government is one of enumerated rather than plenary powers.[54] The Ninth Amendment is most easily understood as a response to the warnings expressed by people like Alexander Hamilton, James Wilson, and James Madison that an explicit listing of rights (if it contained no such disclaimer) would imply a "negative pregnant"— the idea that all not here forbidden to government is permitted—thus undermining the principle that the federal government is to be limited to its enumerated powers.[55] (Incidentally, as an argument against adding a bill of rights this argument was unpersuasive, for the Constitution already contained a listing of rights, particularly in Art. I, Secs. 9 and 10. That is, even without a new bill of rights, the Ninth Amendment was already needed if these warnings were to be addressed.) In any case, I argue below that Ely does not need a Ninth Amendment argument in his effort to persuade readers that the Constitution contains a textual arrow pointing toward extratextual rights. However, since other scholars have by now followed Ely's lead in building defenses for extratextualism on the Ninth Amendment, I shall also address more fully the meaning of that amendment; but I reserve that discussion for the end of this chapter, where it is more germane.

As to the Fourteenth Amendment, on the other hand, there seems to be no reasonable denying (the *Slaughterhouse Cases*[56] to the contrary notwithstanding) that the language of the privileges or immunities clause does create a constitutional shield around whatever are the substantive fundamental rights of U.S. citizenship, and it thus protects those rights from assault by state government.[57] If it is the Supreme Court's job to interpret the legal text—including this clause—then it would indeed seem that the people of the United States in 1868 authorized the Supreme Court[58] to identify those rights fundamental enough to rank as "privileges or immunities of citizens of the United States." Thus, the argument here seems to have moved in a circle: Textualism appears to point to extratextualism. Or, to put it another way, perhaps the privileges or immunities clause of the Fourteenth Amendment did away with the legal question/political question distinction for cases involving state governments (the government level where the vast majority of controversial decisions arise). Or, to put it Ely's way, to "interpret" this Fourteenth Amendment clause is to accept the responsibility of interfering with the state government's political discretion, on behalf of unwritten and unimplied-by-the-text (i.e., "noninterpretive") rights.

There are some scholars who try to avoid this dilemma by following Raoul Berger in assigning to the privileges or immunities clause a meaning so narrow that it merely duplicates the due process and equal protection clauses of the same amendment.[59] That reading, however, certainly does not come from the words. Nor does it follow the meaning assigned in the earliest case (1873) interpreting the clause.[60] And it is a meaning disfavored by at least two common guides to constitutional construction:

1. If possible, words of the Constitution ought to be assumed to have a meaning, a raison d'être.

2. Any deliberate choice by the framers (including a choice for open-ended as against precise and narrow language) ought not to be ignored.

This reflection on the Fourteenth Amendment privileges or immunities clause produces the conclusion that the interpretivist versus non-interpretivist (or textualist versus extratextualist) distinction per se is not really a tenable basis on which to condemn the Court's unwritten fundamental-rights jurisprudence. Even though the phrase "substantive due process" may indeed be an oxymoron, nonetheless what the Court purports to do under the banner of substantive due process (aided or not by the Ninth Amendment) it could reasonably claim it was entitled to do under a not particularly strained interpretation of the privileges or immunities clause.

For this reason, Ely abandons—or transcends—the interpretivist/ noninterpretivist dispute and sets about locating appropriate constraints on the power of the judiciary. His book argues essentially that it is appropriate for the Supreme Court to assert unwritten fundamental rights only when those rights enhance that representative, democratic political process which the written text of the Constitution surely aims at establishing. To put it another way, he defends one particular judicial-power-constraining reading of the text.

This chapter will present an alternative judicial-power-constraining reading of that text. It must first be conceded that if one looks at the Constitution merely as a *text* one would not know how to weigh the force of the words of the privileges or immunities clause—which seems to tell judges to make policy—against the force of those parts of the text that seem to put policymaking power into the hands of electoral majorities. But the U.S. Constitution is more than a group of words; it is not just any text. It establishes a certain kind of political regime, and its import as a regime-founding document can be fully grasped only with attentiveness to its underlying political theory. Ely understands this need but identifies the primary theme of the regime as enhancing democratic representation. This chapter does not deny the centrality of the representative process in the American regime, but it argues that the impetus for seeking textual constraints on judicial power can be more successfully grounded in the tripartite division of powers found in the structure of the Constitution. In separating into two branches "legislative power" and "judicial power" and in its delineation of differing selection processes and respective subpowers for each branch, the Constitution is expressing a certain understanding of the proper role for judges within the American polity. Within that role, judicial power is meant to be constrained expressions of the popular will.

In Defense of (Yet Another) New Typology

The task here is not to elaborate or critique Ely's argument. It is rather to suggest that the goal of constraining judicial power by some expression of the sovereign popular will[61] is a worthy goal. It has roots as deep as the political question versus legal question doctrine; it is a goal that goes further than the term "textualist" toward explaining the much-discussed jurisprudence of Justice Hugo Black; and it is a goal that deserves attention because policy-setting power in the hands of life-tenured judges really is somewhat at odds with the structure of government set forth in the U.S. Constitution. I am suggesting here a reconceptualization of judicial scholarship that would refocus analysis away from the textualist/extratextualist dichotomy and would become attentive to the degree of constraint that particular jurisprudential theories impose on judicial power. This is not to be equated to the old judicial activism versus self-restraint conception, for that was concerned with self-restraining in regard simply to *degree* of judicial impact on public policy. What I am arguing is that, in selecting among possible interpretations of a given, opaque piece of the constitutional text, judges should look for ways in which principles contained within the rest of the text or in the text as a whole can guide their discretion, thereby constraining their power. This approach might be thought of as a text-guided interpretivism or, if it were not so awkward, a textualist textualism.

Justice Black, for instance, was no self-restraintist; he was happy for Court decisions to have an enormous influence on public policy. But he wanted judicial flexibility constrained by pinning the meaning of the privileges or immunities and due process clauses to the words adopted by the people in the Bill of Rights.[62] He argued that the formulations endorsed by justices like Felix Frankfurter and Benjamin Cardozo—reading the text of the Fourteenth Amendment as authorizing judges to decide which procedural rights for accused criminals were "implicit in the concept of ordered liberty"[63] or were required by "immutable principles of justice"[64] were faulty because they implied "that this Court is endowed by the Constitution with boundless power." Black condemned this reading because it "subtly convey[ed] to courts, at the expense of legislatures, ultimate power over public policies in fields where no specific provision of the Constitution limits legislative power"; and it could "be used . . . to license this Court . . . to roam at large in the broad expanses of policy and morals and to trespass, all too freely, on the legislative domain."[65]

Although less of a constraintist than Justice Black when applying the due process clause to the question of obligatory procedures for criminal defendants, Justice Frankfurter, too, felt that some constraints on the range of judicial discretion were needed. His choice when confronted with the truly open-ended privileges or immunities clause was far more drastic than that of Justice Black (who would have constrained its reach by the Bill of Rights). Justice Frankfurter, like Justice Samuel Miller long before him,[66] when faced with the awesome degree of latitude apparently conferred by the privileges or immunities clause, chose simply to shut his eyes—that is, to see no conferral of any power, or any other meaning, in the clause.[67] On the surface, Justice Frankfurter's willingness to ignore the privileges or immunities clause looks like an abnegation of judicial power: He is saying that this clause if taken seriously gives us judges unbounded discretion to override the choices of legislative majorities, so we must instead reduce the clause to a nullity. Further reflection (the kind of reflection applied by Justice Black), however, reveals that a power in the hands of judges to throw out, on their own, a piece of the Constitution adopted by the sovereign people amounts to a far more profound usurpation of judicial power than enforcing the privileges or immunities clause would be.

A constraint-minimizer-to-constraint-maximizer scale of jurists might look suspiciously similar to one measuring the range from a "clause-bound-interpretivist"[68] to a noninterpretivist. The difference between the scales, however, is significant. Justice Frankfurter, no less than Justice Black, was an interpretivist. But the latter chose interpretations more constraining of judicial discretion, because of his views on the appropriate relation between a democratic polity and its life-tenured judges—that is, because of his political theory.

Compared to extremists of the Raoul Berger variety, Justice Black as well as Justice Frankfurter, like John Ely, would fall somewhere in the middle range on a judicial constraint scale; they were judicial discretion, as well as judicial constraint, *optimizers*. Those scholars like Raoul Berger who try to confine justices by the specific, conscious original intent of the framers would fit at the extreme, constraint-*maximizing* (or discretion-minimizing) end of the scale. And the self-proclaimed noninterpretivists, such as Thomas Grey or Arthur S. Miller would appear at the constraint-*minimizing* (or discretion-maximizing) extreme of the scale.

At this point, moreover, the degree-of-constraint scale would be useful in highlighting differences among noninterpretivists. Noninterpretivist Michael Perry builds into the judicial role some traditional nontextual constraints, such as the rule that judges' opinions ought to be rationally justified by neutral and general principles.[69] By contrast, noninterpretivist Arthur Miller rejects even these traditional judicial-role constraints, wanting total discretion for a lifetime-appointed Council of Elders to decide cases in accord with justice simply, apart from what the conventional law may or may not have previously said on the subject.[70]

The purpose here is not to introduce yet another category of jargon (constraint-maximizer, discretion-minimizer) into American jurisprudence—far from it. I argue rather that the dispute over the degree to which judges' opinions are guided by textual or nontextual considerations is to a certain degree beside the point. The critical question pertains really to the dispute over constraints on judicial power, and it is a core question of political theory: What kind of regime do Americans have and/or what kind of regime ought Americans to have? The question, then, over which judicial-constraintists and judicial-discretionists are most fundamentally divided is the very question that animated John Marshall's political question doctrine: To what degree should judges' power be hemmed in by some expression of the will of the people?

Thus, after Ely's book exposed the weaknesses of textualism per se as a constraint, certain scholars sought out constraints elsewhere. Michael Perry found some (as just described) in the traditional concept of judicial power itself, which is in a sense traceable to the text of Article III; but he also found some in the power of our elective Congress to make exceptions to federal court jurisdiction. He devoted a good deal of attention to defending the appropriateness of using this legislative power as a check on judicial power.[71]

In the same vein, a recent book by John Agresto defends additional checks by the political branches.[72] Beyond Congress's jurisdiction-limiting powers, Agresto (taking pages from the histories of Abraham Lincoln and Franklin Roosevelt) insists on the legitimacy of outright defiance by Congress of Supreme Court readings of the Constitution.[73] According to Agresto, Congress has just as much right to read the Constitution its way as the Supreme Court has to prefer its own version. Thus, it is perfectly legitimate for Congress to pass laws that directly and intentionally defy Supreme Court statements of rules of constitutional law.[74]

Lincoln came up with this theory when faced with the extreme crisis of the *Dred Scott* decision. But he limited it to those constitutional positions that had not yet taken firm root in judicial doctrine, that had not been "fully settled," that had not been "affirmed and re-affirmed through a course of years." For those rules that *had* been repeatedly reaffirmed by the Court, Lincoln, at least, felt that they should control "the general policy of the country, subject to be disturbed only by the amendments of the Constitution."[75] Agresto pointedly refrains from endorsing Lincoln's limit on the congressional power of defiance.[76]

Thus, Agresto takes on the calculated risk of loosening the bonds of supreme law (read as judicial interpretation) as a check on congressional power in order to promote a set of effective checks on judicial power. What I would describe as a somewhat dangerous unleashing of a spirit of lawlessness, he would defend as in keeping with the overall scheme of the American constitutional structure—namely, one of checked power where no one branch is trusted to go unchecked by the others.

What Can the Constitution Contribute?

At this point it may be useful to examine the structure of the Constitution, for any light that it may shed on the matter of appropriate constraints on judicial power. The Constitution does create a pretty clear hierarchy of authority. At its peak is the procedural hypermajority that counts as "the people" for Constitution-adopting, -amending, and -ratifying purposes. This group—for ratifying purposes, most commonly those people represented by two-thirds of each house of Congress and then by majorities in both houses of three-fourths of the states—is extremely difficult to mobilize. Thus a very extreme degree of gradualism was initially imposed on the process by which our fundamental law is to be reformed.

From that hypermajority comes the written rules that are to govern the lawmaking majority—those groups with adequate numbers and political energy to move policies through both houses of Congress and the executive branch. That lawmaking majority then produces the statutes and regulations that govern individual citizens. The lawmaking majority, of course, is not a simple majority; it results from varieties of ways of counting majorities: first in staggered and districted election systems, then in two separate legislative houses, and then by an overridable (by a two-house hypermajority) executive veto. Thus, further gradualism was built into the lawmaking process.

The enforcement of the Constitution—the fundamental rules of the hypermajority (the people)—on the lawmaking majority was entrusted, at least implicitly, to the federal courts. They are authorized (Art. III, Sec. 2, cl. 1) to decide cases "arising under the Constitution" and are told to treat as supreme law those federal laws that are in fact "in pursuance" of the Constitution (Art. VI, Sec. 2).

From Madison's notes on the Constitutional Convention, we know two facts about this judicial power to enforce the Constitution against the national lawmaking majority. First, although it is not spelled out in the text of the Constitution, we know that most of the framers who were vocal on the subject expected the federal courts to exercise this power.[77] Second, we know that the framers voted down (more than once) the suggestion that the Supreme Court share the president's veto power. The addition of a judicial vetoing group, which was referred to as a Council of Revision, would have changed the Constitution in two ways:

1. Judicial vetoing could have been done on *any* policy ground, not just the ground that the supreme law had been violated.

2. Judicial vetoes done in this manner would have been overridable by a two-thirds vote in Congress.

Both of these were rejected at the Constitutional Convention.[78]

The Constitution's system of checks on the Court's interpreting power gives one check to the hypermajority—constitutional amendment—and several to the lawmaking majority:

1. the power over the size of the Court;

2. the power over new appointments to the Court—shared between the president and the Senate;

3. the power of impeachment for flagrant abuses; and

4. the power to make exceptions to and regulations of the Court's jurisdiction.

These are extremely blunt instruments, as Agresto's recent book stresses, and unsuitable for altering particular unpopular Supreme Court decisions.[79] They also operate gradually, although—as Charles Black argues—not terribly gradually.[80] (Black calculated the average modern Supreme Court justice's tenure at 13.5 years—just about as long, he noted, as two terms on the Federal Trade Commission.)[81] These imprecise, unwieldy, and gradualist tools for channeling the Court's interpretive choices are all that the Constitution puts into the hands of the elective branches who represent the lawmaking majority. One reactive, direct check on the Court—the lowering of judicial salaries—is expressly forbidden (Art. III, Sec. 1). The only other check is the self-restraint meant to stem from the oath taken by "all judicial officers" (Art. VI, Sec. 3) "to support this Constitution."

It thus appears that the authors of the Constitution deliberately chose to keep from the hands of the lawmaking majority any direct, precise power to overrule the Court; to limit their checks on the judiciary to blunt, uncertain, and gradual techniques; and to have the primary constraint on the judiciary stem from its conscientious reading of the law.[82] This constitutional scheme would seem to be at odds with the view (e.g., Agresto's) that it is legitimate for Congress deliberately to flout judicial readings of the Constitution, for the Constitution seems to go some lengths to attenuate the inevitable linkage between the political force of majority will and the outcome of Court decisions. This pattern of constitutional choices, then, would seem to militate against the quest for more precise political constraints on the Court's interpretive power.

Alternatively, can the text of the Constitution be said in some manner to provide constraints on judicial power—the kind of constraints that Justice Black and John Ely sought there? Ely argues yes. His book defends the enhancing of an egalitarian, representative political process as the guideline-setting goal for judicial review, not on the grounds that this process is favored by Ely's own political theory, but rather that it is the political theory implicitly endorsed by the whole Constitution. Thus, he describes his process-oriented argument as "the ultimate interpretivism."[83]

The extratextualists can challenge Ely with the reminder that the text nonetheless includes clauses like the privileges or immunities clause that seem to license judges to roam all over the map of social policy, striking down any law that evokes in them a powerful feeling of, "But this is wrong."[84] And Ely's book appears not to have an answer for the extratextualists because it does not give an account of his own desire to find constraints in the text.[85] Yes, one can find them if one wants to constrain judicial discretion, but one can also find discretion-enhancing clauses if one sets out to look for them.

In other words, Ely's argument is essentially as follows: The Constitution sets up a representative form of government; the Supreme Court is not very tightly bound to the representative process; so let's look for ways to constrain its discretion, in order that the Court's power will be limited to enhancing the representative process. One could as easily argue a contrary view: The Constitution provides a series of checks on majoritarian, legislative power; the Supreme Court can provide such a check; so let's look for ways to enhance its discretion in order to let it do more checking. I attempt in the following discussion to show a way of choosing between these two arguments.

The answer to Ely's extratextualist critics—as to why, in the United States, one ought to look for constraints on judicial discretion—is provided in some of Justice Black's opinions. His approach to the problem is more subtle than his deceptively simple rhetoric. When Justice Black condemns his colleagues' more freewheeling reading of the due process clause, his opinions repeatedly appeal to the traditional distinction between legislative and judicial power (i.e., to the core of the old political question doctrine). He says that his opponents "appropriate for this Court a broad power which we are not authorized by the Constitution to exercise." Their version "subtly conveys to *courts, at the expense of legislatures*, ultimate power over public policies in fields where no specific provision of the Constitution limits legislative power." It might be used "to license this *Court* . . . to roam at large in the broad expanses of policy and morals, and to trespass, all too freely, on the *legislative* domain." It is one thing for "courts proceeding within clearly marked constitutional boundaries [to] seek to execute policies written into the Constitution."[86] But it is quite another matter for them to "roam at will in the limitless area of their own beliefs as to reasonableness and actually set policies, a responsibility which the Constitution entrusts to the *legislative* representatives of the people."[87]

The U.S. Constitution does, after all, vest judicial power in the Supreme Court; it vests legislative power elsewhere. (Contrast Art. I, Sec. 1 with Art. III, Sec. 1.) The framers consciously opted not to set up a Council of Revision as they called it, or a Council of Elders as Arthur Miller calls it. "Judicial power" does not necessarily mean (contra Raoul Berger) a power limited to the narrowest possible reading of the specific, conscious original intent of the lawmaker, but it does mean *a power to interpret some expression of the sovereign will.* Unless and until our Constitution is amended in a way that expressly adds to the Court's judicial power a power to declare fundamental rights out of its own will, the extratextualists' argument will remain unconvincing. The federal courts, qua *courts*, were not given a power to override legislation in defense of rights nowhere implied by the constitutional text. It is in the Constitution's division between legislative and judicial power that one can locate the obligation to seek constraints on judicial discretion—constraints that must be found in some textual expression, implicit or explicit, of the popular will.

Some examples may clarify my meaning. There are many opaque phrases in the Constitution: due process of law, equal protection of the laws, the privileges or immunities of citizens, a republican form of government. The jurist exercising judicial restraint would be guided by the desire to displace as few politically selected rules as possible. Thus, a justice like Frankfurter would read "due process" in a judicially self-restrained, but discretion-maximizing way: The clause permits whatever procedures are reasonable. Most state-adopted procedures would therefore be upheld, but the judge who becomes nauseated by such egregious measures as coercive police-mandated stomach pumping can declare them unreasonable.[88] Similarly, the self-restraintist might invoke what I would view as a distorted version (albeit an old one) of the political question doctrine and declare certain clauses of the Constitution—like "republican form of government"—judicially unenforceable.[89]

The constraintist, on the other hand, would look to the constitutional text itself for the suggested bounds of such concepts as "privileges or immunities of citizens" or "due process of law" or "a republican form of government." Tying due process to the criminal procedure outlined in the Bill of Rights might be one example; finding First Amendment liberties to be part of the privileges of citizenship might be another. The constraintist, when faced with state legislative apportionment questions (instead of ducking them as self-restraintists have wanted to do), might try to be guided by Section 2 of the Fourteenth Amendment (supplemented by the Fifteenth and the Nineteenth) instead of ignoring it as the Court did in 1964.[90]

Equal protection is harder to elaborate in constraintist terms. One constraintist route is that of Justice William Rehnquist, who takes his guidance from the well-known historic background of the Fourteenth Amendment and would consequently limit the clause to banning racial discrimination. Other constraintists might find that too broad or too narrow a reading. They might read in the history of the same text (e.g., the contemporaneous Freedmen's Bureau activities) a concern to ban only *invidious* racial discrimination—racial discrimination against outgroups.[91] Or they may read in the textual history (specifically the choice to employ broad language and to omit mentioning race or slavery) a broader concern about invidious prejudice against "discrete and insular minorities," or prejudice against relatively powerless groups whose distinctive traits are both accidents of birth and unrelated to the primary goal of the legislation (e.g., statutes barring women from practicing law).[92]

Finally, the constraintist must address this problem: The wording of the Ninth Amendment (as also discussed earlier in this chapter) appears at first blush to present an embarrassment to the constitutional theory of judicial constraint. For that amendment would point construers of the Constitution specifically *beyond* the enumeration of rights "in the Constitution" in order to locate those "others retained by the people." One can obey this textual command, however, without adding nonjudicial ammunition to the power of federal judges.

The command of the Ninth Amendment—like the announcement in its structural partner, the Tenth—can be made sense of only with a look to history. In the historical context of the Ninth Amendment, the negative pregnant was understood to be an authoritative rule of construction. Thus, many Federalists argued against a Bill of Rights for fear that any express list of rights carried the implication that all other rights were thereby abolished (see note 55 for this chapter). The question must be addressed, however, *which* rights the authors and ratifiers understood themselves to be securing against implied abolition or "disparagement." That answer, too, comes from the historical origins of the amendment.

The history of the Ninth Amendment indicates specifically that the rights on behalf of which the amendment was put forth were those rights expressly "retained by the people" in state constitutions. George Mason first proposed a Bill of Rights in the final week of the Constitutional Convention, and was met with Roger Sherman's reply: "The State Declarations of Rights are not repealed by this Constitution; and being in force are sufficient." To this Mason countered, "The Laws of the U.S. are to be paramount to State Bills of Rights."[93] Mason's concern makes considerable sense in light of the supremacy clause (Art. VI, cl. 2), the list of rights in Article I, Sections 9 and 10 (and in occasional other places in the unamended document), and the rule of the negative pregnant. The supremacy clause precluded the possibility that the state bills of rights could check federal power. Moreover, the negative pregnant rule (in the absence of a Ninth Amendment) would not only cause the short and inadequate list of rights in Article I, Section 9 (and in the rest of the unamended document)[94] to be the only rights safeguarded against federal power, but also would cause the short and inadequate list of rights against *state* power in Article I, Section 10 (via the supremacy clause) to wipe out existing *state* constitutional safeguards against abuses of state power. Thus, the Ninth Amendment was needed to protect against the otherwise logical inference that rights previously secured against state governmental power were now to be "denied." With the Ninth Amendment in place, judges in the states could continue on the basis of textually secured higher law rights to exercise properly *judicial* review, as understood within the framework of separation of powers here elaborated.[95]

Conclusion

A judiciary determined to take the constitutional text seriously as a constraint on its own discretion would not necessarily be an inactive judiciary. Nor would its decisions be mechanistically predictable in the format of a computer program. Nor would it aim to *maximize* constraint on its own discretion by following the extreme rule that judges could nullify only those laws and executive acts that conflicted with the specific, narrow, conscious intention of the Constitution's authors. Such a rule misconceives the nature of constitutions as establishing broad and adaptable principles rather than narrow policy results, and thus misconceives judges' role as enforcers of constitutions.

What a text-constrained judiciary would be, however, is one that—by optimizing the constraints on its own discretion and, within that optimal level, by choosing to be guided by text-derived norms—honored the Constitution's concern for separation of powers and for the ultimate sovereignty of the people.[96]

Notes

1. *Marbury v. Madison*, 5 U.S. (1 Cranch) 137 (1803), at 170, 166, and 177.

2. It was reiterated as early as 1814 in *Brown v. United States*, 12 U.S. (8 Cranch) 110, and explicated at considerable length in the 1838 case of *Rhode Island v. Massachusetts*, 37 U.S. (12 Peters) 657—from which Taney, who wrote the later, more well-known explication of the principle in *Luther v. Borden*, 48 U.S. (7 Howard) 1 (1849), incidentally, dissented. The justices in 1838 were united in the principle but in disagreement as to its application to the instant case.

3. The 1838 *Rhode Island* case. The issues were first set forth in the debate in dicta between Justices Iredell and Chase in *Calder v. Bull*, 3 U.S. (3 Dallas) 386 (1798). The Court announced no consensus on the political question doctrine until *Marbury*.

4. *Rhode Island*, at 736 and 737. Emphasis added. Justice Baldwin's reference to "settled principles" of jurisprudence explicitly included the well-established rules that governed courts of equity as a matter of judicial custom. He did not intend his remarks to preclude common law jurisprudence in the federal courts.

There is, as well, a second feature that can render an issue a "political question." Even if it might be "in its nature" judicially decidable, if the Constitution nonetheless commits authority over it to one of the political branches, the courts are not to decide it. That aspect of the doctrine is not a concern of this chapter.

5. See the Preamble of the Constitution.

6. The argument that voting, where such an oath is constitutionally mandated for elected officials, does amount to consent to the Constitution was frequently put forth by the Garrisonian abolitionists, who—believing the Constitution to be pro-slavery—on that score refused to vote. This argument does provide something of an answer to the deprecations by, e.g., Alexander Bickel and John Ely of the *Marbury* picture of judicial review as upholding the will of the people against actions of the people's mere agents. Cf. John Ely, *Democracy and Distrust* (hereinafter cited as DD), pp. 11–12. Alexander Bickel, *The Least Dangerous Branch* (hereinafter cited as LDB), pp. 16–17. On the Ely–Bickel side, perhaps it should be conceded that many of that majority of "the people" who vote every four years probably have not read the Constitution.

7. I added the part about implicit consent of the heirs of the framers, through voting. It is also the tale told by Alexander Hamilton in *Federalist #78*.

8. *Marbury*, at 176–79.

9. The fact that judicial interpretation of laws involves a considerable range of discretion (although not one, properly speaking, as wide as that available to lawmakers) was implicitly acknowledged as long ago as Hamilton's *Federalist #78* (well before the advent of the school of Legal Realism) in his discussion of the duty of a judge faced with "unjust and partial laws" that nonetheless are not "infractions of the Constitution." Judicial power, Hamilton argued, would be of benefit "in mitigating the severity and confining the operation of such laws."

10. *Dred Scott v. Sandford*, 60 U.S. (19 Howard) 393 (1857).

11. This crisis began with *Lochner v. New York*, 198 U.S. 45 (1905), and included critical reaction to *Adkins v. Children's Hospital*, 261 U.S. 525 (1923), and *Morehead v. New York ex rel. Tipaldo*, 298 U.S. 587 (1936).

12. *Brown v. Board of Education of Topeka*, 347 U.S. 483 (1954).

13. Lino Graglia, following Alexander Bickel, pinpoints *Brown* as the beginning of the (very activist) judicial era of our time. Lino Graglia, "In Defense of Judicial Restraint," pp. 158–60. Bickel made the point in his 1962 book, LDB, p. 244, and again in 1970 in *The Supreme Court and the Idea of Progress* (hereinafter cited as SCIP), pp. 7–8. These scholars are identifying an era of judicial behavior, while I am linking that era to an era of judicial scholarship. In my view the two coincide because the Warren and Burger Courts' era of active judicial policymaking produced a number of policies pleasing to liberal judicial scholars whose legally trained intellectual consciences nonetheless

produced discomfort at the degree to which judges were making rather than interpreting law. To cope with this dissonance these legal scholars began to spin out new theories justifying, critiquing, and/or explaining what was going on.

14. Alexander Bickel, "The Original Understanding and the Segregation Decision."

15. Cf. *Strauder v. West Virginia*, 100 U.S. 303 (1880).

16. Bickel, "Original Understanding," p. 58. Emphasis added. Raoul Berger, in his book *Government by Judiciary*, develops the same evidence, but comes to a contrary conclusion about the propriety of the Warren Court's decision.

17. Bickel, "Original Understanding," pp. 59–64.

18. The Bickelian notion that ours is a constitution of aspiration is developed at some length in three recent books. John Agresto, *The Supreme Court and Constitutional Democracy* (hereinafter cited as SCCD), pp. 52–55 and ch. 6; Sotirios Barber, *On What the Constitution Means*, pp. 33 ff.; and Gary Jacobsohn, *The Supreme Court and the Decline of Constitutional Aspiration*. The phrase "open-texture" is from Bickel, *The Morality of Consent* (hereinafter MC), pp. 29–30. See also Willard Hurst, "The Role of History," pp. 55–60.

19. "If the fourteenth amendment were a statute, a court might well [be] . . . foreclosed from applying it to segregation in public schools. The evidence of congressional purpose is as clear as such evidence is likely to be." Bickel, "Original Understanding," p. 59.

20. Bickel, LDB, and SCIP, and MC.

21. This was the year following *Cooper v. Aaron*, 358 U.S. 1 (1958), signed by all nine justices, in which the Court reaffirmed the *Brown* holding and declared itself "supreme in the exposition of the law of the Constitution." *Cooper*, at 18.

22. Henry M. Hart, "The Supreme Court—Foreword: Time Chart of the Justices."

23. Herbert Wechsler, "Toward Neutral Principles of Constitutional Law."

24. Wechsler, "Neutral Principles," pp. 6, 10, 12, 15–17.

25. Hart, "Time Chart," at p. 99 n. 34.

26. Hart, "Time Chart," at p. 99.

27. Bickel, LDB, pp. 235 ff. and also ch. 4. See also Bickel, MC, p. 25, to the effect that the Court's obligation "to give us principle," bounded by the need that it be rigorously reasoned and that the justices consider both "history and changing circumstances," originates in "the Constitution as the Framers wrote it." And more generally, Bickel, MC, pp. 25–30. Also, Bickel, SCIP, pp. 86–87, clarifies that Bickel's references to the Court's use of the method of "moral philosophy" was an effort to describe an approach to constitutional interpretation: "The justification must be that the *constitutional judgment* turns on issues of moral philosophy"—i.e., "the method of reason familiar to

the discourse of moral philosophy, and in *constitutional adjudication*, the place only for that'' (as specifically contrasted to policy preferences either of the justices or of the public). Emphasis added in both text and note.

28. Charles Black, *The People and the Court*, p. 48. (The preface, dated 1959, establishes this work as contemporaneous with the Hart and Wechsler pieces. See notes 22 and 23.)

29. Another influential work of this period was Gerald Gunther's critique of Bickel, ''The Subtle Vices of the 'Passive Virtues'—A Comment on Principle and Expediency in Constitutional Law.''

30. E.g., Black, *People and the Court*; Bickel, LDB, ch. 4; Gunther, ''Subtle Vices of the 'Passive Virtues.' '' A number of books of more recent vintage continue to address this older activism versus self-restraint debate— e.g., Jesse Choper, *Judicial Review and the National Political Process*; Stephen Halpern and Charles M. Lamb, eds., *Supreme Court Activism and Restraint*; and Michael Perry, *Morality, Politics, and Law* (hereinafter MPL), pp. 170–72, 175–79.

31. *Griswold v. Connecticut*, 381 U.S. 479 (1965).

32. Justice John M. Harlan rested his *Griswold* concurrence, at 499–502, in large part on his dissent in *Poe v. Ullman*, 367 U.S. 497 (1961), at 522, 539–55. There, at 541, Harlan argued that the due process clause of the Fourteenth Amendment embraced all of the fundamental (unwritten) rights that the Art. IV, Sec. 2 ''privileges and immunities of citizens'' clause had protected for persons who change state residency. (He offers no explanation why, within the Fourteenth Amendment, it is the due process rather than the ''privileges or immunities of citizens of the United States'' clause that gives this protection.) He specifically insisted that to limit the due process clause to procedural matters would be a foolishly ''extreme instance of sacrificing substance to form.'' *Poe*, at 549–51.

The *Griswold* concurrence of Justice Goldberg carried the support of Chief Justice Warren and Justice Brennan, at 486, and if one adds the concurrence of Justice White, at 502, one arrives at a total of five justices who at least implicitly endorsed substantive due process.

33. *Griswold*, at 507–27, Black dissenting, and at 527–31, Stewart dissenting.

34. *Roe v. Wade*, 410 U.S. 113 (1973), at 167–68, Stewart concurring. See also *Eisenstadt v. Baird*, 405 U.S. 438 (1972), where Stewart switched to the side he had opposed in *Griswold*.

35. *Roe*, at 152–53.

36. I reserve the phrase ''substantive due process'' for the creation by the Court of unwritten fundamental rights, even though one could argue that the Court had long been using that doctrine for the ''written'' rights (both express and implied) of the First Amendment. I would argue that the application of First Amendment rights against state governments is legitimate not as a matter of substantive due process, but either because these are certainly ''privileges or immunities of citizens of the United States'' (see discussion of this clause

in the next text section) or because these are rights essential to a democratic lawmaking process and thus are "due" to Americans as procedural "due process." The merger of these two arguments is a central theme in Ely, DD.

37. *Griswold*, cited in note 31.

38. *Eisenstadt*, cited in note 34.

39. Other scholars criticize the Court for pronouncements of positive rights to (rather than from) certain government actions (i.e., rights to certain entitlements). See, e.g., Agresto, SCCD, pp. 11–12; Nathan Glazer, "Towards an Imperial Judiciary"; Archibald Cox, "The New Dimensions of Constitutional Adjudication"; Donald L. Horowitz, *The Courts and Social Policy*. Cf. Stephen Halpern, "On the Imperial Judiciary and Comparative Institutional Development and Power in America." This criticism strikes me as essentially a critique of the amount of impact judges have over public policy (or a critique of "activism," as it is often called) rather than a critique of the source of judicial authority, which is the focus of this book. See above, text for note 30.

40. The idea that constitutionalism expresses a will by the majority for self-restraint appears in the work of a number of judicial scholars—e.g,, Black, *People and the Court*, pp. l05–9, 117–19, 178–82; Bickel, MC, ch. 1; Agresto, SCCD, pp. 52–55; and Laurence Tribe, *The Constitutional Structure of American Government*, pp. 9–11.

41. Besides, *Griswold* was concurred in by Justice Harlan, widely known as an opponent of "judicial activism"; and since many scholars were busying themselves with the activism versus restraint question, they did not give *Griswold* much heed. See above, text for note 30. (As should by now be clear, the concern of this book is not degree of influence over public policy by the judges, but the source of judicial authority and the degree of discretion in that authority.)

42. *Roe*, cited in note 34.

43. E.g., ibid., at 153: "The right of privacy, whether it be founded in the Fourteenth Amendment's concept of personal liberty [i.e., the due process clause] . . . , as we feel it is, or, as the District Court determined, in the Ninth Amendment's reservation of rights to the people, is broad enough to encompass a woman's decision whether or not to terminate her pregnancy."

It is worth noting in this context that not even one of the justices who currently oppose the idea that there is a constitutional right to seek an abortion wishes to abandon the doctrine that the due process clause licenses judges to decide which rights are fundamental for Americans. See *Akron v. Akron Center*, 462 U.S. 416 (1983), O'Connor with White and Rehnquist dissenting. These justices do not oppose the judicial assertion that there is a fundamental right under the Fourteenth Amendment to privacy in reproductive matters; they simply argue that state concerns for protecting fetal life should be viewed as compelling enough to override the fundamental right. *Akron*, part II of dissent, at 459–61. Thus, they would continue to protect the Court's (i.e., their own) power to declare other unwritten rights to be fundamental whenever the justices see fit.

44. John Ely, "The Wages of Crying Wolf: A Comment on *Roe v. Wade*."
45. Berger, *Government by Judiciary*.
46. Thomas Grey, "Do We Have an Unwritten Constitution?" and "Origins of the Unwritten Constitution," "The Original Understanding and the Unwritten Constitution," and "The Uses of an Unwritten Constitution."
47. Walter Murphy, "The Art of Constitutional Interpretation," pp. 130–59, especially 135–47 and 155–59.
48. Suzanna Sherry, "Founders' Unwritten Constitution."
49. Michael Perry, *The Constitution, the Courts and Human Rights* (hereinafter cited as CCHR), especially ch. 4. His more recent book, Perry, MPL, shifts in the view of what should limit judges—from congressional restraints to judicial self-restraint—but continues to endorse what he now calls "non-originalism" in defense of a roughly Dworkinian jurisprudence. Details on his more recent book appear in Chapter 1 above.
50. Laurence Tribe, *The Constitutional Protection of Individual Rights*, ch. 15 and especially p. 893.
51. Philip Bobbitt, *Constitutional Fate: Theory of the Constitution*, especially chs. 7–12.
52. Arthur S. Miller, *Toward Increased Judicial Activism: The Political Role of the Supreme Court*.
53. With the possible exception of Miller, this group that I have called extratextualists would fit the category that William Harris dubs "transcendent structuralist" in "Bonding Word and Polity," p. 41.
54. Cf. Ely, DD, pp. 34–41, with Perry's critique in CCHR, pp. 22–24.
55. James Wilson, in Jonathan Elliott, *The Debates in the Several State Conventions on the Adoption of the Federal Constitution*, vol. 2, p. 436; Alexander Hamilton, *Federalist #84*; James Madison: "My own opinion has always been in favor of a bill of rights; provided it be so framed as not to imply powers not meant to be included in the enumeration," Letter to Thomas Jefferson, October 17, 1788, in vol. 5 of *The Writings of James Madison*.
56. *The Slaughterhouse Cases*, 83 U.S. (16 Wallace) 36 (1873).
57. Perry, CCHR, pp. 23 and 61–75—following Raoul Berger—attempts the denial, but his denial ignores the deliberate choice of open-ended language for the provision and the very open-ended description of the concept of "privileges and immunities of citizenship" in the leading federal case at the time, *Corfield v. Coryell*, 6 Fed. Cases 546, no. 3230 (1823). (See further discussion of this case in Chapter 1.) Justice Harlan's classic defense of substantive due process in *Poe* anticipated Ely's privileges or immunities clause argument by quoting directly from *Corfield* to explain what "substantive due process" protects. In fact, Harlan in that dissent at least implicitly suggests most of the arguments later developed by extratextualist scholars. See *Poe*, at 539–45.
58. At least, that is, as a back-up mechanism for failures of omission by Congress; see Sec. 5 of the Fourteenth Amendment.
59. See Berger, *Government by Judiciary*; and e.g., Michael Perry, CCHR, pp. 61–62.

60. *Slaughterhouse Cases.* I disagree with the Court's reading of the clause in that decision, as well.

61. Ely finds an expression of the sovereign popular will in the structure of government established by the constitutional text and in the political process it implies.

62. *Adamson v. California*, 332 U.S. 46 (1947), Black dissenting, at 68–72.

63. *Palko v. Connecticut*, 302 U.S. 319 (1937), 325.

64. *Adamson*, at 60, Frankfurter concurring.

65. Ibid., at 75, 90, Black dissenting. Black was making a dual argument: (1) The historic intent of the framers of the Fourteenth Amendment was compatible with his, and not Frankfurter's, reading; and (2) Frankfurter's reading would have the bad institutional consequence of producing limitless judicial power. When Black's historical argument was persuasively challenged, he did not abandon his interpretation. See Charles Fairman, "Does the Fourteenth Amendment Incorporate the Bill of Rights? The Original Understanding"; *Rochin v. California*, 342 U.S. 165 (1952), at 174–77, Black concurring; and *Duncan v. Louisiana*, 391 U.S. 145 (1968), at 166, Black concurring. For further discussion of the role of history in the jurisprudence of Justice Black, see Chapter 2.

66. *Slaughterhouse Cases*, cited in note 56.

67. *Adamson*, at 61–62: "*I put to one side the Privileges or Immunities Clause* of that Amendment. *For the mischievous uses to which that clause would lend itself* if its scope were not confined to that given by . . . the *Slaughterhouse Cases*, see the deviation in *Colgate v. Harvey*, 296 U.S. 404 [1935], overruled by *Madden v. Kentucky*, 309 U.S. 83 [1940]." Emphasis added; citation omitted.

In my own opinion, the *Colgate* reasoning on the privileges or immunities clause is much more impressive than that in *Madden*. But it is probably useful to note the dissent in *Colgate*, at 445, by Justice Stone (with Brandeis and Cardozo):

> The reason for this reluctance to enlarge the scope of the [privileges or immunities] clause . . . [beyond the *Slaughterhouse Cases* view that it did no] more than duplicate the protection of . . . other provisions of the Constitution, [is that i]t would enlarge judicial control of state action and multiply restrictions upon it to an extent difficult to define, but sufficient to cause serious apprehension.

Similarly the *Slaughterhouse Cases* shied away from allowing the language of the privileges or immunities clause to carry any real meaning. Justice Miller writing for the Court explained that to take the words at face value would be to "constitute this court a perpetual censor upon all legislation of the states, on the civil rights of their own citizens, with authority to nullify such as it did not approve." *Slaughterhouse Cases*, at 409. So instead, the Court read the clause as securing only those rights created by the relation between the citizen and the federal government—rights that predated the Fourteenth Amendment

and that were already enforced by the supremacy clause (Art. VI, Sec. 2). See *Crandall v. Nevada*, 73 U.S. (6 Wallace) 35 (1868)—cited in the *Slaughterhouse Cases*, at 409—which predated the Fourteenth Amendment. See also discussion in Ely, DD, pp. 22–30 and 193–200.
68. The term is from Ely, DD, ch. 2.
69. Perry, CCHR, pp. 25–27. Later he was to add supplementary norms of judicial self-restraint. Perry, MPL, pp. 170–72, 175–79.
70. Miller, *Toward Increased Judicial Activism*.
71. Perry, CCHR, pp. 126–45.
72. Agresto, SCCD.
73. Agresto, SCCD, ch. 5. Defiance, that is, of the rules of law pronounced by the Court. Like Lincoln, Agresto would insist that the executive and legislative branches must cooperate in imposing the Court-ordered particular result on the specifically involved litigants. Besides the examples of Lincoln and Roosevelt, Agresto is also very much influenced by the judicial history of federal civil rights laws. See, e.g., Agresto, SCCD, pp. 126–27; *The Civil Rights Cases*, 109 U.S. 3 (1883); *Heart of Atlanta Motel, Inc. v. United States*, 379 U.S. 241 (1964); and *Katzenbach v. McClung*, 379 U.S. 294 (1964).
74. Agresto characterizes this not as defiance, but as a power "to force reconsideration" by the Court—a power "repeatedly to call for reexamination and reconsideration." Agresto, SCCD, pp. 126, 130. Eventually, one presumes, the Supreme Court would get to decide again on a law that Congress had repassed after it had been declared void, but, in the meantime, much mischief could be done—e.g., innocent people might spend years in jail. Agresto does not view the matter from that angle because he has in mind judicial mischief—i.e., errors of interpretation by the Supreme Court that need correcting. Still, to the degree that his advice became accepted, congressional flouting of Supreme Court reasoning would be understood as legitimate and normal day to-day behavior (rather than as a response to an extreme crisis, as it was with the *Dred Scott* decision and the Great Depression). It is very difficult to imagine that this would not undermine the general respect for law in the United States.
75. Abraham Lincoln, *Collected Works*, Speech at Springfield, June 26, 1857, in vol. 2, p. 401. Cited in Agresto, SCCD, pp. 128–29.
76. Agresto, SCCD, pp. 128–29 n.
77. Max Farrand, ed., *The Records of the Federal Convention of 1787*, vol. 1, pp. 97–98, 109, vol. 2, pp. 73, 76, 78, 93, 298–99, 376, 440. For a more guarded assessment, see Leonard Levy, "Judicial Review, History, and Democracy: An Introduction."
78. Farrand, *Records*, vol. 2, pp. 73–80, 298. Cf. Agresto, SCCD, at 134–35.
79. Agresto, SCCD, ch. 5.
80. Black, *People and the Court*, pp. 179–81.
81. Black, *People and the Court*, pp. 179–81.

82. Of course, if Congress disagreed with the Court's reading of one of its own statutes, Congress could simply rewrite the law. To the extent that the Constitution implies a power of federal judicial review, however, it seems to create a deliberate distance between the lawmaking majority and the Court, so that only the hypermajority with Constitution-amending power can act directly and precisely to undo a Court decision.

83. Ely, DD, pp. 87–102.

84. Philip Bobbitt's defense of what he calls "ethical judicial review" seems to match this description. See Bobbitt, *Constitutional Fate*, chs. 7–12.

85. Ely's earlier essay, "Wages of Crying Wolf," p. 947, did hint at an answer: *Roe* is "a very bad decision . . . because it is bad constitutional law, or rather because it is *not* constitutional law and gives almost no sense of an obligation to try to be." Emphasis in original. His later book does not really follow up on this lead.

86. *Adamson*, at 70, 75, 90, 91–92, Black dissenting. Emphasis added.

87. Ibid., at 91, Black quoting his own dissent from *Federal Power Commission v. Natural Gas Pipeline Co.*, 315 U.S. 575 (1942), at 599, 601 n. 4. Emphasis added.

88. *Rochin v. California*, 342 U.S. 165 (1952).

89. *Colegrove v. Green*, 328 U.S. 549 (1946); *Luther v. Borden*, cited in note 2.

90. See *Reynolds v. Sims*, 377 U.S. 533 (1964), at 593–94, Harlan dissenting.

91. See *Regents of the University of California v. Bakke*, 438 U.S. 265 (1978), at 390–92, 396–98, Marshall separate opinion.

92. Cf. *Craig v. Boren*, 429 U.S. 190 (1976); *Bradwell v. Illinois*, 83 U.S. (16 Wallace) 130 (1873).

93. Farrand, *Records*, vol. 2, pp. 587–88.

94. E.g., the right of trial by jury in Art. III, etc.

95. Russell L. Caplan, "History and Meaning of the Ninth Amendment," argues independently for this same reading of the Ninth Amendment. He provides there a much richer look at the historical materials, including the particularly telling early version of the Ninth and Tenth Amendments as proposed in the Pennsylvania ratifying convention:

> That Congress shall not exercise any powers whatever, but such as are expressly given to that body by the Constitution of the United States: nor shall any authority, power, or jurisdiction, be assumed or exercised by the executive or judiciary departments of the Union under color or pretence of construction or fiction; but all the rights of sovereignty, which are not by the said Constitution expressly and plainly vested in the Congress, shall be deemed to remain with, and shall be exercised by, the several states in the Union, according to their respective constitutions; and *that every reserve of the rights of individuals, made by the several constitutions of the states in the Union, to the citizens and inhabitants of each state respectively, shall remain inviolate, except so far as they are expressly and manifestly yielded or narrowed by the national Constitution.*
>
> Caplan, "History and Meaning," pp. 251–52, citing Elliot's *Debates*, vol. 2.

96. This separation of powers argument was anticipated by Thomas Grey when he launched the modern defense of extratextualism or "non-interpretivism" in 1974. He countered it by asserting that the case-by-case evolution of decision rules by judges is an "entirely *traditional judicial* task" of common law courts. And then he posed this rhetorical question: "If common law development is an appropriate judicial function, falling within the traditionally accepted judicial role, is not the functionally similar case-by-case development of constitutional norms appropriate as well?" Grey, "Do We Have?" p. 715. Grey elaborated in a footnote his belief that common law judges are applying rather than making law: "The law in question consists of the generally accepted social norms applied in the decision of the cases, norms that are . . . best seen as 'part of the law.' " "Do We Have?" p. 715 n. 48. His point is that the identification and elaboration of consensual social norms, or customary judicial norms, has traditionally been understood in the Anglo-American legal system as a legitimate part of the judge's function.

Grey then went on to acknowledge a problem: "[T]he supremacy of constitutional law over legislation, when contrasted with the formally inferior status of common law, makes a great difference." "Do We Have?" p. 715 n. 48. But he insisted that court *authority* to override legislation on the basis of unwritten higher law is a question essentially separable from the question whether applying nonstatutory law to a case is a judicial function. And then he asserted, without claiming to prove, that the framers did intend this authority for the federal courts. Here is where Grey mistook the message of the Constitution.

As W. W. Crosskey noted in the course of his extensive elaboration of the framers' understanding of the common law role of federal courts, to grant that the Art. III reference to "laws of the United States" included common law rulings does *not* entail granting that the courts' power of judicial review can make federal common law rights override federal statutory rights. W. W. Crosskey, *Politics and the Constitution in the History of the United States*, vol. 1, p. 622.

5

Judicial Review and Democratic Theory: Guardian Democracy versus Representative Democracy

As explained in the preceding chapter, public law scholarship of the past dozen years has been increasingly dominated by a school of thought known variously as "extratextualist," "noninterpretivist," "supplementers," or "fundamental rights jurisprudence."[1] The highly reputable scholars in this group differ among themselves on a variety of constitutional law doctrines, but they are unified by their guiding normative principle concerning the role of the federal judiciary in the American political system. They all agree that it is appropriate for the Supreme Court to announce as "fundamental rights" particular rights that are implied nowhere in the constitutional document (neither in a particular clause nor in the overall structure of the document), and to strike down actions by elected government officials that conflict with these "extratextual" rights.

In the viewpoint of this book, the jurisprudence of these scholars promotes the development of a political system distressingly similar to the rule "by a bevy of Platonic Guardians" once condemned by Judge Learned Hand.[2] While Chapter 4 critiqued extratextualism on the ground that it deviates from the tripartite structure of government set forth in the U.S. Constitution, Chapter 5 now turns to the political theory undergirding that structure. The purpose, then, of this chapter is to delineate in systemic terms the political theory that appears to underlie this extratextualist jurisprudence[3] and to contrast that political theory with the one that underlies the more traditional jurisprudence

125

of *Marbury v. Madison*[4] and its doctrinal progeny (termed variously "textualist," "interpretivist," "originalist," or "preservativist").[5] In other words, these two alternative constitutional theories belong respectively to alternative political theories, and each of those political theories describes a kind of political system or regime. This chapter will delineate these alternative regimes with specific concern for the normative question of the role of the people (or of their elected representatives) in the alternative theories of judicial review. Putting it most bluntly, to what degree does the theory of judicial review proffered by these opposed groups of scholars leave a place in our political system for "government by consent of the governed"?

This analysis of the contrasting political theories is prefaced by an effort to show its needfulness. Initially, the claim that judicial history legitimates unwritten-law fundamental rights jurisprudence is critically examined; next, a counterargument is presented to the effect that history per se provides inadequate legitimation; and then an argument is developed that the choice between extratextualism and textualist jurisprudence ultimately must be made on the basis of competing political theories.

The examination of competing political theories presented here yields the conclusion that the ethical norm often presented as orienting the moral compass of the fundamental rights jurists—equal respect and concern for all people—is probably heeded more in the political theory of the traditional jurisprudence of their opponents than in their own. Moreover, an examination of the history, wording, and structure of the Constitution yields the conclusion that the political system it establishes, and the political theory immanent in that system, fits more comfortably with textualist jurisprudence than with fundamental rights jurisprudence.

Unwritten Fundamental Rights and the Tradition

As indicated in earlier chapters (especially at the beginning of Chapter 3), two leading public law scholars named Thomas Grey[6] and Walter Murphy[7] several years ago produced highly influential accounts of the importance and especially the durability of an unwritten-law tradition in the exercise of American judicial review. More recently their arguments have been reaffirmed in the work of Suzanna Sherry.[8] The scholarship of this group, which tends to support the defense of unwritten rights by the contemporary Supreme Court, has been significantly refined by Gary Jacobsohn. He has demonstrated persuasively that the natural justice rules believed to be judicially enforceable by the founding generation were limited to the minimal Lockean principles of securing life, liberty, and property, and equality before the law, against arbitrary governmental action;[9] that the framers and early jurists understood these minimal principles to have been embodied in the constitutional text;[10] that there was, thus, for them no conflict between a commitment to positive constitutional law and to natural (moral or ethical) rights;[11] and that this generation understood there to be a difference between the totality of "justice" or "good public policy," on the one hand, and minimal natural rights obligations, on the other hand. Jacobsohn has done an able job of providing the doctrinal context of early judicial statements that influenced the work of Murphy and Grey.[12] His explanation has to a substantial degree repudiated the view that the natural rights commitment of the framers sanctions the jurisprudence put forth by a number of modern scholars[13] who would have the Court constitutionalize the norms of currently fashionable moral philosophy (i.e., the teachings of John Rawls, a prominent neo-Kantian).[14]

Ambiguities of History

Jacobsohn's analysis, however, cannot be sustained for the decades beyond those immediately following the founding. First, as was documented in Chapter 1, slavery cases during the antebellum period revealed all too nakedly the limits of this natural rights cum positivism jurisprudence. It was one thing for justices to stretch the constitutional text in favor of a natural right they wanted to find there, such as a right against the legislative "devesting" of property. (John Marshall stretched the contracts clause to do it in *Fletcher v. Peck*,[15] and *Dartmouth College v. Woodward*;[16] Joseph Story implied that the right was an inference from the guarantee of a republican form of government.[17]) It was quite another for justices to uphold as law what they knew to be indisputably within the sphere of even the most minimal natural rights when they also knew it to be the intent of the Constitution's framers and ratifiers to deny those rights. Even though the constitutional text was arguably unclear on the matter, when it came to slavery, Justices Story and Marshall (not to mention Roger Taney and his ilk) failed miserably to uphold the natural rights in which they confessed themselves to believe.[18]

Second, cases after the antebellum period—and Murphy concedes

an exemption for that period[19]—do confirm the Grey–Murphy thesis.
At least Murphy's cautious version is amply demonstrable: Both before
and after the slave cases, American judges frequently applied a jurisprudence of natural rights.[20] There is more to question in Grey's
stronger claim that unwritten-law jurisprudence was the dominant
mode all along:

> *Marbury* is a most *atypical* constitutional case, and an inappropriate
> paradigm for the sort of judicial review that has been important and
> controversial throughout our history, from *Dred Scott* to the *Legal Tender
> Cases* to *Lochner* to *Carter Coal* and on to *Brown v. Board of Education*,
> *Baker v. Carr*, and the Death Penalty and Abortion cases in our own
> day.[21]

The cases cited by Grey and Murphy indicate that, although Grey
overstates the typicalness of unwritten-law jurisprudence (some of
which overstatement consists of unduly narrowing the concept of
interpretivism so as to exclude from it desegregation, procedural due
process, reapportionment, and death penalty cases), one ought to
concede the point that there are in Supreme Court history ample
enough examples of vague allusions to the spirit of our free institutions
to amount to a bona-fide alternative tradition of unwritten-law jurisprudence. That tradition is not limited to a combination of the cases
scholars generally associate with *Lochner v. New York* (1905)[22] and the
sexual privacy cases,[23] although this is an impression conveyed by
constitutional law textbooks and courses. One can find numerous
examples of it in majority and minority opinions stretching from 1798
to the present.[24]

This descriptive fact, although embraced by Grey and Murphy, is a
source of some distress to scholars more inclined than they to constrain judicial power. And the latter group is not limited to those who
disapprove of the more-or-less Rawlsian moral philosophy that would
form the foundation of the unwritten law that the Court might enact if
freed from the bounds of the constitutional text and structure.[25] As
policy one might have no quibble with the general line of results the
unwritten-law scholars seem to favor and yet might nonetheless object
seriously to the political theory implied by an endorsement of unwritten-law jurisprudence. As Ronald Dworkin has argued, it is one's
political theory that determines one's view of what should bind the
judges;[26] the intent of the framers (however one defines "framers") as
to the legally determinative status of their intentions in writing partic-

ular clauses cannot decide that status for us.[27] A belief that the framers' intentions ought to be honored (or, alternatively, supplemented) cannot persuasively be grounded only in those intentions; it needs to be buttressed by a political theory.

Nonetheless, the political theory implicitly endorsed by Murphy and Grey apparently includes the premise that the framers' intent as to the role of judges ought to be honored or at least taken into account, for these scholars clearly expect their review of the historic record to lend legitimacy to this unwritten-law jurisprudence.[28] Both of them seem to claim that one can garner evidence of the framers' intent not only in judicial history, but also in the textual expression of the Ninth Amendment.[29]

History as Legitimation

While the responsible scholar must concede the Murphy–Grey thesis as to the historic *existence* of a long line of Court opinions appealing to unwritten law, it is quite another matter to jump to the conclusion that this fact *justifies* such jurisprudence. For these opinions may have been the product of inferior judges, or of weak moments in the careers of superior judges. A historic series of mistakes does not, in and of itself, prove that the mistakes were not mistakes.[30] As to the Ninth Amendment, the mere fact that it was written into the text and ratified does not tell us what the amendment meant to its framers. In order to speak to us, historic facts need to be interpreted.

The historic fact that the Ninth Amendment was put into the Constitution does not legitimate unwritten-law jurisprudence, at least not if historic understanding of that amendment is to be our guide. For the long line of unwritten-law adjudications, which Grey summarizes[31] and which Murphy amply details,[32] does not *mention* the Ninth Amendment for more than 170 years. From 1791 through 1964,[33] in all the dozens of judicial invocations of fundamental unwritten values that went on, no federal court thought to invoke the Ninth Amendment as support for that enterprise. Moreover, the antebellum period produced an extraordinarily imaginative flowering of pro-natural-rights interpretations of the Constitution from abolitionists trying to invoke the Constitution "properly read" as authorization to free the slaves.[34] None of these abolitionists (whom Robert Cover called the "utopian" constitutional theorists) was utopian enough to dream up the use to which the Ninth Amendment would be put in 1965—as a repository of all the fundamental human rights that are unabridgeable by government.[35]

Thus, a careful look at the treatment of the Ninth Amendment by people temporally close enough to know how the ratifying generation understood it reveals that even those judges and constitutional theorists with the strongest incentives to view the Ninth Amendment as a charter for unwritten-law jurisprudence did not do so.[36] Even an exhaustive survey of the Ninth Amendment by a sympathetic proponent of it writing in 1955 could uncover only 14 times in all reported state and federal cases that litigants had even thought to invoke the Ninth Amendment.[37] The first of these was not until 1908 (more than 100 years after the amendment was ratified), the second in 1925, and the rest from 1936 on. These constitutional afterthoughts were routinely ignored or rejected by the judges who heard them.[38]

What then of the judicial tradition itself? Can recourse to fundamental (unwritten) principles really be viewed as in any sense illegitimate when Supreme Court justices so frequently and over such a long course of time resorted to it? Well, Grey to the contrary notwithstanding,[39] these opinions in the unwritten-law tradition simply read—at least to the modern reader—as unconvincing, poorly crafted opinions.[40] Presumably, Murphy and Grey would reply that we react that way because we have been conditioned by our *Marbury*-oriented law courses and textbooks to view the textually grounded opinion as the only good opinion. It is also possible, we could reply to them, that the reason our textbooks skimp on the cases in the extratextual tradition is that they were poorly reasoned, unconvincing opinions. One gets the sense in reading them that the justices—lacking either the time, energy, or ability to find a convincing argument—appealed in desperation (because they desperately craved the policy result) to the "spirit" or "fundamental principles" of our institutions. *Dred Scott*,[41] *Lochner*,[42] and *Adkins*[43] are notorious in this regard. For the reader who would like a closer look at the genre, the *First Legal Tender Case* (1871)[44] seems typical enough. It was overruled within one year.[45]

Indeed, the decisions that relied on unwritten-law principles tended to get overruled[46] *unless* there was readily available a well-reasoned, textually oriented alternative basis for the decision. For example, Professor Murphy suggests that *Ex Parte Young* (1908)[47] could alternatively have been premised on the view that the Fourteenth Amendment modified the Eleventh. Similarly, the guarantee clause is available for the reapportionment decisions;[48] and the privileges or immunities clause, or Charles Black's (ultimately textual) structural argument,[49] or John Ely's due process of lawmaking argument[50] is available to sustain the "substantive due process" or "substantive equal protection" cases that protect against state abridgment of the right to vote, the right to travel, and the rights of speech, press, and freedom to and from religion. Omitted from this list is an alternative textual foundation for the desegregation decisions because I believe the Court's use of the equal protection clause there is not at all a strained interpretation.[51] (If history is any predictor—and it may not be, given the current drift of legal scholarship[52]—the prognosis is not good for the sexual privacy cases, on account of their lack of connection to "citizenship" as such.)[53]

In sum, it may well be more than just a contemporary obsession with *Marbury*'s popular-sovereignty-grounded textualism that causes our textbooks to de-emphasize this line of cases. This group of opinions may well be alien to the version of democratic theory embedded in the structure of government established by the Constitution. The American people, including judges and judicial scholars, may well have a deep enough commitment to that understanding of representative democracy to cause these precedents sooner or later to be rejected.

As a matter of historic fact, Murphy and Grey are on solid ground in drawing attention to a long series of unwritten-law opinions. But the history of what happened to these opinions belies the claim that this was a respected tradition, let alone the typical tradition.

Unwritten Fundamental Rights Jurisprudence

In any case, these articles by Murphy and Grey fail to discuss the prior question: What ought to be the status of judicial tradition, or history, in determining the canons of constitutional interpretation? If there are conflicting judicial traditions that compete for legitimacy, one needs a standard other than history itself to settle the conflict. (History can say which prevailed, but not which *ought* to have prevailed.)[54] Murphy and Grey do not explore this matter because the historic tradition they uncover supports the jurisprudence they favor. Their work, to a substantial degree, amounts to a marshalling of this support.

Contemporary Fundamental Rights Jurisprudence

There is another group of constitutional scholars—a very wide-ranging one—who do not rely on history for their arguments, but who end up in the same place (i.e., endorsing a fundamental rights jurisprudence). It would be impossible to provide a comprehensive list of these scholars,[55] for new ones seem to hit the presses every month. There are two types of them. One type takes its cue from the premise that justice is important in any decent society.[56] Judges are in a position in the United States to help society attain justice. Therefore, these scholars argue, judges should declare void any law that is not just.

Another type takes particular phrases of the Constitution or depic tions of the overall scheme of government created by the Constitution and then interprets them at such an abstract level that they become a mandate to judges to strike down any law that conflicts with justice.[57] This notion of justice is described variously as every person's right to equal concern and respect (e.g., Ronald Dworkin and Kenneth Karst[58]), respect for human dignity or for the inherent worthiness of every human being,[59] or simply a deeply felt sense of political right and wrong.[60]

The purpose of this chapter is certainly not to contest the claim that justice is good or that there is an inherent worthiness to every human being. Rather, the point here is to elaborate and critique the political theory implied by this jurisprudence.

Original Intent in Fundamental Rights Jurisprudence

First of all, fundamental rights jurisprudence seems to discount the authoritativeness of the well-known rejection (twice, in fact) at the Constitutional Convention of the proposal to add to the Supreme Court's powers those of a Council of Revision in order to empower the Court to strike down laws that may be "unjust," "unwise," or "destructive" and "yet may not be so unconstitutional as to justify the judges in refusing to give them effect."[61] The grounds for this discounting might be either that the deliberate and well-known intent of the framers no longer matters[62] or that this intent was later modified by constitutional amendments, including particularly the Ninth (e.g., Murphy) and the Fourteenth with its privileges or immunities clause (Bobbitt), equal protection clause (Karst), and due process clause (the Supreme Court in the sexual and familial privacy cases).

The latter version would maintain that the Ninth and/or Fourteenth Amendments implicitly authorized the Supreme Court to be a Council of Revision. In this approach, historic intent still counts.[63] But this chapter has already noted (in the preceding section) the contemporaneous evidence rendering dubious any claim that historically there was an understanding of the Ninth Amendment as a sweeping grant of judicial power. The Fourteenth Amendment is a much more difficult case.

Candor compels one to acknowledge that the broad sweep of the wording in Section 1 of the Fourteenth Amendment—irrespective of the conscious, specific intentions of its framers and ratifiers (assuming those were ascertainable)—tempted litigants right from the start to argue that rights fundamental to a free society (which in the United States is generally meant as a synonym for "the good society") were now protected from state abridgment. Under this section, litigants relying at first primarily on the privileges or immunities clause but later—under the Court's leadership—moving over to the due process clause and even later to the equal protection clause asserted a wide variety of unwritten rights. Some claimed a right against state-imposed monopolies (*Slaughterhouse Cases*);[64] some claimed a right of educated, taxpaying adult citizens to vote irrespective of gender (*Minor v. Happersett*);[65] some claimed a right of those qualified by training, knowledge, and character to practice law irrespective of gender (*Bradwell v. Illinois*);[66] some claimed a right against minimum-wage and maximum-hours laws (*Adkins v. Children's Hospital* and *Lochner v. New York*);[67] some claimed parental freedom in child-rearing (*Meyer v. Nebraska* and *Pierce v. Society of Sisters*);[68] some claimed a right against state-mandated vaccination (*Jacobson v. Massachusetts*);[69] and some claimed a right against state-mandated sterilization (*Buck v. Bell* and *Skinner v. Oklahoma*).[70] Not all of these litigants won. But their readings of the Fourteenth Amendment were taken seriously enough that most of these cases produce at least some division at the Supreme Court. And much of this litigation occurred within the lifetime of Fourteenth Amendment ratifiers.

Unless one restricts the words of the Constitution to the narrow, concrete, specific intentions of the framers—a position that very few scholars besides Raoul Berger[71] consistently and seriously endorse— one has to grant that the words of the text themselves establish certain broad core purposes or principles. And it seems undeniable that many well-educated, legally trained persons near the time of the ratification of the Fourteenth Amendment believed that those broad principles had constitutionalized all the rights fundamental to a free society, or at least to the traditional, Anglo-American conception of a free society (another of our parochial synonyms for "the good society"). It must be granted that this at least is one plausible reading of the text.

It is not, of course, the only plausible reading of the text. One can argue that "equal protection of the laws" creates only a principle against statutory race discrimination, or only a principle against invidious race discrimination (hurting the weaker minority), or only a principle against legal categorizations that are the product of unreasoned group prejudices. One can argue that the due process clauses reach only *procedures* with which people are executed (deprived of life), incarcerated (deprived of liberty), or fined (deprived of property). And one can argue that the privileges or immunities clause protects only rights specifically bearing on citizenship within the American form of government—that is, within a representative democracy with a written Constitution that contains an itemized Bill of Rights. These, too, are plausible readings of the text, but they are readings that constrain judicial power against legislation much more than the fundamental rights reading does.

The Political Theory of Fundamental Rights Jurisprudence

On behalf of the fundamental rights reading, one can marshal the importance of moral reasoning in any society and the justices' institutional position, which facilitates tranquil, reasoned reflection.[72] In this reading the justices speak as the voice of moral reason and are given authority to check majority impulses because the electoral majority may behave tyrannically. The people (i.e., ordinary citizens) acquiesce in this system because they know that they may, on any given day, find themselves among the victimized minority. If the Court ever gets too wild, there remains the remedy of impeachment via activation of the elected representatives of the people. For less egregious cases there remain the more gradual remedies of electoral influence over Court appointments, legislative regulation of jurisdiction, and constitutional amendment. Short of these extremes, the electoral majorities must submit to judicial will and hope for the best. In this political theory of a "good" representative democracy, distrust of electoral majorities weighs heavily. A frequent added ingredient of the theory is the claim that supposedly representative (i.e., electoral) institutions are elitist and unrepresentative anyway. While the Court is not depicted as any *more* representative, it is viewed as a useful check on those branches driven by forces more vulgar than moral reasoning, such as the crass drive for reelection.

The role of a written constitution in this system is analogous to the role of statutes in the common law system. Judges can fill in the spaces that statutes do not cover and can alter statutes while purporting to interpret them. As the legislature can then override judicially created common law, so the public through its constitution-amending procedural hypermajority can override judicially created constitutional law.

The political system just described is not a terrible system; and one might not mind living in such a regime, as long as the justices produced more-or-less palatable decisions. Moreover, in light of the elitist training and prior political experience of Supreme Court justices, such palatability is a reasonable expectation.

Nonetheless, in my view, what I have just described is not—properly speaking—the political system established by the U.S. Constitution.[73] Although a plausible case can be made that it is, a better case can be made that it is not. Why is it that justices bother with arcane and intricate legal reasoning to support their decisions? Why do they not just make announcements along the following lines?

> Our reading of clauses a, b and c of the Constitution requires that we declare void any unjust law (or any law that violates human rights, or that conflicts with human dignity). This law is unjust for the following reasons: [Here would follow elegant treatises of moral as distinguished from legal reasoning.][74]

If it is really the judges' job to function as moral guardians of the nation, why do they make such a fuss about precedent? Injustice would seem to be injustice, whether precedented or not.

If the answer to these queries proceeds along the lines of fooling the people in order to get them to accept this necessary moral guardianship, that response exhibits a thoroughgoing contempt for the notion of equal concern and respect for every human being. Thomas Grey alternatively (and more reputably) seems to be arguing that the justices should reason along these lines more often and more openly.[75] I think the justices wisely resist this suggestion, for the Constitution itself points in a different direction.

The Political Theory of Textualist Jurisprudence

There are many reasons to believe the Constitution does not endorse fundamental rights jurisprudence. First, the debates at the Constitutional Convention regarding the Council of Revision (noted above) indicate the expectation that judicial review would proceed on the basis of the Constitution as written higher law rather than on the general

unwisdom or injustice of statutes. Second, the wording of the supremacy clause (Art. VI, cl. 2), authorizing judicial review over state laws,
refers specifically only to conflict with national laws, treaties, or "this
Constitution." The wording of Article III, Section 2 giving federal
jurisdiction accords it (apart from diversity controversies) only in cases
arising under the Constitution, national laws, or national treaties. It is
highly implausible that the authors or ratifiers of these clauses expected that they were thereby empowering judges to strike down
statutes on the general grounds of injustice. Third, the original Constitution's specific list of forbidden types of laws (bills of attainder, etc.)
in Article I, Sections 9 and 10 militates against the claim that judges
were expected to throw out all unjust laws. Fourth, the public reception
of pre–1800 natural rights judicial review was markedly more hostile
than the public reception of post-*Marbury*,[76] written-law judicial review.[77] And fifth, the wording of the privileges or immunities clause of
the Fourteenth Amendment (in my judgment, the strongest textual
foundation of the ultimately weak fundamental rights position) seems
to indicate by its focus on U.S. citizenship that political rights (as
distinguished from societal traditions, human dignity, or abstract justice) delimit the content of the protected category.[78]

Some scholars still believe it matters what political system the
constitutional text established. The political theory underlying a text-
guided jurisprudence is a familiar one. It gives priority to the written
Constitution and, to some degree, to what the founding generation
understood the text to mean. It is the tale told by *Marbury* and by
Federalist #78. In it the people in their role as electors of representatives are the ultimate sovereign. They adopt the fundamental rules of
the game by consenting to a written version of those rules, so that all
people will know what they have agreed to. This consent is given, at
least in the first instance, by a specially elected body of representatives. Governing authorities are the people's deputies, assigned to
carry out the rules. If government agents violate the rules, judges
enforce them by judicial review: They declare void the rule-breaking
statutes.

It is true that all members of the government are duty bound to
enforce the rules, but members of the judiciary have a special responsibility in that regard; it is "emphatically" their "province and duty"
(as Marshall noted in *Marbury*). In this political theory the particular
responsibility of the judiciary to enforce the rules is justified by the
judges' specialized training as construers of law and also by the
institutional structure that removes them from electoral pressures. The

absence of those pressures reduces the incentives for judges to distort the rules in their own self-interest.

In this political system the values of individual autonomy and equality of respect for each human being are built into the *base* of the system via popular consent to the fundamental rules in the Constitution-amending process, rather than guarded as policy outcomes by a tiny elite removed from popular control. This system honors more fully than the other does the ultimate moral authority of the will of the people, understood as expressed through those elected representatives who operate within the constitution-amending process. Judges are bound to look to the text of the Constitution—that is, to the will of the sovereign people—for the rules that they enforce.

This picture is not so fictional as its ancient lineage may make it seem. An obvious problem with it, however, is that we have no institutional mechanism for formally gathering mass popular consent to the rules.[79] As Paul Brest poses this critique, why should the opportunity for meaningful community debate over public values be limited to 1787 and 1866—the "rare occasions of constitution revolution"?[80] As others[81] have phrased the critique, everyone who ostensibly (through constitutional ratification or amendment) consented to the clauses generally litigated has long been dead. This concern underlay Jefferson's well-known interest in holding national constitutional conventions every 20 years (an interest he seems never to have promoted in any serious way, perhaps because he was a sitting president in 1807).

There are some answers to this critique (although they are perhaps not fully satisfying). For one thing, the assertion that the ostensible voice of the people is really no more than the dead hand of the past underrates the degree of historical continuity that life in any society presupposes. To some degree the rule of law always creates bonds of a shared culture between living and dead.[82] A substantial number of the laws people live under were adopted by legislatures elected entirely by persons now deceased, but that fact does not produce a demand that all statutes be repassed annually or biennially. Popular acquiescence to laws—*as long as* it occurs within a political system that allows the majority institutionalized control over legislatures—can properly be viewed as consent to those laws.[83]

Although the United States does not hold regular constitutional conventions, it does allow people freedom to leave if they are dissatisfied with the system, and it does give the public in its role as elector of Congress, of state legislatures, and of potential constitutional conventions the opportunity to amend the Constitution. For St. George

Tucker, writing in 1803, these two institutional features were enough from which to conclude that people had "consented" to the Constitution whenever they refrained from amending it.[84]

During the three antebellum decades, the Garrisonian abolitionists emphatically proclaimed that every vote for any government office in the United States was an act of consent to the Constitution, for the Constitution (Art. VI, Sec. 3) explicitly mandates that all such officials swear an oath to support the document.[85] Obdurately opposed to the slavery compromises in the Constitution, this faction of abolitionists refrained (as a point of honor) from voting. One could, of course, argue that even today the act of voting continues to imply citizen consent to the constitutional system. And the suggestion that "the framers" might be understood to include all Americans who have refrained from attempting to amend the Constitution has even been made (perhaps not altogether seriously) in recent legal scholarship.[86]

Such suggestions fail to persuade, however, because the difficulty of amending the Constitution—its leaden bias toward the past—is notorious.[87] In other words, the voting majority may very well wish to express nonconsent to a part of the constitutional text, or to a Supreme Court interpretation of that text, but the obstacles of the amendment process force the public to live with the unpopular text or unpopular interpretation until opposition to it has not just captured majority sentiment but has become truly overwhelming (dominating two-thirds in each house of Congress and majorities in both legislative houses in three-fourths of the states).[88]

Still, these suggestions that the public does consent to the Constitution by participating in the voting system and by refraining from amending the document can be refined to make them more persuasive, by taking into account the broader *politics* of constitutional amendment. It is well known that the Supreme Court sometimes makes abrupt turns in its interpretations of particular clauses. It is not so widely recognized that two very prominent recent instances of these turns can be explained as judicial responses to constitutional amendment politics. The Supreme Court radically changed the meaning of the equal protection clause in regard to gender discrimination between the 1960s[89] and 1971.[90] This shift followed on the heels of overwhelming endorsement of the Equal Rights Amendment in the House of Representatives.[91] The Supreme Court's shift on child labor regulation in the 1930s[92] is widely attributed to judicial fear concerning FDR's Court-packing plan. That plan never got very far in Congress; but a child labor amendment to the Constitution had achieved a two-thirds vote in both houses of Congress in 1924 (with no time limit on state ratification), and FDR's election spurred a renewal of state ratification activity in the 1930s.[93] The Supreme Court did not announce its shift on child labor until 1941;[94] by that time, the impact of FDR's appointing power had produced unanimity. But the key votes were already shifted by 1937,[95] shortly after FDR's landslide made state ratification appear a more viable possibility.

In fact, it is not unreasonable to add the president's appointment power, combined with congressional power over the size of the Court, to the consent-garnering calculus of Constitution politics. The Court produces an interpretation of the Constitution. The public experiences its impact for a while and reacts. If the interpretation is intensely and widely unpopular, it is likely to become a matter of electoral debate influencing congressional and presidential elections (e.g., the Lincoln–Douglas debates concerning *Dred Scott*,[96] Nixon's campaign for a "law and order" Court, Reagan's promise to appoint "pro-life" justices), and ultimately judicial appointments. It is of course true that every presidential or senatorial election contains a multiplicity of issues and thus, even if voter awareness were higher than it is, virtually never would present a clear mandate to appoint and confirm a particular kind of judge. On the other hand, if a long series of elections produces a long series of judicial appointments—long enough to wreak a dramatic transformation in the Supreme Court's approach to a particular electorally controversial doctrine—it is hard to resist the conclusion that the voting public has expressed its will as to the meaning of the Constitution.

Still, commitment to "government by consent of the governed" has to include agreement with Abraham Lincoln's concession that once a Supreme Court decision has been "fully settled"—that is, once it has been "affirmed and re-affirmed through a course of years"[97]—it eventually does become in a practical sense part of the Constitution. For if the voters over a long course of years refrain from using constitutional politics to try to alter it, they ought to be viewed as exercising a sovereign power of choice. This assertion admittedly is a two-edged sword, for noninterpretivists can and do argue that popular acquiescence in extratextual decisions of the Supreme Court means that the public (post facto) has consented to those rules as well as to rules derived from the text. All that can really be said in reply is that human beings are fallible. The citizenry and government of the United States permitted a system of chattel slavery to endure for decades even though this system surely did run counter to principles embodied in the Fifth Amendment due process clause; to Article I, Section 10 prohibitions on titles of nobility, bills of attainder, and ex post facto laws; and to any minimally significant meaning of the "republican form of government" that was supposed to be guaranteed to the states by Article IV, Section 4. The Supreme Court sometimes does announce decisions that are contrary to constitutional principles, properly understood. The public sometimes acquiesces in them for extended periods. This chapter argued earlier that in time these decisions have generally been overturned. But there always remains the possibility that over a long course of years a judicial "amendment" to the Constitution will simply be accepted by the voting public and by its representatives as a matter of national legal custom. This is not a phenomenon that the Constitution desires, as it were. But the nature of human fallibility makes it an inevitable possibility.

A distinction here is important. The Constitution provides a formal amending process in Article V (one that the American public shows little interest in altering). This Article V procedure appears to establish a different, higher, more binding status for amendments formally adopted than for those that occur through judicial interpretation with or without public acquiescence. Long acquiescence in *Plessy v. Ferguson* (1896)[98] had a markedly less powerful hold on the Court than would have been true of a hypothetical Fourteenth Amendment clause saying, "Nothing in this amendment shall be construed to forbid legislatures from mandating separation of the races in public places." The latter would be the public voice speaking (via elected representatives) as formally, as solemnly, and as forcibly as it can; the former (long acquiescence in a particular Court reading of the Constitution) is the public speaking tentatively, provisionally, and until circumstances change. When the voting and lobbying portion of the public speaks through constitutional politics (succeeding in pushing a proposed amendment through both houses of Congress in reacting to Court decisions; continually electing presidents who plan to move Court interpretations in a certain direction), it is in a sense speaking to the Court, saying, "We read the Constitution differently. Please reconsider." If the Court refuses to reconsider, the voting public may become dissatisfied to the point that a successful amendment will result.

The distinction can be developed by a concrete example. The Court has made a number of "mistakes" in the sense of distorting the apparent meaning of the constitutional text. One such mistake was *Plessy v. Ferguson*. Another was to "incorporate" First Amendment freedoms (via a long series of decisions) into the due process clause of the Fourteenth Amendment instead of into the privileges or immunities clause of the same amendment, where such incorporation would make more textual sense. The latter mistake survived and remains part of our national legal custom. The former did not survive. *Roe v. Wade*,[99] in terms of the argument presented here, is another textual mistake; but it—or at least its legacy of a fundamental right to procreative privacy—may well survive and become part of constitutional law, just as due process clause incorporation has. If so, this would mean that the people through constitutional politics had tacitly consented to it, but such tacit consent is in principle not so binding on the Court as explicit consent (through amendment) would be.

The argument thus far has been that there is a subsystem of constitutional politics operative within the American political system. Within the variegated processes of constitutional politics the American voting public and its elected representatives in Congress, state legislatures, and potential constitutional conventions[100] provide consent (of a tacit but meaningful variety) to the American constitutional document by refraining, over the course of years, from attempting to amend that document. Constitutional politics is a rather sloppy system; its results cannot be neatly calibrated, unlike the results of a yes/no referendum on the Constitution or its parts. It has been aptly characterized in the public law literature as an ongoing dialogue between the judiciary and the branches elected by the voters.[101] Still, its amorphous, ongoing quality does not make it any less real as a set of devices for garnering the consent of the living to the U.S. Constitution. And the fact of that consent—however amorphous, fluid, and difficult of measurement— does provide a nonfictional foundation for the *Marbury* theory of textual judicial review adumbrated above.

The core difference between the role of the judge in this political system and in the system of the fundamental rights jurists is that in this system the judges are duty bound to interpret the written Constitution, not morality or up-to-date public opinion—in the words of Professor Owen Fiss, "The legal text, not the moral or social texts."[102] The judges look to the written text because it is the expressed will of the people—expressed through the tacit consent system of constitutional politics—that this text be the highest law of the nation. Justices' selection among plausible interpretations of the text—and there always is a range of choice or we would not need judges—will of course be colored by their sense of morality or justice. And it is also appropriate for them to consider the constitutional politics going on around them.

One hopes and expects that, among plausible interpretations of the text, judges will always choose the more just one.

The inscription over the entrance to the U.S. Supreme Court reads, "Equal justice under law." It does not read, "Justice from the minds of our chosen moral guardians." Those who purport to be guided by the norm of "equal respect and concern" for all people would be well advised to heed the differences of democratic theory indicated by that distinction.

Notes

1. Thomas Grey in "Do We Have an Unwritten Constitution?" and "Origins of the Unwritten Constitution" coined the first two terms, and then argued in "The Original Understanding and the Unwritten Constitution" for replacing them with the third. Paul Brest in "The Fundamental Rights Controversy: The Essential Contradictions of Normative Constitutional Scholarship" coined the fourth.

2. Learned Hand, *The Bill of Rights*, p. 73. Paul Brest in "Fundamental Rights," p. 1106, makes the telling point that the real aspiration may be to exercise such rule, since a number of the most prominent judicial scholars once clerked at the Supreme Court and may dream of attaining seats there. This, however, cannot be the whole explanation, because some of the scholarship to which I refer is produced by political scientists—i.e., nonattorneys (e.g., Murphy).

3. In fact this "fundamental rights" scholarship as Brest in "Fundamental Rights" calls it, or "natural law" scholarship as Lief Carter in *Contemporary Constitutional Lawmaking* (hereinafter cited as CCL) somewhat misleadingly calls it—although now probably the largest school of judicial criticism—is perhaps not the fastest growing one. The up-and-coming judicial scholarship seems to be that of the Critical Legal Studies (CLS) movement and their theoretical allies, who argue for the essential indeterminacy of all legal texts. The work of this group, at least as it applies to constitutional law, is treated in Chapter 6.

4. *Marbury v. Madison*, 5 U.S. (1 Cranch) 137 (1803).

5. Lief Carter coined this last term (preservativist) to describe those scholars who accord "binding authority to the text of the Constitution or the intentions of the adopters" and who believe that "the only proper constitutional decision . . . is significantly guided by one or more of these sources." Carter, CCL. Chapter 5 defends a text-oriented version of this point of view, which he labels "discredited" CCL, p. 41. The term "preservatist"—like that of "originalist," sometimes favored by Paul Brest as in "The Misconceived Quest for the Original Understanding"—lumps together textualism and inten-

tionalism into one blend. Chapter 1 explicated the important differences between these two theories. Both textualism and intentionalism typically, however, are propounded in opposition to "fundamental rights jurisprudence." For that reason, their differences fade into less significance for purposes of this chapter.

    6. Grey, "Do We Have?" and "Origins."

    7. Walter Murphy, "The Art of Constitutional Interpretation."

    8. Suzanna Sherry, "The Founders' Unwritten Constitution."

    9. Gary Jacobsohn, "E.T.: The Extra-textual in Constitutional Interpretation" (hereinafter cited as ET).

    10. These norms find expression in Art. I, Sec. 9, cls. 2, 3, 4, and 8; Art. I, Sec. 10, cl. 1; and Art. IV, Sec. 4 (guarantee clause).

    11. Gary Jacobsohn, "Hamilton, Positivism, and the Constitution."

    12. Jacobsohn, ET; and Gary Jacobsohn, "Modern Jurisprudence and the Transvaluation of Liberal Constitutionalism."

    13. E.g., Ronald Dworkin, *Taking Rights Seriously* and "The Forum of Principle" (hereinafter cited as FP); Walter Murphy, "An Ordering of Constitutional Values"; and David Richards, "Sexual Autonomy and the Constitutional Right of Privacy."

    Ronald Dworkin does not explicitly endorse unwritten-law jurisprudence. But he argues that those who do are really interpretivists who simply interpret the text as having imposed (or as presupposing) very abstract values such as justice. Dworkin, FP, p. 427. This description, of course, also fits Dworkin himself. See Jacobsohn, "Modern Jurisprudence," for detailed exposition. In other words, Dworkin collapses the difference between interpretivism and noninterpretivism and reads "constitutional text" as though it said "correct moral theory." For further details, see discussion of Dworkinism in Chapter 1.

    14. John Rawls, *A Theory of Justice.* For additional discussion of the founding generation, see Chapters 1 and 3.

    15. *Fletcher v. Peck*, 10 U.S. (6 Cranch) 87 (1810).

    16. *Dartmouth College v. Woodward*, 17 U.S. (4 Wheaton) 518 (1819).

    17. *Terrett v. Taylor*, 9 Cranch 43 (1815), at 52; and *Wilkinson v. Leland*, 2 Peters 627 (1829), at 657. See the detailed discussion of this set of Marshall–Story decisions in Chapter 1.

    18. A revealing example is Marshall's opinion in 1825 in *The Antelope Case* (in which Story concurred), 23 U.S. (10 Wheaton) 66, at 120–21.

> That [the slavery trade] is contrary to the law of nature will scarcely be denied. That every man has a natural right to the fruits of his own labor, is generally admitted; and that no other person can rightfully deprive him of those fruits and appropriate them against his will, seems to be the necessary result of this admission. But from the earliest times war has existed, and war confers rights in which all have acquiesced. . . . That which has received the assent of all, must be the law of all. Slavery, then has its origin in force; but as the world has agreed that it is a

legitimate result of force, the state of things which is thus produced by general consent, cannot be pronounced unlawful.

Marshall's belief in natural rights and his constitutional (and legal) positivism clashed; the latter won. Cf. Murphy "Art," pp. 142–43. See the more detailed discussion of the slavery cases in Chapter 1.

19. Murphy, "Art," pp. 142–43.
20. Murphy, "Art."
21. Grey, "Do We Have?" p. 709. Emphasis added.
22. *Lochner v. New York*, 198 U.S. 45 (1905).
23. *Griswold v. Connecticut*, 381 U.S. 479 (1965); *Eisenstadt v. Baird*, 405 U.S. 438 (1972); *Roe v. Wade*, 410 U.S. 113 (1973); *Planned Parenthood of Central Missouri v. Danforth*, 428 U.S. 52 (1976); *Carey v. Population Services International*, 431 U.S. 678 (1977); *Akron v. Akron Center for Reproductive Health*, 462 U.S. 416 (1983).
24. And Murphy, "Art," has done so.
25. Murphy's debt to Rawls is made explicit in Murphy, "Ordering of Constitutional Values," p. 746.
26. Dworkin, FP, pp. 478, 488–500; Ronald Dworkin, "Law as Interpretation," pp. 545–46.
27. Indeed, H. Jefferson Powell has argued persuasively that the framers' intent as to which "original intent" binds future generations focused on the meaning of the constitutional text and *not* on the conscious purposes of authors or ratifiers. See H. Jefferson Powell, "The Original Understanding of Original Intent."
28. Grey, "Do We Have?" pp. 715–16, and "Origins," pp. 847–79, but cf. his admission of the inconclusiveness of his historical argument at p. 893.
29. Grey, "Do We Have?" p. 176; Murphy, "Art," pp. 140, 154, 157. See also John Ely, *Democracy and Distrust* (hereinafter cited as DD), pp. 14 and 38.

Murphy in "Art," pp. 138, 140, 147, 154, 156, and "Ordering," p. 712, also invokes the Preamble to support this jurisprudence. He does acknowledge a fundamental indeterminacy as to the framers' intent—Murphy, "Art," p. 194, n. 142—but he cannot believe it is totally irrelevant. If it were, why would he spend so much energy digging up the past?
30. A similar error of reasoning from sheer "is" to "ought" pervades Lief Carter's tale of the Martian trying to make sense of the U.S. Supreme Court. Since every principled standard for evaluating the Court has been dishonored by the Court at one time or another—Carter, CCL, pp. 22–25—Carter concludes that no principled standard for evaluating the Court is available. He recurs instead to an emotionally grounded standard: Does the Court opinion produce in its audience a felt sense of "intersubjective zap," as a good rock concert does? If so, it is a good opinion. (He admits, at CCL, p. 8, to swiping the term "intersubjective zap" from Peter Gabel and Duncan Kennedy, "Roll Over, Beethoven.")

31. Grey, "Do We Have?" pp. 707–8.
32. Murphy, "Art."
33. The innovation occurred in *Griswold*.
34. See William Wiecek, *The Sources of Antislavery Constitutionalism in America 1760–1848*; and Robert Cover, *Justice Accused*.
35. Cover, *Justice Accused*, pp. 156–58.
36. Grey has also argued, in "Origins," that the founders understood the word "Constitution" in the Art. III and Art. VI authorizations of judicial review to include an amalgam of unwritten law consisting of tradition, common law, and natural law. For a critique of that argument as it would apply to the post-1789 period, see Chapter 3. For a critique of Grey's views of the Constitutional Convention debates, see Jacobsohn, ET, pp. 22–27, 33–34.
37. Bennett Patterson, *The Forgotten Ninth Amendment*, pp. 29–32.
38. The cases cited by Patterson were *State v. Michel*, 46 So. 430 (1908), asserting a right to vote in both Democratic and Republican party primaries; *Clay v. City of Eustis*, 7 F. 2d 141 (1925), right against annexation of new territory to prior bonded indebtedness of the city; *Alexander v. TVA*, 297 U.S. 288 (1936), right against disposition of electric power by the U.S. Government; *Johnson v. Board of Commissioners*, 75 Pac. 2d 849 (1938), right to sell 3.2-percent alcohol beer; *Tennessee Electric Power Co. v. TVA*, 306 U.S. 118 (1939), right to acquire and use property free from competition by U.S. Government; *Ex Parte Kirth*, 28 F. Supp. 258 (1939), right of asylum in the United States; *Gernatt v. Huiet*, 16 S.E. 2d 587 (1941), right to be free of a state-government unemployment compensation program; *Commonwealth & Southern v. SEC*, 134 F. 2d 747 (1943), right to be free of a U.S. Government order to alter corporate structure; *United Public Workers v. Mitchell*, 330 U.S. 75 (1947), right to participate in electoral campaign process; *Woods v. Miller*, 333 U.S. 138 (1948), power of states to regulate rent; *National Maritime Union v. Herzog*, 78 F. Supp. 146, aff'd. mem 334 U.S. 854 (1949), right to participate in collective bargaining associations irrespective of political affiliation with communists; *United States v. Painters' Local*, 79 F. Supp. 516 (1948), right to unlimited contribution to candidates and spending on electoral campaigns; *Whelchel v. Mcdonald*, 176 F. 2d 260 (1949), right of trial by jury of peers in court-martial process; *United States v. Fujimoto*, 102 F. Supp. 890 (1952), right to associate to advocate forcible overthrow of government. Patterson also cites *Youngstown Sheet and Tube v. Sawyer*, 103 F. Supp. 569 (1952), as an instance in which a district judge alluded to the Ninth Amendment in asserting that the American constitutional structure is one of enumerated and delegated powers; but this is, in fact, an instance of the traditional view of the amendment and does not support Patterson's argument that the Ninth Amendment creates a judicially enforceable set of unwritten individual rights.
39. Grey, "Do We Have?" p. 708, argues that overextended textualism is often responsible for weak arguments. For instance, he characterizes Marshall's textual argument in *Fletcher* as a "strained interpretation of the

contract clause" exhibiting "flimsiness." But cf. Wallace Mendelson, "Was Chief Justice Marshall an Activist?" for a contrary view. Grey adds that many judicial "results" would be better justified by explication of "contemporary moral and political ideals not drawn from the constitutional text." Grey, "Do We Have?" p. 706. He does not, however, even attempt to demonstrate that past opinions taking this approach were at all persuasive. Moreover, individual instances of weak textual arguments prove nothing about the legitimacy of extratextualism.

40. I am alert to the dangers in asserting that any text "simply" reads as anything, since interpretive standards vary. However, the eventual judicial fate of these decisions probably tells us something about how they measured up at least to prevailing standards of persuasiveness. Chapter 6 explores in greater detail the matter of the ascertainability of the meaning of a given legal text.

41. *Dred Scott v. Sandford*, 19 Howard 393 (1857).

42. *Lochner v. New York*, 198 U.S. 45 (1905).

43. *Adkins v. Children's Hospital*, 261 U.S. 525 (1923).

44. *Hepburn v. Griswold*, 75 U.S. (8 Wallace) 603 (1870).

45. *Knox v. Lee*, 79 U.S. (12 Wallace) 457 (1871).

46. An absolutized version of the principle of the right-to-vested-property decisions of Story and Marshall (see notes 15–17 above) was repudiated in 1834 in *Watson v. Mercer*, 33 U.S. (8 Peters) 110: "[I]t is clear that this court has no right to pronounce an act of the State Legislature void, as contrary to the Constitution of the United States, from the mere fact that it devests antecedent vested rights of property." And Marshall's *Barron v. Baltimore*, 32 U.S. (7 Peters) 243 (1833), decision (with Story concurring) seemed to concede that property value (as distinguished from the title to the property, which Marshall had characterized as an executed "contract" in *Fletcher*) was not secured against state infringement. The overruling of the economic substantive due process decisions is a well-known story. *Dred Scott*, of course, was overruled by the Thirteenth and Fourteenth Amendments. It was also flouted by Congress in 1862 with the ban on slavery in all federal territories.

47. *Ex Parte Young*, 209 U.S. 123 (1908). See Murphy, "Art."

48. Ely, DD, pp. 122–25; William Wiecek, *The Guarantee Clause of the U.S. Constitution*, ch. 9.

Also available to justify the reapportionment decisions is the neglected Sec. 2 of the Fourteenth Amendment, which mandates that states who "abridge in any way" the right to vote of adult males shall lose their representation in Congress in proportion to the numbers who suffer such abridgment. Threat of losing congressional representation would surely have provided adequate incentive to states to reapportion. (And, of course, this section would be read as having been modified by the Fifteenth, Nineteenth, and Twenty-sixth Amendments.)

49. Charles Black, *Structure and Relationship in Constitutional Law*.

50. Ely, DD.

51. Cf. Grey, "Do We Have?" p. 712; Michael Perry, *The Constitution, the Courts, and Human Rights* (hereinafter cited as CCHR), pp. 62–69; and Raoul Berger, *Government by Judiciary*. For an interpretation that agrees with mine, see, e.g., Ralph Winter, "The Growth of Judicial Power," pp. 40–41.

52. Even as it moved in the *Webster* decision toward abandoning *Roe*'s protection of abortion, the Supreme Court clung to its power to declare that procreative privacy nonetheless is a "fundamental right" (which can be abridged only where the state can demonstrate a compelling interest in abridgment). *Webster v. Reproductive Health Services*, 109 S.Ct. 3040 (1989), at 3044–46; *Roe*, cited in note 23.

53. Cf. Kenneth Karst, "Foreword: Equal Citizenship."

54. To a substantial degree the standard that Grey in "Do We Have?" seems to invoke is desirable political outcome. He suggests that without noninterpretive review we would have to throw out many cases whose results we like. As indicated above, I believe he exaggerates the point. Perry in CCHR follows Grey down this same misguided path.

55. See review of some of them in Chapter 4; and in Brest, "Fundamental Rights."

56. E.g., Arthur Miller, *Toward Increased Judicial Activism*; Perry, CCHR.

57. This school was characterized as Dworkinian in Chapter 1, but it includes a wide range of scholars besides Ronald Dworkin: E.g., Walter Murphy, "Art" and "Ordering," in his references to the Preamble, the Ninth Amendment, and the structural concept of "constitutionalism"; Philip Bobbitt, *Constitutional Fate*, in his references to the Ninth Amendment, the privileges or immunities clause, and the ethos of limited government created by the U.S. constitutional structure; or Kenneth Karst, "Foreword: Equal Citizenship," in his references to the equal protection clause.

58. Karst, "Foreword: Equal Citizenship."

59. Murphy, "Ordering."

60. Bobbitt, *Constitutional Fate*, e.g., p. 160.

61. James Wilson, speaking on July 21, from Max Farrand, ed., *The Records of the Federal Convention of 1787*, vol. 2, p. 73.

62. E.g., Miller, *Toward Increased Judicial Activism*.

63. In this reading of the Fourteenth Amendment, Congress too would have a veto over any unjust state law, by virtue of Sec. 5 of the Fourteenth Amendment. The relationship between national and state power per se is not a concern of this book.

64. *Slaughterhouse Cases*, 83 U.S. (16 Wallace) 36 (1873). The litigants used all the clauses of Sec. 1 of the Fourteenth Amendment for their argument, but the justices who agreed with them (in dissent) emphasized the privileges or immunities clause.

65. *Minor v. Happersett*, 88 U.S. (21 Wallace) 162 (1875). These litigants relied on the privileges or immunities clause.

66. *Bradwell v. Illinois*, 83 U.S. (16 Wallace) 130 (1873). The privileges or immunities clause was the basis of the claim.

67. In *Lochner*, at 53, the Court ruled that the right to be free from maximum-hours legislation is part of the "liberty of contract," which is "part of the liberty protected by [the due process clause of] the Fourteenth Amendment." The attorneys for Lochner had not pinpointed this textual locus in their brief: They had argued with a broad sweep that the maximum-hours law was "not a reasonable exercise of the police power" because it violated the Fourteenth Amendment by "impairing essential rights and principles" to an unnecessary degree. Ibid., at 48–52. By the time of *Adkins*, at 535–38, attorneys following the signposts of *Lochner* structured their successful attack on minimum-wage laws along the lines of the due process clauses. They used the due process clauses of both the Fifth and Fourteenth Amendments. Because a federal law was involved, they had to use the Fifth Amendment; but they relied also on a variety of Fourteenth Amendment precedents.

68. *Meyer v. Nebraska*, 262 U.S. 390 (1923); *Pierce v. Society of Sisters*, 268 U.S. 510 (1925). In *Meyer* the attorneys spoke in broad terms of "the rights guaranteed by the Fourteenth Amendment"; the Court granted their claim with specific reference to the protection of "liberty" in the due process clause. The attorneys in *Pierce*, at 520, emphasized that the law under challenge invaded "the exercise of fundamental rights comprehended in an essential individual liberty," against which invasion "the Fourteenth Amendment was . . . designed to protect." The Court followed its due process clause reasoning of *Meyer*, specifically relied on that precedent, and spoke in terms of unreasonable legislative invasion of the liberty and property that "the Fourteenth Amendment guarantees." *Pierce*, at 534–35.

69. *Jacobson v. Massachusetts*, 197 U.S. 11 (1905). Here the plaintiff made primarily a due process clause argument—that compulsory vaccination of adults violated liberty to an unnecessary degree—but he also invoked the Preamble, the spirit of the Constitution, the privileges or immunities clause, and the equal protection clause. Ibid., at 14–15. The Court, speaking through Justice Harlan, gave short shrift to the Preamble and spirit-of-the-document arguments—ibid., at 14–22—but devoted most of the opinion to refuting Jacobson's liberty/due process clause argument. Unlike most of the Fourteenth Amendment opinions of this period, this one—probably because of the first Justice Harlan's own preferences—did treat the privileges or immunities argument as a serious one, although it found Jacobson's claim unpersuasive. Ibid., at 37–38.

70. *Buck v. Bell*, 274 U.S. 200 (1927); *Skinner v. Oklahoma*, 316 U.S. 535 (1942). In *Buck* the attorney relied on the due process and equal protection clauses (and lost); in *Skinner* both clauses plus the Eighth Amendment were employed, but the Court majority (of seven) relied solely on the equal protection clause. Chief Justice Stone, concurring, urged the alternative foundation of the due process clause; and Justice Jackson, also concurring, wanted to rely on both of these clauses.

71. Berger, *Government by Judiciary*.

72. E.g., Brest, "Fundamental Rights," pp. 1082 and 1106; Michael Perry, *Morality, Politics, and Law: A Bicentennial Essay*, pp. 147–48.

73. The described system is, however, the political system that operates, in fact, when the Court embraces the view that the due process clause authorizes it to identify fundamental, nonprocedural rights without any textual anchor in the Constitution. Thus, this system was in operation from 1905 (*Lochner*) to 1937 (*West Coast Hotel v. Parrish*, 300 U.S. 379). It arguably was reinstituted in 1965, with *Griswold*, although Douglas's majority opinion purported (unpersuasively) to be relying on a textually implied right (of "marital privacy"). It certainly was reinstituted in 1973, with *Roe*, where the Court majority rested the right of sexual privacy frankly "in the Fourteenth Amendment's concept of personal liberty and restrictions upon state action."

74. This imaginary pronouncement is not far from what the Court produces in the sexual/familial privacy cases. E.g. Harlan's dissent in *Poe v. Ullman*, 367 U.S. 497 (1961), at 542–44 and 549–53; Powell's plurality opinion in *Moore v. City of East Cleveland, Ohio*, 431 U.S. 494 (1977). In these, the Court claims not to be discerning abstract rights or justice but to be constrained to following traditional American values—i.e., "this Nation's history and tradition." *Moore*, at 503. Still, these cases do cast the Court essentially as our moral guardian; and to the extent that they proliferate, the Court is endorsing essentially the political system I claim the Constitution does not establish.

75. Grey, "Do We Have?"

76. *Marbury*, cited in note 4.

77. See Chapter 3 for detailed elaboration of this point.

78. A caveat is in order here, because American statesmen of the late-eighteenth to mid-nineteenth centuries viewed economic rights as much more directly "political" than we of the late twentieth century tend to. Perhaps this outlook stemmed from the Lockean premise that people form governments in order to protect their property. Thus for Justice Washington, when as a circuit court judge in 1823 he was defining "the privileges and immunities of citizens of the several states" (Art. IV, Sec. 2), to participate as a citizen included participation in the public economic sphere—i.e., the right to share in "protection by the government, with the right to acquire and possess property of every kind . . . subject nevertheless to such restraints as the government may prescribe for the general good." *Corfield v. Coryell*, 6 Fed. Cases 546, no. 3230 (1823). (Washington also included the right to vote in his list of citizen privileges.) Perhaps the right of participation in the public life of the community best expresses the core of what was meant by citizenship. (See Leslie Friedman Goldstein, "Death and Transfiguration of the State Action Doctrine," for exploration of this point.) If this is a correct reading, it is difficult to infer therein a right to privacy, except for the particular instance of the right to privacy concerning one's political associations. See, e.g., *NAACP v. Alabama*, 357 U.S. 499 (1958).

79. There is another problem that has become "obvious" to the poststructuralist eyes of contemporary scholars: How does one discern the meaning of a legal text? If one cannot—if it is all up for grabs, as it were—then the notion that the Constitution has expressed anyone's will in a determinable way is hopelessly mistaken. I believe that this "problem" has answers (and that Owen Fiss, "Objectivity and Interpretation," accurately depicts as "nihilist" the assertion that this problem has no answer), but that discussion is reserved for Chapter 6.

80. Brest, "Fundamental Rights," p. 1107.

81. E.g., Ely, DD, 11.

82. James Boyd White, "Law as Language," pp. 442–43.

83. One can, of course, question whether American institutions do not too often permit well-entrenched minorities to block change that the majority prefers. This, in fact, was probably the political situation in Connecticut that gave rise to the *Poe* and *Griswold* litigations. It was not the political situation surrounding *Roe*. If minority veto, however, were the typical problem, it is not at all clear that judicial veto could very frequently provide a solution. It did, for instance, with reapportionment; but dozens of examples do not exactly flood one's consciousness. The political situation that is typified by the NRA's opposition to gun control legislation is not amenable to judicial solution.

84. St. George Tucker, ed., *Blackstone's Commentaries with Notes of Reference to the Constitution and Laws of the U.S. and of the Commonwealth of Virginia*, vol. 1, app. p. 173; vol. 2, p. 370 n. 4; vol. 2, p. 90 "Note K."

85. Sotirios Barber, *On What the Constitution Means*, pp. 45–62, 114–15, 119, 181, 211–14, provides an interesting gloss on the institutional requirement of an oath to support the Constitution. The oath can be understood as a promise to restrain one's future behavior in line with constitutional strictures. Barber argues that, whenever citizens restrain themselves in the sense of reining in unconstitutional impulses in order to promote constitutional values, such people are "reaffirming" the supremacy of the Constitution. This is an intriguing argument; but it does seem to overlook the degree to which people restrain themselves not because the law (constitutional or statutory) prohibits *x*, but rather because of the internalized belief that *x* is simply wrong.

86. J. B. White, "Law as Language," p. 418.

87. John Agresto, *The Supreme Court and Constitutional Democracy*, pp. 107–11.

88. Walter Dellinger, "The Process of Constitutional Amendment," has noted that the attention to states in the amendment process makes it possible for states containing as few as 4 percent of the population to block an amendment or for states with barely more than 40 percent of the population to ratify an amendment. This calculation poses what are essentially hypothetical problems, for the states never align in that mathematical pattern; but it does draw our attention to the nonplebiscitary character of our "representative democracy." The "people," for purposes of constitutional amendment—like

the "majority," for purposes of election of the president by the electoral college—are counted as members of state organizations. To describe elections as majoritarian and the amendment process as hypermajoritarian, although accurate in certain dimensions, does cause this piece of the picture to be overlooked.

89. *Hoyt v. Florida*, 368 U.S. 57 (1961); and *State v. Hall*, 385 U.S. 98 (1968).

90. *Reed v. Reed*, 401 U.S. 71 (1971). See also *Taylor v. Louisiana*, 419 U.S. 522 (1975). The Court was still vacillating a bit in 1971 and 1972, prior to congressional (House plus Senate) adoption of the ERA, for it handed down two decisions without opinion in which it upheld lower court permissions for sex discrimination. *Williams v. McNair*, 401 U.S. 951 (1971); and *Forbush v. Wallace*, 405 U.S. 970 (1972). But *Reed*, decided after the House voted by a better than 20–1 margin for the ERA, signaled a definite and dramatic shift against permitting gender discrimination in law—a shift that the Court retrospectively acknowledged to have taken place in its opinion in *Craig v. Boren*, 429 U.S. 190 (1976).

91. See Leslie Friedman Goldstein, "The ERA and the U.S. Supreme Court," for details.

92. Cf. *Hammer v. Dagenhart*, 247 U.S. 251 (1918); *Bailey v. Drexel Furniture*, 259 U.S. 20 (1922); and *National Labor Relations Board v. Jones and Laughlin Corp.*, 301 U.S. 1 (1937); and *United States v. Darby Lumber Co.*, 312 U.S. 100 (1941).

93. Clement Vose, *Constitutional Change*, pp. 243–52.

94. *Darby*, cited in note 92.

95. *NLRB v. Jones & Laughlin*, cited in note 92.

96. *Dred Scott*, cited in note 41.

97. Abraham Lincoln, *Collected Works*, vol. 2, p. 401.

98. *Plessy v. Ferguson*, 163 U.S. 537 (1896).

99. *Roe*, cited in note 23.

100. The only occasion on which state ratifying conventions were used for a constitutional amendment was for the anti-Prohibition Twenty-first Amendment. Dellinger, "Process of Constitutional Amendment," p. 18.

101. Alexander Bickel, *The Supreme Court and the Idea of Progress*, p. 91; and Jonathan Casper, "The Supreme Court and National Policy-making," pp. 62–63.

102. Fiss, "Objectivity and Interpretation," p. 740.

6

Indeterminacy and Constitutional Theory: A Critique of CLS and Company

Until this point, all of the material in this book has proceeded on the assumption that the members of a national community can come to a shared understanding of the meaning of its basic legal texts. If such a shared understanding were impossible, then textualism too would be impossible, for a text that had no ascertainable meaning (or an infinity of meanings, which boils down to the same thing) could not possibly serve as a guide to judicial practice. A school of legal theorists of growing influence during the 1980s has been insisting on precisely that impossibility. Some of these legal theorists—those who adhere to the Critical Legal Studies (CLS) movement—have received substantial media attention and law review space in the past few years, but espousal of the central jurisprudential thesis of the CLS school extends far beyond the confines of CLS membership.[1] This central thesis is the essential indeterminacy of law in general, and of American constitutional law in particular, and the consequent inability of law to constrain raw judicial power. Accordingly, the law's incapacity to restrain judges is understood as a phenomenon intrinsic to legal texts. It is not that there are inadequate external sanctions for the wayward judge; rather, the argument is that even the dutiful judge is in principle unconstrained by legal texts, for all legal texts and especially the constitutional text have indeterminate meanings.

This chapter puts forth a critique of four influential versions of the indeterminacy thesis—those of Mark Tushnet (a professor at Georgetown Law School and a prodigious CLS scholar); Paul Brest (now dean of Stanford Law School, not officially designated a CLSer but someone who has defended a number of favorite CLS arguments); Sanford Levinson (profesor at the University of Texas Law School and express critic of CLS,[2] but sometimes criticized by others as sharing their alleged "nihilism"); and Lief Carter (professor of political science at the University of Georgia, who has authored a book-length exploration[3] of the linkages between some of the arguments propounded within CLS and those of pragmatic philosophy, critical social theory, and recent literary theory).

The critique of the indeterminacy thesis that is proffered here is premised on the view that the text of the U.S. Constitution can, should, and usually does constrain judicial, as well as other political, power. The degree of constraint defended here fits the approach that Paul Brest has labeled "moderate textualism." By "moderate textualism" I mean that approach to constitutional interpretation which is guided first by the text of the document but which reads the text in light of the following elements:

1. the broad principles understood by the founding (or amending) generation to be embodied therein;

2. the political structure established by the text;

3. the aspects of American political and legal history that have shaped the text; and

4. the contemporary (i.e., modern) moral understanding of the principles embodied in the text.

It is a nonrigid approach, but it is nonetheless textually guided. If it is impossible for legal texts, or in particular the constitutional text, to have a determinate meaning, then textualism *could* not operate as a constraint on judicial power. Consequently this chapter attempts to answer the indeterminacy proponents' claims (as a necessary precondition for the possibility of the textualism that this book defends.)

Riddles of the Liberal Tradition

It has been fashionable of late in certain circles of legal scholarship to invoke and discuss the weakness of "liberal political theory" or "the liberal tradition," and to argue that the indeterminacy of the Constitution is grounded in the incoherence of liberal theory. This line of discussion is particularly characteristic of CLS writers, of whom the most prolific constitutional law analyst is Mark Tushnet. In at least one article[4] Paul Brest, too, attacked liberal political theory as plagued by "ambivalent, if not contradictory" tensions. Certain salient features of the liberal tradition will be examined here prior to an analysis of the scholarship of Brest and Tushnet that attacks it.

Locke's Liberalism

By everyone's account the contribution of the political thought of John Locke to the American liberal tradition has been enormous and pervasive. In Locke's influential *Second Treatise*, humans in a "state of nature" are described as free and equal, and possessing the innate and inalienable rights to life (self-preservation), liberty (the means of self-preservation), and property (one's own body and those parts of nature with which one has "mixed" one's own bodily labor). People's natural reason tells them that they have these rights, that they should not interfere with the parallel rights of others, and that the protection of rights is everyone's prerogative. When it becomes necessary to judge concrete cases, however, individuals' judgments are always warped by their self-interest, colored by their powerful, instinctive passion for self-preservation.[5] Moreover, nature produces a minority of individuals who are just plain "quarrelsome and contentious."[6] For both these reasons (the contentiousness of the few, and the bias of selfishness), the state of nature turns out to be very insecure and filled with danger.[7] Consequently, people contract with one another to form a society. They give up their natural liberty to that society in order to gain more security for the preservation of their life and property. The security that makes society preferable to the state of nature consists in three things:

> First, . . . an *established*, settled, known *law*, received and allowed by common consent to be the standard of right and wrong, and the common measure to decide all controversies. . . .
> Secondly, . . . *a known and indifferent judge*, with authority to determine all differences according to the established law. . . .
> Thirdly . . . *power* to back and support the sentence when right and to give it due *execution*.[8]

The form of the lawmaking authority (whether it be one, a select few, or the majority) is to be determined by majority rule at the moment of the formation of the social contract: The contracting that is taking place is a contract to abide by the will of the societal majority in this initial government-constituting decision. The contract itself provides security against the fears of the nonsocial state, because rights in the nonsocial state would have to be enforced by single individuals pitted against other individuals. Because all in nature are equal, the victory of the good—in Locke's terms, "the rational and industrious"[9]—is never certain, and the few contentious troublemakers can make life miserable for the rest. In society the force of numbers brings security and safety. There the rational and industrious majority of humankind can flourish because society's members have all agreed to unite their forces to form the backbone of the executive power in support of the agreed-on legislative authority. The quarrelsome and contentious are thus effectively outnumbered and overpowered. Government authority, then, in Locke's *Second Treatise* is a combination of *will* (the initial consent and then generally "tacit consent" thereafter)[10] and *force* (the force of numbers).

The notion of inalienable natural rights as an ultimate check on force figures prominently in Locke's rhetoric and retains a kind of abstract moral power, but it attains concrete impact only as majority will backed by the power of revolutionary majority force. Only if government power becomes so abusive that the people who number a majority feel threatened in their life and property will they be energized to the point of making an "appeal to Heaven"—that is, resorting to revolutionary resistance.[11] And the threat of such an appeal is the only real check on government power.[12] The implicit normative grounding of this lodging of power in majority will is Locke's apparent assumption that most people are by nature industrious and rational rather than quarrelsome and contentious. Although Locke describes all as naturally biased by selfishness and the "greater part" of humankind as "no strict observers of justice and equity," most people nonetheless are rather peaceable, more disposed to suffer even an occasional injustice than to risk life or limb in resisting governmentally secured order.[13]

For purposes of discussing the Lockean-liberal contribution to American constitutional theory, what is central is that the "settled, known law" is one the majority can recognize and in support of which it can rally its force. If the people could not agree on what the law is, they would be no better off than in the state of nature. Here the agreed-on judge takes on importance, for the agreed-on judge can obviate the inevitable disputes over *how* the settled, known law applies to particular cases. Again in Locke's theory, the effective law becomes a matter of *will* and *force*: The will of the judge settles the dispute, and the majority force backs his or her judgment. It does not matter that the judge's will, like everyone else's, is biased by selfishness;[14] what matters is that the outcome is free from uncertainty. Disputes are settled and the settlement is effective (by force of numbers). People can live in peace and security.

The debt of American liberal theory to Locke's *Second Treatise* is evident, of course, in our Declaration of Independence. After the break from England, however, American political thinkers tried in a variety of ways to cope with the potential for majority tyranny that permeates Lockean theory.[15] A variety of techniques were produced: One strand emphasized the traditional concern for republican virtue and need for moral training to keep the majority mindful of the public good;[16] another strand blended together some new and distinctively American techniques. That other strand was the liberalism of the framers.

Federalist Liberalism

This distinctively American liberal theory is sometimes called Madisonian, but it is probably more aptly characterized as an amalgam of ideas propounded by a group of influential political writers and activists during the epoch of national political transition from 1776 to 1803 (the year in which judicial power to nullify unconstitutional presidential or congressional action was announced by the Supreme Court and widely accepted by the American public). These ideas were all defended in the collection *The Federalist Papers* (of which Madison was only one of three authors) and so should perhaps be labeled Federalist liberal theory.

The new theory propounded at least three new techniques for checking or preventing majority tyranny. First, the populace is purposefully diversified and dispersed over a large and variegated territory, which fact makes less probable the formation of a stable majority coalition. Because the coalition is unstable from one issue to the next, everyone is tomorrow's potential ally, and thus all should recognize that it is expedient and prudent to avoid oppressing anyone or any group.[17]

Second, the governing elite is subdivided; each subdivision is kept responsive to a different slice of the majority—for example, the Senate to a majority represented as states, the president to the majority represented by electoral college votes, and so on. Thus, again, differing majority coalitions keep each other in check; and in addition, the personal ambitions within each segment of the governing elite are pitted against each other. This is accomplished by the system of shared powers among the three national branches, which has come to be called "checks and balances."[18]

Third and finally—and central to this chapter—a system that combined the Lockean elements of will-in-the-sense-of-consent and the certainty of a settled, known law was developed to empower judges to check both abusive power by the other governing branches and tyrannical power responsive to majority sentiment. The check on other branches was clearly compatible with Lockean theory—a small "friendly amendment—but the check on the majority was a substantial and distinctively American innovation.

As described in Madison's *Federalist #39*, judicial power to decide whether the terms of the written-down social compact are ever being violated by the governing authorities is "clearly essential" to prevent an "appeal to the sword." This idea, although quite reminiscent of Locke's *Second Treatise*, was an improvement on Locke's theory because it now allowed a check on abuses by government long before accumulation of the egregious excesses required for triggering revolutionary resistance. Judicial review provided a peaceful substitute for Lockean revolution.

By contrast, the idea that judicial review allows for a check on *majority will, itself*—to keep it in accord with the terms of the original written social compact to which each individual has in principle consented—was something new.[19] This was not an aspect of judicial review that received much attention in early discussions of the institution. Instead, influential framers such as James Iredell, James Wilson, and John Marshall[20] tended to focus on the potential of judicial review as a check on governmental abuses of power.[21] Only Alexander Hamilton detailed the benefit to be derived from judicial review as a check on majority tyranny:

> This independence of the judges is equally requisite to guard the Constitution and the rights of individuals from the effects of those ill humors, which the arts of designing men, or the influence of particular conjunctures, sometimes disseminate among the people themselves, and which, though they speedily give place to better information, and more deliberate reflection, have a tendency, in the meantime, to occasion dangerous innovations in the government, and serious oppressions of the minor party in the community. Though I trust the friends of the proposed

Constitution will never [question] . . . the right of the people to alter or abolish the established Constitution . . . yet it is not to be inferred from this principle, that the representatives of the people, whenever a momentary inclination happens to lay hold of a majority of their constituents, incompatible with the provisions in the existing Constitution, would, on that account, be justifiable in a violation of those provisions; or that courts would be under a greater obligation to connive at infractions in this shape than when they had proceeded wholly from the cabals of the representative body. Until the people have by some solemn and authoritative act, annulled or changed the established form, it is binding on themselves collectively, as well as individually; and no presumption, or even knowledge of their sentiments, can warrant their representatives in a departure from it, prior to such an act.[22]

In instances like this, "where legislative invasions of [the Constitution] had been instigated by the major voice of the community" judges "would require an uncommon portion of fortitude."[23] For that need, a judicial tenure was designed to secure judges from the pressure of majority will, so they would be free to guard these "rights of individuals" to which the people had agreed. The Lockean elements of a unified will that gives force to the "settled, known law" are present here, but a gaping hole in Locke's theory has been patched by the American Federalist innovation: Through judicial review based on a written, consented-to Constitution, even occasional tyrannical majorities can be checked.[24] The Federalist liberal innovation improves on Locke's necessary assumption that the majority consists in general of "good guys"; the founding generation by the late 1780s had experienced what they believed to be oppression at the hands of legislatures responsive to majority sentiment.[25] American Federalist theory benefited from these experiences by developing governmental mechanisms aimed at checking unjust majorities.

Assessment of Liberal Legal Theory

While the innovation of writing down and making enforceable the limits on majority power was no cure-all, it did improve liberal theory by making available a genuine, if imperfect, constraint on majority tyranny. Writing down the agreed-on rules does diminish the uncertainty people would be left with if their only guidance were the natural justice admonition: Do the right thing.

Despite the sophisticated Derridean,[26] Nietzschean,[27] Heideggerian,[28] structuralist,[29] or legal realist[30] criticisms that can be brought to bear on the preceding statement, it nonetheless iterates a truth that resonates powerfully with felt experience. If, for instance, all drivers had to take a drivers' education class before being licensed and if all roads—instead of formal speed limits—simply posted the admonition "Drive safely," certain outcomes are highly likely:

1. A much greater diversity of speeds would prevail on each particular road than under the current system.

2. Each driver would feel much less certainty about what speed was expected than is currently the case.

3. The imposition of sanctions on violators would be far less predictable and far more variegated than is currently the case.

These outcomes may not be true as a matter of sheer logic, but there seems to be something in the way language operates on human thinking and behavior patterns that does cause them.[31] In other words, the human desire for certainty and predictability that conduce to a sense of security does seem to create a preference for expressly articulated, or written-down, generalized rules (laws). This is the Lockean insight, and it is retained as a foundation in the Federalist liberal system.

However, neither the Lockean nor the Federalist version of liberal theory is a panacea. Neither claims to turn humans into superhumans, to eliminate selfishness or bias in human judgment. This is why even settled, known laws (or mere "parchment barriers," as Madison put it in *Federalist #48*) do not suffice in either scheme. Judges and executors of judgment are needed, because—however clearly articulated any given rule—human beings (biased by self-interest) always run the risk of disagreement when applying that rule to their own concrete cases. From the point of view of those disagreeing humans, the judgment of the judge appears as *will* backed up by the *force* of numbers. This remains true in both the Lockean and the Federalist schemes.[32]

In liberal theory it does not matter that people cannot ascend to a superhuman perspective to determine if the judge in a particular case is "right" according to some grand scheme of natural justice. If the judge is wrong enough and often enough, people "cannot but feel what they lie under" and will revolt.[33] Most judges, legislators, and executives are smart enough to avoid that outcome, and thus people are protected from that degree of tyranny (i.e., the degree wherein the majority feel threatened in their lives, liberties, and properties.) In sum, what liberal theory advocates is a system of government in which people feel *secure* from violent threats on their lives, liberties, or property. It does not guarantee that every judge in every decision will make the right decision, according to some idealized standard of right reason. Thus Madison, in describing the human dilemma in *Federalist #51*, was posing an enduring riddle, not purporting to solve it.

> If men were angels no government would be necessary. . . . In framing a government which is to be administered by men over men, the great difficulty lies in this: you must first enable the government to control the governed, and in the next place oblige it to control itself.

The basic operative assumption is the nonangelic character of humans—humans whose judgment is bound to be partial. That is to say, Federalist (like Lockean) liberal theory assumes that the people exercising checks on others are always doing so on the basis of imperfect, limited, all-too-human judgment.

Critics of Liberal Theory

Two of the prominent critics of liberal theory who emphasize the indeterminacy of law as its weak link are Mark Tushnet and Paul Brest. Each of them, however, rejects liberal theory by the maneuver of demanding much more perfection from judges than liberal theory ever supposed judges or anyone else could have. In other words, when Professor Tushnet or Professor Brest suggest that the constitutional text is too indeterminate to provide the kind of check on judicial power that liberal theory demands, they are vastly overestimating the certainty demanded by liberal theory or by its conception of "the rule of law." These assertions are defended below, with Professor Tushnet's arguments being treated first and then Professor Brest's, although at times their arguments overlap and at those points are treated together.

Mark Tushnet

According to Tushnet, something called "constitutional theory" attempts to provide a normative, albeit noncoercive check on raw judicial power by articulating standards for evaluating and guiding judges' pronouncements on constitutional law.[34] The theory presumably operates by the mechanism of offering judges the sociopsychological rewards and punishments of scholarly, professional, and even self approval or disapproval.[35] Tushnet believes that liberal theory, in a sense, established a need for constitutional theory once the legal realists of the 1930s convinced legal scholars that constitutional law alone provided no restraint on judicial will.[36] Since liberal theory assumes human selfishness, it assumes the need to check power exercised by mere humans. If law in itself would not restrain judges, a theory explaining how judges *should* treat law then needed to be developed. Hence, constitutional theory.

One of the constitutional theories that Tushnet takes up is precisely the idea that the text of the law *is* what should constrain judges—and when the text is too opaque, then the framers' intent concerning that text. This theory, which he calls "interpretivism," amounts to a normative rejection of the legal realists' empirical claim. In short, it says that if the judges are not acting bound by the law they are doing something wrong and should mend their ways. In other words, the core maxims of interpretivism are that judges should aspire to apply the settled, known law as distinguished from their personal policy preferences (private will), and that in constitutional law the settled, known law is the text of the constitutional document, to be elucidated (when necessary) by the intent of the people who wrote and/or ratified the textual passage in question.

Although Tushnet acknowledges in passing the idea (defended in this book) that a legal text might constrain a judge, he passes by it so quickly that one has to conclude he considers it next to impossible. Apparently persuaded by the legal realists that the idea of textual constraint is an impossible myth, he collapses interpretivism into "intentionalism" and proceeds to critique intentionalism. Intentionalism fails, he argues, for a number of reasons. First, if narrow, specific, conscious intent of the framers (à la Raoul Berger's argument) were all that could guide judicial review, then such a wide range of legislative and executive forms of tyranny would be permitted that judicial review would be close to useless.

Second, the argument defended in Chapter 1 of this book—that one should look not to specific intentions of the framers, but rather to broader principles suggested by the language of the text—is dismissed by Tushnet on several grounds. Tushnet flatly asserts that there is no historical evidence of a conscious intent by the framers that their posterity be guided by their broad legal principles rather than their narrow conceptions.[37] Tushnet's argument by assertion fails to persuade, however, because it ignores a substantial body of scholarly literature defending the contrary assertion—namely, that the most influential among the backers of the Fourteenth Amendment did intend for the equal protection clause to establish a broad principle of equal treatment that could take on new applications as American society evolved over time.[38]

Apart from the historical question, Tushnet identifies a level-of-generality problem in the suggestion that the text should be read as representing not narrow conscious policy intentions, but broad principles of law. The level-of-generality problem poses, for example, these questions: Does the principle of "equal protection of law" forbid only government action that fits one of the following descriptions? And if so, which one?

1. It transgresses rights itemized in the 1866 Civil Rights Act.

2. It singles out blacks for harmful treatment.

3. It singles out any racial group (including whites) for harmful treatment.

4. It is essentially the product of unreasoned group prejudice, unduly ignoring individual skills and aptitudes (e.g., sex discrimination).

5. It arbitrarily limits individuals' opportunities in the race for success—for instance, by structuring children's educational opportunities on the arguably arbitrary basis of the neighborhood where their parents reside?[39]

Tushnet suggests that choosing among such options, or choosing some principle that would tell us x institution in contemporary society is the functional equivalent (for constitutional purposes) of y institution in the framers' society, is perforce arbitrary. By such choices, he argues, "interpretivism reintroduces the discretion it was intended to eliminate."[40] Similarly, an effort to think oneself back into the framers' world in order to discern the true import for them of the text they adopted requires an ultimately subjective, creative hermeneutic accomplishment. Because it is creative, he says, it is discretionary and thus does not provide "the constraints on judges that liberal constitutional theory demands."[41]

Tushnet seems to assume that if the judge is allowed discretion as to either the level of generality at which to define the legal rule, or the sense to make of the legal text in a setting where a *range* of plausible meanings is available, then the judge is exercising sheerly arbitrary and legally unconstrained power. Tushnet does acknowledge that there are limits to what will be viewed as plausible readings of the constitutional text, but he sees these as the product of societally based constraints on what the judges do. (In other words, they are socialized to believe in certain values rather than others; judges are selected through a political process that favors certain attitudes over others.) To Tushnet the fact that judges share a certain consensus—for example, the belief that the U.S. Constitution does not demand socialism— is not a fact that comes from the duly adopted law. To him it is instead a product of the exercise of power by one social group (the elite who produce judges) over another (the nonelite).[42]

The essence of Tushnet's argument against textualism is thus twofold. First, he insists that the range of discretion available to a judge faced with a text as opaque as the U.S. Constitution is so complete it leaves the judge with a degree of unchecked power that is forbidden in the liberal tradition. Second, he admits that within the American community there really are limits to how the text will be interpreted. He suggests, however, that these limits do not come from the law or from the public majority who originally supported the law. Rather, they come from the intellectual hegemony of a particular dominant elite in our society. Both strands of Tushnet's arguments are flawed.

The first is flawed because it attributes utopian expectations to the liberal tradition that were never there. Tushnet hypothesizes a "liberal theory" that—to speak metaphorically—wants robots for judges, and computer programs for laws (or for legal theory). Neither Lockean nor Federalist liberal theory aspires to remove human discretion; both theories recognize that even well-intentioned humans do disagree about how rules apply to particular cases. This is why judges are needed to settle disputes. The articulated rules eliminate many potential disputes by producing law-abiding behavior;[43] but at some point an umpire is needed, and this is where the judge comes in. What the judge provides is not discretion-free reasoning (a human impossibility) but a resolution of the dispute, and an increment of additional clarity as to how the rule applies.[44] Neither Locke nor the Federalists expected that judges would become angels on the moment of appointment.

Moreover, Locke is characteristically tough-minded on the subject of the rule of law: He first insists that the rule of law is needed for nontyrannical government; but next he defines "prerogative" as the power of "the prince" to act *against* the law, when necessary, for the public good (defined as the preservation of the people's lives, liberties, and properties); and then he concludes that in the hands of a good and wise prince the frequent exercise of this prerogative is an excellent thing. The people will know whether the public good is being served or not; the rule of law per se is rendered incidental. For Locke, as long as the general run of people do not feel tyrannized, tyranny is avoided. Majority acquiescence in public policy is all that his liberal tradition requires. The *people* are the ultimate check on government power, not law per se.

Nor does the Madisonian, or Federalist, version of the liberal tradition offer any further support for Tushnet's insistence that liberal theory expected an idealistic degree of tight constraints on judicial discretion. Here is Madison in *Federalist #37* explaining the inevitable problem of vagueness in all legal texts and the inevitable need for judges to, in effect, construct the details of the law as they apply it from case to new case:

All new laws, though penned with the greatest technical skill and passed on the fullest and most mature deliberation, are considered as more or less obscure and equivocal, until their meaning be liquidated and ascertained by a series of particular discussions and adjudications. Besides the obscurity arising from the complexity of objects and the imperfection of the human faculties, the medium through which the conceptions of men are conveyed to each other adds a fresh embarrassment. . . . [N]o language is so copious as to supply words and phrases for every complex idea, or so correct as not to include many equivocally denoting different ideas. Hence it must happen that however accurately objects may be discriminated in themselves, and however accurately the discrimination may be considered, the definition of them may be rendered inaccurate by the inaccuracy of the terms in which it is delivered. And this *unavoidable* inaccuracy must be greater or less, according to the complexity and novelty of the objects defined. . . . [The] three sources of vague and obscure definitions: indistinctness of the object, imperfection of the organ of conception, inadequateness of the vehicle of ideas . . . must produce a certain degree of obscurity.[45]

Tushnet first hypothesizes a wildly unrealistic degree of certainty demanded by liberal theory in order for law to count as determinate enough to check judicial power, and then on that basis concludes that law is not determinate. But his assumption that a moderate degree of determinateness in the law does not count is in fact at odds with the liberal tradition and, moreover, denies the patent reality of political life.

As to the second strand in Tushnet's argument, he acknowledges that in theory there might be a society in which its members share a common world view and thus have a shared understanding of the community's legal texts. Such a society would be the unified, small classical republic, where civic moral education was emphasized and people were trained to subordinate private advantage to the public good[46]—just the kind of society whose premises were rejected by the liberal tradition. At this point, though, Tushnet mistakes theory for reality. He insists that, because in liberal theory each person is by nature a free individual who is not socially molded, it cannot be true that actual liberal society consists of individuals who share common, societal, "public" values. Instead, to the degree that judges do share values and lawyers do share common expectations of what judges will do with particular legal texts, those facts reflect *not* a society's shared understanding of the meaning of its constituting law and legal tradition,[47] but rather one class's domination of other classes. "It is only in consequence of the pressures exerted by a highly developed deeply entrenched, homeostatic social structure that judges seem to eschew conclusions grossly at odds with the values of liberal capitalism."[48] Tushnet comes to this conclusion only because he begins with it. There is nothing in his analysis to preclude precisely the opposite conclusion—namely, that, at least in terms of the big picture, Americans do have a shared understanding of the meaning of the Constitution.[49]

Tushnet attempts to counter this last criticism by saying that, if there were a societal consensus in the United States on the meaning of the fundamental law, there would be no need for judicial review, since the higher law would not get violated by legislatures.[50] Again he makes this criticism from the perspective of an unrealistically utopian assumption. People may very well agree on the existence of a particular rule but differ in their understanding of how it applies to their own cases, where their private passions are most likely to color their judgment. This is precisely the point at which the Lockean insight of the need for an umpire is most useful. To acknowledge that need is not ipso facto to deny the existence of societal consensus.

Paul Brest

Professor (and recently Dean) Paul Brest, unlike Professor Tushnet, takes more seriously the possibility of a constitutional law guided by "textualism" as distinguished from sheer "intentionalism";[51] but he, too, concludes ultimately that *all* theories defending particular modes of judicial review are fatally defective when measured against the supposed demands of Madisonian liberal theory.

> All are vulnerable to similar criticisms based on their indeterminacy, manipulability, and ultimately their reliance on judicial value choices that cannot be "objectively" derived from text, history, consensus, natural rights, or any other source. No theory of constitutional adjudication can defend itself against self-scrutiny.[52]

As Brest understands Madisonian theory, it presents an unresolvable dilemma: Majority power is intrinsically in tension with individual rights, and there is "no point of equipoise" from which to decide which should prevail in any given case.[53] The rule of law, as an alternative to rule by the subjective value choices of judges, may be wholly illusory; and the supposed ideal of "scientific objectivity in legal interpretation," which Brest attributes to nameless "determinant commentators," is an absurdly impossible "fantasy."[54]

Brest's claim would be relatively noncontroversial if he were discussing only extratextual—or as he puts it, "non-originalist"—theories of judicial review. For, since those theories reject the authority of the constitutional text, they leave the judge with no guidance other than the judge's understanding of contemporary fundamental values.[55] The problem with those theories—as Brest honestly acknowledged[56]—is that, if there really were a contemporary consensus on unwritten fundamental values, there would be no reason at all to expect that judges are more attuned to those values than are majoritarian legislators.[57] He admits that "fundamental values" jurisprudence inevitably allows a small elite of judges to impose their views on the populace.

Brest argues, however, that moderate textualism cannot escape this subjectivist dilemma either. He first describes "moderate textualism" as a sensible alternative to "strict textualism." The latter (something no actual person seems ever to have defended) would be more or less an absurdity, "unable to handle the ambiguity, vagueness, and figurative usage that pervade natural languages"; but the former—moderate textualism—at least employs a sensible methodology and produces sensible results. "A moderate textualist takes account of the open-textured quality of language and reads the language of provisions in their social and linguistic contexts." It closely resembles moderate intentionalism "in methodology and results," looking for the purpose of the constitutional provision "at a relatively high level of generality" in the sense of attempting to discern "what the adopters' purposes might plausibly have been."[58] Although moderate textualism can easily accommodate most of contemporary free speech and equal protection doctrine, Brest argues that it must "strain" the text to justify a number of other very basic doctrines in modern constitutional law.[59] Brest labels as "originalism" the combination of textualism and intentionalism, and he then explains the moderate version of originalism.

Moderate originalism—because original sources alone usually "cannot resolve the controversy before the court," due to the opaqueness of the text and the multiplicity of possible applications of the broadly understood purposes of the text—supplements these original sources by looking to "custom, social practices, conventional morality, and precedent."[60] Although this is a "perfectly sensible strategy of constitutional decision-making," the hard truth is that the idea of textual constraints embodied in the strategy is "simply illusory," a matter of mistaken "faith."[61] In fact, argues Brest, modern equal protection doctrine on such matters as gender and voting rights has not been in any real sense "guided" by the constitutional text:

> The text is wholly open-ended. . . . At most, the Court can claim guidance from the general notion of equal treatment reflected in the provision. I use the word "reflected" advisedly, however, for the equal protection clause does not establish a principle of equality; *it only articulates and symbolizes a principle defined by our conventional public morality.* Indeed, because of its indeterminacy, the clause does not offer much guidance even in resolving particular issues of discrimination based on race. [62]

In essence, Brest's indeterminacy argument has three dimensions:

1. The constitutional text is indeterminate because it embodies a variety of conflicting values,[63] at the bedrock of which lies the conflict between majority rule and minority rights that pervades Madisonian liberal theory.[64]

2. There is no definitive answer to be found in either the constitutional text or in our political tradition for the appropriate level of generality at which to define the legal principle to be derived from the text.[65]

3. For these reasons, the moderate textualists (who claim to be constrained by the text, and even believe themselves to be so)

are, as an empirical matter, inevitably guided by their subjective preferences just as much as are the jurists of the extratextualist or nonoriginalist persuasion—which is to say, for all practical purposes, totally. When it comes to deciding the hard cases in constitutional law, "no defensible criteria exist."[66]

Like Professor Tushnet, Professor Brest does concede the existence of an "interpretive community" of jurists; and like Tushnet, Brest denies that their consensus on the rules of the legal game reflects a societal consensus on the range of plausible meanings of the constitutive document. Instead, like Tushnet, Brest suggests that this range of interpretive consensus shows nothing more than the rule over society by a small elite.[67]

Brest's core argument has developed into an empirical claim—namely, that key provisions of the Constitution operate on the judge more as an inspiring symbol than as a principled guide. Both he[68] and Tushnet[69] acknowledge that their perspective in making this claim is external rather than internal. That is, they admit that judges may *feel* constrained by the constitutional text, but both scholars believe that the really effective constraints come from the social group in which the judges are found and from the norms prevalent in that group. (In other words, the judges receive psychological and social rewards of both material and nonmaterial kinds for behaving in certain ways.) This argument, however, has taken its proponents in a circle. If it is one of the norms of the social group "judges" that the text *should* constrain them, and if judges are in fact constrained by the norms of their social group, then how can it be that the text does not constrain judges?

Brest's way out of this ratiocinative circle is to appeal to certain historic facts. Tushnet's—by contrast—is to acknowledge that, even if some historic facts (not the ones in Brest's discussion) seem to show the limits of the argument for textual indeterminacy, this apparent weakness in the argument can be countered by hypothesizing new facts. Because Tushnet's defense is easier to parry, I take it up first.

Tushnet acknowledges the point (emphasized by various textualist scholars)[70] that parts of the constitutional text do indeed seem very clear-cut and do appear to guide in definitive ways the behavior of judges, lawyers, and potential litigants. He then takes up one example: the clause specifying a minimum age for candidates for the U.S. presidency. Tushnet spins out an elaborate, hypothetical fantasy in which someone might challenge the prevailing meaning of this clause;

he does so all for the purpose of showing that the clause has not been tested only because no powerful social group has yet arisen whose interest would be served by challenging the accepted view of it.[71] The group that he hypothesizes is a religious group. This is an important fact, and one that points directly to the problem with Tushnet's argument. The story illustrates the importance of ideas in shaping human behavior; but Tushnet fails, in this instance, to acknowledge the Constitution's own force as a constituter—as a shaper—of beliefs within the American community.[72] Thus, it is not an accident no group has arisen to insist that 30-year-olds should be allowed to seek the presidency; potential members of such groups are all raised in a society where the dominant legal opinion is unified as to the meaning of the text that forbids such candidacy, and it is reasonable to conclude that the clarity of the text itself has powerfully contributed to such unanimity.

The history and clauses utilized in Brest's argument require a much more detailed answer. Brest points to four very central, very much respected doctrines of modern American constitutional law and argues that none of them readily comports with the text of the Constitution. He cites the following doctrines:

> (1) the incorporation of the principle of equal protection into the fifth amendment, (2) the incorporation of provisions of the Bill of Rights into the fourteenth amendment, (3) the more general notion of substantive due process [more general than that involved in fundamental rights decisions of the ilk of *Lochner v. New York*[73] or *Roe v. Wade*[74]], including the minimal rational relationship standard, and (4) the practice of judicial review of Congressional legislation established by *Marbury v. Madison*.[75]

He claims that these doctrines all "strain" the text, that a textualist can justify these doctrines only with "serious difficulties," and that one cannot establish with any certainty that the text was the *origin* of these doctrines.

Because Brest is correct that the textual basis of these doctrines is not immediately obvious, it is worth explicating them one by one. As every law-schoolboy knows, the Constitution does not spell out a judicial power to invalidate unconstitutional congressional statutes. Even without resort, however, to the records of the Constitutional Convention or *The Federalist Papers* for the ample evidence they provide of a supportive framers' intent, one can argue that the constitutional text "invites" this practice.[76] It is obvious from a number of features of the text that the Constitution contemplates being treated by all officialdom (not just judges) as above and in control of statutes. In this sense, the constitutional text clearly indicates its own status as higher law. Should judges be bound by their own (as distinguished from Congress's and/or the president's) views as to which statutes comport with this higher law? Several features of the text—a concept of "the judicial power" that was at least in the air, if not totally dominant by 1787;[77] the "in pursuance thereof" phrase in the supremacy clause; the requirement that judges swear loyalty to the Constitution; the grant of judicial power to examine cases "arising under this Constitution"; and the establishment of an extracongressional amending power—all invite the conclusion that judges should have this power. These textualist claims, however, cannot prove that the text is the *reason* that John Marshall defended the power of judicial review in *Marbury v. Madison.*[78] It would be silly to deny that the text interacts with political and other forces in complicated ways; but it also seems silly to deny that the text was a major force in producing the power of national judicial review, that it had a much more formative influence than one of merely inspirational symbol.

Similarly, the text can be seen as an operative force in the "minimal rationality" doctrine that Brest calls "the more general notion of substantive due process." This refers to the rule that a law, in its substance, must bear at least some rational relationship to some aspect of the public good (for example, health, safety, prosperity, morality, or overall well-being). The text of the due process clauses says that people may not be deprived of liberty without "due process of law." How can the rule requiring a connection between a law's substance and the public good be a mandate of due process? The answer is that the legislative and administrative branches of government—in order to be acting in accord with the "process of law" that is "due" to Americans—must be acting in their *public* capacity. If, for example, they are acting simply out of private greed or to inflict revenge on personal enemies (i.e., in the only kinds of ways imaginable where there would be *no* rationally believable connection to any aspect of the public good), they are not acting in the proper office of legislator or executor and therefore have no legitimate authority for depriving others of liberty.[79] Although the textual connection is not obvious at the proverbial first glance (probably because the very idea of substantive due process in its extreme versions has ripped the concept away from its textual moorings), a bit of reflection reveals the connection;

and a textual foundation for this minimal notion of the doctrine is not particularly implausible.

The textual moorings of the other two doctrines cited by Brest are a much more complicated matter. The Fourteenth Amendment protects against state abridgment "the privileges or immunities of citizens of the United States"—a phrase that would seem normally to refer to citizen rights identified as such by the Constitution of the United States—and the Constitution itemizes citizen rights primarily in the Bill of Rights.[80] But this apparent textual meaning (as is well known) was rejected by the Supreme Court in *The Slaughterhouse Cases* of 1873,[81] and then gradually worked its way back into constitutional law by a step-by-step path according to which the Court held most of the Bill of Rights to be implied in the Fourteenth Amendment due process clause. This is indeed a strained textual reading. Nothing in this bizarre actual history, however, indicates any textual difficulty in reading the privileges or immunities clause as calling for Bill of Rights incorporation. The Court has chosen not to proceed that way; but a century-long parade of dissenting justices—from the first Justice Harlan to the late Justice Black—did so, and a contemporary textualist might comfortably do the same.[82]

The most powerful judicial argument for this textualist reading of the privileges or immunities clause was written by Justice Black in the 1947 *Adamson v. California* case.[83] Part of his dissent consisted of an original intent argument, but part of it was a textualist argument that spoke to the nature of the judicial role under the American constitutional scheme of tripartite separation of powers. Black argued against his colleagues' "fundamental fairness" reading of the due process clause and their ignoring of the privileges or immunities clause. He insisted that vague due process formulas like "fundamental fairness" or "ordered liberty" provide judges with blank slates on which to inscribe their own views of public policy. In contrast, the judicial role properly understood is that of applying a policy adopted by the people. Black believed that the policy adopted by the people in the Fourteenth Amendment is that of requiring state governments to honor the Bill of Rights and that this policy is amply evident in both the text and history of the amendment.

Justice Black's personal views do not make the answer to Professor Brest on incorporation any more complete; the text of the privileges or immunities clause itself provides the complete answer to the incorporation question. But Justice Black exemplifies the possibility of a seriously textualist jurisprudence even in the late twentieth century.

And it was Justice Black—preeminent textualist—who authored one of the most puzzling of constitutional doctrines: the rule that the Fifth Amendment due process clause, which was addressed to the federal government in 1789, "incorporates" the principles of the Fourteenth Amendment equal protection clause, which was addressed to the states in 1868. Like most commentators, Professor Brest erroneously ascribes this incorporation to the 1954 *Bolling v. Sharpe*[84] opinion of Justice Earl Warren.[85] This error is understandable, for when Justice Warren explained in *Bolling* simply that he found it "unthinkable" to hold the federal government to a lesser desegregation standard than that required of states by the Fourteenth Amendment, he relegated an important citation of *Korematsu v. United States*[86] to a footnote (a footnote often omitted from casebooks).[87] The majority of justices[88] serving on the Court for *Bolling*, however, were cognizant of its links to the *Korematsu* precedent, for they had been members of the Supreme Court in 1944 when Justice Black produced the Court opinion for *Korematsu v. United States*.

It was in *Korematsu*, a Fifth Amendment due process case—rather than in a Fourteenth Amendment equal protection clause case—that Justice Black produced the doctrine that any racial classification in the law is "constitutionally suspect" and will be subjected to "the most rigid scrutiny." Racial classification will be allowed only if justified by compelling necessity.[89] For purposes of this discussion, the egregious results of that case can be put aside;[90] the point of interest here is its doctrine. Justice Black, the Court's most outspoken textualist, authored the leading statement to the effect that the anti-discrimination principle of the Constitution infuses not only the post–Civil War Fourteenth Amendment but also the much older Fifth Amendment.

Was he abandoning his textualism and giving a nod in the direction of contemporary morality? On the contrary, *Korematsu* can be viewed as part of Justice Black's career-long effort against what he liked to call "natural law" theories of the due process clause. He used the phrase "natural law" to mean unwritten law, guided not by the text but rather by the justices' own ideas of right reason or justice. In injecting into the Fifth Amendment due process clause the rule that racial classifications are suspect, Justice Black believed he was upholding a principle of law that had been present in the text of the Constitution (even if dishonored in practice) since 1791. He explained retrospectively, in 1965, that he understood *Bolling v. Sharpe* (and implicitly *Korematsu*) to have "merely recognized what had been the understanding from the beginning of the country . . . that the whole

Bill of Rights, including the Due Process Clause of the Fifth Amendment, was a guarantee that all persons would receive equal treatment under the law."[91]

Despite the pervasive floutings of this principle by the federal government, whose early legislation cannot honestly be described as color-blind, there is some textual support for this reading by Justice Black. Both the bill of attainder and titles of nobility clauses of Article I, Sections 9 and 10 can be comfortably read as embodying the principle that Americans are to receive penalties and privileges not on the basis of birth, but on the basis of behavior. In this sense, laws that deprive persons of liberty on the sheer basis of race would violate procedures of law "due" to Americans as a result of Article I. Still, if historic practice is taken at all seriously, one must conclude that the founding generation did not seem to view racial discrimination as forbidden by the Fifth Amendment.[92]

However, one need not accept Justice Black's view of the 1790s "understanding" of the Fifth Amendment in order to believe that as a textual (if not a historical) matter the due process clause of this amendment requires a condemnation of racial discrimination in laws. The phrase "due process of law," like the phrases "unreasonable searches and seizures" or "cruel and unusual punishments," seems to imply a concept that would evolve with societal changes. "Due process" would seem to include not only the old common law procedural rules (for example, requirement of notice, hearing, guilt beyond a reasonable doubt, etc.), but also more contemporary understandings of obligatory procedure. There is more than ample textual evidence that the American understanding of the procedure "due" after 1870 did not embrace racial discrimination. The post–Civil War alteration of the Constitution (not only by the Fourteenth but also by the Thirteenth and Fifteenth Amendments, which unlike the Fourteenth Amendment did refer directly to slavery and to denial of rights on the basis of race) textually inscribed a national—not just a judicial—transformation of consciousness on racial justice. In the post–Civil War national consciousness expressed in the constitutional document, racial discrimination was rejected as a legitimate part of the legal process. That it took a long time for all the nation's lawmakers and all its judges to catch up to this constitutionally inscribed aspiration is beside the point. One need not agree with Justice Black's eighteenth-century history to accept the idea that the constitutional text by 1870 had altered—even for national law purposes—the legal process henceforth to be due to Americans.

Justice Warren, writing for a unanimous Court in *Bolling v. Sharpe*, did not really care about this argument; for him, right reason or sheer fairness was enough. He did not need supportive details from the text. But others who concurred in his opinion for the sake of presenting a unanimous front in the explosive school segregation cases may well have been of a more textualist disposition. Certainly Justice Black was.

Up to this point, the argument has demonstrated that it is possible to present a textualist defense for the constitutional doctrines Paul Brest identified as presenting the most difficult challenge to textualists.[93] In the course of the argument, it has also been revealed that Justice Black, the most outspoken textualist on the Court, was motivated by a political theory: He wanted to provide a textualist content to the open-ended provisions of the Constitution in order to keep judges from roaming freely all over the map of public policy. He wanted to constrain judicial power. One could argue that this essentially political desire did not come from the constitutional document, but one can also make the opposite claim. At a minimum, the constitutional text contemplates that there will be three essentially differing kinds of government power: a legislating, an executing, and a judging power. By attempting to provide concrete textual content to the otherwise wholly plastic privileges or immunities clause, Justice Black argued that he was being true to the textual, or textual/structural, phenomenon of division of powers.[94]

At this point, it is appropriate to concede two points to Professors Tushnet and Brest. It is true that the Constitution embodies a variety of values or legal principles that, in extremis, are in tension with each other. One example can be found within the First Amendment itself: To the degree that the government goes out of its way to provide special leeway under the laws for the "free exercise of religion," it is to the same degree inevitably providing law "respecting an establishment of religion." There is no getting around the fact of the need for balancing of competing legal concerns. (One could spin out lists indefinitely: the prohibition on involuntary servitude versus the power to raise and support an army, etc., etc.) Judges in any legal system must do this. Similarly, judges must choose the appropriate level of generality at which to apply any given legal rule. These choices are real facts; judicial discretion is a real fact. It is not at all clear, however, why Brest believes that, rather than being mere facts about the nature of law, these facts lead him to suppose that the rule of law may be "entirely illusory."[95] It seems that, like Tushnet, he reaches this point only by assuming a much more robotlike, mechanistic view of the meaning of ''rule of law'' than ever made sense in the first place.

Aesthetics and Political Vision

Whereas Professors Tushnet and Brest emphasize difficulties within the Madisonian liberal tradition and its purported conception of the rule of law and elucidate these difficulties by pointing both to the multiplicity of values in our Constitution and the level-of-generality flexibility available to judges (a flexibility earlier pointed out by the legal realists), another group of contemporary legal scholars pose an even more radical critique.[96] They move outside the discourse of the legal tradition and argue that every legal text, like every linguistic text and even every human experience (as in the phrase ''the social text''), is open to interpretation to a degree that is hopelessly indeterminate. ''Hopeless'' here carries the meaning that representative democracy is at least partially fraudulent because—however much legislators or constitution writers may *try* to constrain later judges and executors of the ''rules laid down''—it is inevitable that these interpreters of the words will in the act of interpreting create meaning that was not in the mind of the authors or ratifiers of the law. The flavor of this critique is captured in the following two quotations, the first from a law journal article written in 1950 by Felix Cohen and the second written in 1982 by Robert Gordon, a prominent CLS jurist:

> Perhaps if we look closely enough, a sentence never means exactly the same thing to any two different people. For no two minds bring the same apperceptive mass of understanding and background to bear on the external fact of a sound or a series of marks. Indeed, I doubt whether any sentence means exactly the same thing to me the first time I hear it that it means the tenth or the hundredth time.[97]

> [W]hat we experience as ''social reality'' is something that we ourselves are constantly constructing; and . . . this is just as true for ''economic conditions'' as it is for ''legal rules.'' If I say that's a bus taking people to work, I'm obviously doing much more than describing a physical object moving through space; my statement makes no sense at all except as part of a larger cultural complex of shared meanings: it would mean little or nothing to you if your culture were unfamiliar with bus technology, with ''work'' as an activity performed in a separate place outside the family compound, or indeed with ''work'' as distinct from ''play'' or ''prayer.''[98]

The impossibility of transcending—or perhaps one should say, the senselessness of expecting to transcend—the context-shaped world (or worlds) of discourse that all humans inhabit is a theme on which one sees a convergence among the writings of Critical Legal Studies;[99] various contemporary sociologists of knowledge;[100] the theorists of the Frankfurt School, most notably Jurgen Habermas; in some interpretations, Hans Georg Gadamer;[101] Michel Foucault; Martin Heidegger; John Dewey; Ludwig Wittgenstein; Jacques Derrida and his followers among American literary critics;[102] Stanley Fish and his followers;[103] and, probably the most influential because of the relative clarity of his presentation, Richard Rorty.[104] As is evident in the above quotation from Felix Cohen, this theme has been around for a long time in the United States, but it is of increasing influence lately.[105]

The very fact of this scholarly convergence appears to have deeply impressed two other advocates of indeterminacy in jurisprudence: Sanford Levinson and Lief Carter. Each has produced an account of "constitutional lawmaking" that attempts to incorporate this philosophic theme. Rather than emphasizing alleged flaws in the "liberal tradition," these scholars focus squarely on the problem of the radical indeterminacy of all interpretation. Levinson's "Law as Literature" article[106] and Lief Carter's 1985 book *Contemporary Constitutional Lawmaking*[107] share a number of themes.[108] Both attack a model of traditional jurisprudence. For Levinson, the target is the Langdellian theory that law is a textual science—the science of how to extract meaning from written materials such that law would amount to "submission to the commands of authoritative texts."[109] For Carter, the target is something vaguely identified as "conventional jurisprudence."[110] He does not clearly identify it; but like Langdellian science, it is bound up with a belief in "the determinateness of legal texts"[111]— a belief that Carter views as passé.

Both authors rest their case for the indeterminacy of the constitutional text on an acceptance of the premise of the social construction of perception/knowledge, as well as the claim that there is not a unified community of discourse in the United States. If the nation or even the legal community shared a consensus as to what the Constitution means—or even as to how to go about deciding what it means[112]—we as a nation might, with intellectual respectability, view the Constitution as guiding our course; but Levinson and Carter contend that we have no such common discourse about law. Thus, Lief Carter writes,

In pluralistic political communities, where people from different cultural, religious, economic, and educational experiences seek to operate together

through many highly differentiated . . . organizations . . . , we should
expect to find that people frequently disagree on the nature of reality.
The United States is just such a pluralistic political community.[113]

[In contemporary America t]o an unprecedented degree, people make
and live in different worlds.[114]

In Sanford Levinson's parallel description, "there is no reason to
believe that the community of persons interested in constitutional
interpretation will coalesce around one or another . . . approach. . . .
[T]his is the result of a genuine plurality of ways of seeing the world."
We are left with "fragmented and fractured discourse."[115] Neither
writer denies that ordinary communication nonetheless can take place
within the divided, pluralistic American community. People can talk to
each other about chairs and tables, can follow the same culinary
recipes with appropriate success, and so on.[116] But within American
culture, the Constitution is a "numinous document,"[117] one containing
mysteries of meaning. Both Levinson and Carter liken the Constitution
to the Bible.[118] Levinson also likens it to *Hamlet*,[119] and Carter likens
Court interpretations to dramatic performances.[120] The Constitution is
a document that within the prevalent religious, political, and cultural
practices of our nation is susceptible of almost an infinite number of
readings.

Both writers concede, however, that there is such a thing as an
American legal community with certain norms of discourse. For Levinson, these establish the bounds between "on-the-wall" and "off-the-
wall" arguments (although he emphasizes that these bounds shift over
time).[121] For Carter there are "forms and norms of legal reasoning"
and an art to using them well. He sees the legal audience as sharing
certain "minimal standards of legal reasoning" (although he emphasizes that these do not depend on text or original intent).[122] Nevertheless, both writers emphasize, "Legal forms do not seriously limit
judicial choices."[123]

Finally, and perhaps most importantly, both writers turn away from
the discourses of law and politics in hope of finding illumination for the
murky areas of those disciplines. Levinson turns to literary criticism
and then, in his most recent book-length effort, to the idea that
constitutional law might be most usefully understood as we understand
religion.[124] Lief Carter turns to aesthetic philosophy in order to shed
light on what makes for a good Supreme Court performance. He takes
literally the word "performance" and insists that, in principle, Su-

preme Court decisions are best understood as phenomena in the same sociocultural category as a musical concert interpreting a certain score, a dramatic production interpreting a certain script, or a painting, which he views as interpreting experience within a particular community.

These explorations in new directions by Levinson and Carter are not without some benefit.[125] The law is a textual matter; understanding the nature of textual interpretation is important. Supreme Court justices are very much political actors, very much in the national spotlight; the effectiveness of their rhetoric in giving people a sense of the meaning of American traditions is indeed important to the life of the national community.

However, these explorations into allied fields—these efforts to say, "Law is really a species of *x*"—tend to obscure as much as they elucidate. They leave us without any sense of what is distinctive about law qua law. Surely there are important differences between, say, a wildly successful Bruce Springsteen concert and Justice Warren's *Brown v. Board of Education* (1954) opinion, between a particularly moving experience of religious worship and the sense of admiration one feels at reading, say, the first Justice Harlan's dissent in *Plessy v. Ferguson* (1896).[126]

These new explorations—indeed the whole indeterminacy school of law—fail to address the decidedly real experience within American culture that may be rendered as follows:

1. *X*-rule is the law.

2. *X* governs not only my behavior but also that of my neighbor and even that of government officials.

3. Our society is generally better off with this system of the various rules *x*, *y*, and *z* that do indeed govern it than it would be without such rules (which is not to deny that some rules might need changing).

These experiences are not sheerly illusory.

Conclusion

The fact that the indeterminacy advocates seem to obscure at least as much as they clarify has led to a school of counter-arguments. For lack of a better term, these critics of the indeterminacy thesis might be called neo-legal-process scholars. (The "legal process school" is what is said to have dominated U.S. law schools from about 1950 to the mid–1970s—that is, from the decline of Legal Realism to the New Uncertainty. Its hallmark was an emphasis on legal craftsmanship, and it included such scholars as Herbert Wechsler, Henry M. Hart, and Alexander Bickel.)[127] These neo-legal-process scholars would include, for instance, Owen Fiss, James Boyd White, and Frederick Schauer. They insist that law as a distinctive discourse does have norms limiting the range of acceptable argument,[128] that enormous amounts of law within American culture do have a determinate meaning, to citizens as well as legal professionals, and that these sections of the law shape behavior within the nation and constitute the society.[129]

One might step back from this debate between the indeterminacy advocates and the neo-legal-process scholars and conclude that this is not much more than a debate over whether the glass is half empty or half full. Much more than description, however, is at stake.

As a community of citizens, legislators, bureaucrats, and judges that constantly interprets its own laws, Americans constantly both reaffirm and remake those laws. Stability and flux (albeit gradual and imperceptible) are ever-present phenomena in social life. To the extent that the indeterminacy advocates convince citizens—but especially future lawyers, which means future judges—of the meaninglessness of legal constraints, to that extent the law *will* fail to constrain. We human beings by our beliefs and our actions based on those beliefs produce what constraint there is in the law. Many members of CLS look forward to this breakdown of constraint because they want to liberate us from the legal shackles of dirty old liberal capitalism; but their faith that such liberation would free us to move in a New Left direction[130] is (to put it mildly) overconfident. The Nazi pasts of two of the leading modern prophets of indeterminacy—Martin Heidegger and Paul de Man[131]—provide ample evidence for the view that saying, "Everything is possible," does not necessarily point in a New Left direction. (Nor even in an anti-establishment direction, if the accession of Paul Brest to the deanship of Stanford Law School is any evidence.)

The text of the Constitution embodies values that, at the edges, are in tension with each other; but this does not mean that it fails to embody a vision of the good polity. It creates a representative democracy guided by a number of legal principles (principles too familiar to warrant itemization here), and it presumes as its foundation a particular legal culture—a culture the norms of which are familiar to readers of this book. None of this denies that judges exercise discretion, nor that two justices on the Supreme Court might in a given hard case write equally impressive justifications for opposed results.

The more legal scholars argue for indeterminacy, the more indeterminate the Constitution will become. The underside of the claim that meaning is something that is created is the realization that meaning is something that can be destroyed. Ultimately, the American people—including their judiciary—are free to do whatever they want with their constitutional document. By contrast, the more energy legal scholars devote to doing doctrinal analysis that confronts the Supreme Court with its failure to take account of the constitutional document as it is best understood in the light of American political and legal traditions, the better constitutional law will become. What the polity needs at this point is not more insistence on treating the Constitution as a document with indeterminate meaning. What is needed is more well-considered constitutional interpretation. The Burger–Rehnquist Court has produced more than its share of unimpressive opinions and could certainly benefit from the guidance of America's best legal minds.

Scholars like Lief Carter and Sanford Levinson are aware of this need, but their efforts to help by turning away from doctrinal analysis—away, in a sense, from the language of the law—and toward the alternative discourses of aesthetics and religion are not likely to strengthen American legal discourse. Paul Brest, in particular, appears to be floundering for a direction[132] and has lately begun to rework attitudinal research materials that are old hat to political scientists.[133] Yet Brest's excellence at doctrinal analysis shines through even when he purports to be exploring the contradictions of liberal theory.[134] So long as politico-legal practices of the American polity continue, that polity will need well-reasoned analyses of how the various parts of the constitutional text fit together, apply to particular hard cases, and fit into and express the values of the political community (which, however pluralistic, is nonetheless a political community in the sense that its members share a consciousness of belonging to a single polity). This is not a task for religious prophets, nor for dramatic artists, but for wise (in the sense of statesmanlike) judges—judges whose wisdom would benefit from more doctrinal analysis from the likes of Paul Brest and Sanford Levinson.

Notes

1. CLS membership is apparently a matter of self-selection, accomplished by choosing to attend the annual CLS conference. This chapter makes no

attempt to delineate a comprehensive "CLS position," if indeed such a thing exists. Instead I have simply selected a prominent member of the Conference on Critical Legal Studies, Mark Tushnet (identified as a CLS member both in his own writings and in other writers' descriptions), as one of the four jurists whose work is being analyzed here.

This chapter is more concerned with the jurisprudential thesis of indeterminacy than with CLS as such. This thesis has attained such prominence of late that even Chief Justice Rehnquist has begun to address it in his public speeches. See William Rehnquist, "The Nature of Judicial Interpretation."

For a detailed discussion of CLS scholarship, see Mark Kelman, *A Guide to Critical Legal Studies*; and Andrew Altman, *Critical Legal Studies: A Liberal Critique*.

2. Sanford Levinson, "Book Review—Escaping Liberalism: Easier Said than Done."

3. Lief Carter, *Contemporary Constitutional Lawmaking: The Supreme Court and the Art of Politics* (hereinafter cited as CCL).

4. Paul Brest, "State Action and Liberal Theory: A Casenote on *Flagg Brothers v. Brooks*."

5. See in particular pars. 13 and 21 of John Locke, *Second Treatise of Government* (hereinafter cited as ST).

6. Locke, ST, par. 34.

7. Locke, ST, pars. 123–25.

8. Locke, ST, pars. 124–26. Emphasis in original.

9. Locke, ST, par. 34.

10. Locke, ST, pars. 119–122.

11. Locke, ST, pars. 168, 208, 209, 225, and 230.

12. Locke makes it look as though he is imposing several more specific limits on government power, but each of them dissolves upon close inspection. In addition to saying that government may not "destroy, enslave, or designedly impoverish" the people (ST, par. 135), Locke says that rule may not be by "extempory, arbitrary decrees" but must be "by promulgated, standing laws, and known authorized judges" (ST, par. 136); yet he undercuts this restraint with his description of executive prerogative, which turns out to permit the ruler to go "against the direct letter of the law, for the public good," whenever such illegality is appropriate. Moreover, the better the prince, the more often it is appropriate (ST, pars. 164–65). Similarly, Locke's other injunction—that the government may not take any part of a person's property without consent (ST, par. 138)—is eviscerated by Locke's acknowledgment that every government needs the power to tax, which power it legitimately receives from the people's representatives (ST, par. 140). In Locke's definitions, any government established by social contract *is* the people's representative, and thus *may* take parts of the people's property. Finally, the maxim that the sovereign may not give away its own sovereignty to a third party (ST, par. 141) checks a tendency that is for the most part

nonexistent; the sovereign's ever-present self-interest would provide the same check.

I provide such detailed citations both here and in the text because there exists a substantial controversy among Locke scholars over the role of natural law in Locke's thought. For citations of many of the scholars who disagree with this interpretation, the reader may wish to consult Michael Zuckert, "The Recent Literature on Locke's Political Philosophy."

13. Locke, ST, pars. 123, 168, 208, 209, 225, 230.

14. It is true that Locke requires an "indifferent" judge, and at first glance this requirement that the judge not be a party to the dispute suggests a freedom from bias. But Locke immediately undercuts this implication by remarking not only that "men being partial to themselves, passion and revenge is very apt to carry them too far, and with too much heat, in their own cases," but also that "negligence, and unconcernedness [is very apt] to make them too remiss in other men's [cases]" (ST, par. 125). Detachment does not eliminate human bias; it just gives it a different characteristic form.

15. An excellent discussion of these efforts appears in Gordon Wood, *The Creation of the American Republic, 1776–1787*.

16. Although the tone of this strand sets a distinctive contrast to Locke's *Second Treatise*, it is not wholly alien to Locke's thought. See Nathan Tarcov, *Locke's Education for Liberty*.

17. *Federalist #10* and *#51*. These papers, originally signed "Publius," are attributed to James Madison. The other two authors to whom some of Publius's *Federalist Papers* are attributed are Alexander Hamilton and John Jay.

18. *Federalist #47–51* (Madison); and, generally, Max Farrand, ed., *The Records of the Federal Convention of 1787*.

19 Of course, the idea that each individual gave initial consent to the social compact was to some degree a fiction. A great many Americans (arguably the majority) opposed the Constitution of 1787, and they elected representatives to the ratifying conventions who were expected to vote against it. Still, one can say of the founding generation (excluding slaves) at least that they or their recent ancestors had chosen the American community, that they chose to stay during or after the Revolution (when many others left for such places as Canada), and that the political community represented by each state ratifying convention did—as an organized community—consent to the Constitution.

20. Although the three people listed were all early Supreme Court justices, they were also important as framers—Wilson both at the Constitutional Convention and the Pennsylvania ratifying convention, and both Iredell and Marshall in their home state ratification processes (North Carolina and Virginia, respectively), in which the framing of the Bill of Rights was taking place.

21. For more detailed discusssion, see Chapter 3.

22. *Federalist #78* (Hamilton). James Madison, in introducing the Bill of Rights in Congress, indicated a concern that the written Constitution check majority tyranny, but he did not stress the role of judicial review. See *Debates and Proceedings in the Congress of the United States* (hereinafter *Annals*), vol. 1, pp. 454–55 (June 8, 1789).

23. *Federalist #78* (Hamilton).

24. There are limits to the potential of the judiciary in this regard, however. A determined, longlasting overbearing majority cannot be checked, at least not in a system of popular government, as the institution of chattel slavery made painfully evident.

25. For details, see Wood, *Creation*.

26. James Boyle, "The Politics of Reason: Critical Legal Theory and Local Social Thought."

27. Sanford Levinson, "Law as Literature."

28. Richard H. Weisberg, "Text into Theory: A Literary Approach to the Constitution."

29. Thomas C. Heller, "Structuralism and Critique."

30. Mark Tushnet, *Red, White, and Blue.*

31. For a semiotic attempt to explain this "something," see Gerald Graff, " 'Keep Off the Grass,' 'Drop Dead,' and Other Indeterminacies."

32. I do not mean to deny here the force of arguments—e.g., that of Gary Jacobsohn, *The Supreme Court and the Decline of Constitutional Aspiration* (hereinafter cited as *Constitutional Aspiration*)—that the American framers believed they were securing natural rights with their written Constitution. My claim is that the *mechanism* for securing these rights within the liberal tradition boils down to a combination of will and force.

33. Locke, ST, par. 225.

34. Mark Tushnet, "Following the Rules Laid Down: A Critique of Interpretivism and Neutral Principles." Tushnet repeats the essential argument in ch. 1 of *Red, White, and Blue.* See also Mark Tushnet, "Anti-formalism in Recent Constitutional Theory," pp. 1505–6.

35. Owen Fiss, "Conventionalism," offers just such a defense of how judges are in fact checked, although he does not describe in detail any particular theory that checks them.

36. Tushnet, "Following," p. 784, including n. 9.

37. Tushnet, "Following," p. 791, citing Michael Perry, "Interpretivism, Freedom of Expression, and Equal Protection," pp. 297–98.

38. Alexander Bickel, "The Original Understanding and the Segregation Decision." See also Jacobsohn, *Constitutional Aspiration*, at pp. 52–54 and ch. 6; and Michael Kent Curtis, *No State Shall Abridge: The Fourteenth Amendment and the Bill of Rights*.

39. See *San Antonio v. Rodriguez*, 411 U.S. 1 (1973), where the Supreme Court—over vehement dissents—held that such arrangements do not violate the equal protection clause.

40. Tushnet, "Following," p. 802.

41. Tushnet, "Following," p. 804.

42. Tushnet, "Following," pp. 821–27 and n. 135; see also ch. 1 of Tushnet, *Red, White, and Blue.*

43. This point receives a detailed elaboration in Frederick Schauer, "Easy Cases."

44. Madison makes clear in *Federalist #37* that he does not rely on some naively utopian notion of "plain meaning" in laws. See the long quotation therefrom in the text for note 45. Cf. the discussion of the framers' purported "plain meaning" views in ch. 1 of Tushnet, *Red, White, and Blue.*

45. This passage occurs in the sixth-last and fifth-last paragraphs of *Federalist #37.* Emphasis added.

Hamilton too, in *Federalist #78*, conceded the power of the judge to alter statutes in the process of deciding cases. After discussing the judicial power to declare invalid any unconstitutional law, he turned to the subject of "unjust and partial laws" that are nonetheless constitutional. Regarding these, Hamilton suggested (in the fourth-last paragraph) that the judiciary's power of interpretation would be useful for "mitigating the severity and confining the operation of such laws."

46. Tushnet introduced the theme of the American republican tradition in "Anti-formalism," and he more fully elaborates the theme in *Red, White, and Blue.* It is evident that he is personally drawn to this intellectual tradition; but he does not seem to grasp the extent to which this tradition is traceable to Aristotle, whose views he finds particularly alien to American culture. "Anti-formalism," pp. 1534–36.

47. Such an understanding is suggested, e.g., by Owen Fiss, "Objectivity and Interpretation."

48. Tushnet, "Following," p. 824.

49. Lest the phrase "the big picture" be taken as a cop-out, I will provide a concrete example. Not terribly long ago—i.e., in the age of Locke—the notion of toleration of religious differences was understood as properly excluding Roman Catholics. But late-twentieth-century Americans really do share a consensus that views religious toleration as extending to all well-established religious faiths. At the edges of the consensus are questions of whether atheism or the more newly established "cults" are to be tolerated, but the fact that there exist some areas of uncertainty does not preclude the fact of wide areas of societal consensus.

50. Tushnet, "Following," pp. 826–27; Tushnet, *Red, White, and Blue*, ch. 1.

51. He explicates these terms in Paul Brest, "The Misconceived Quest for the Original Understanding."

52. Paul Brest, "The Fundamental Rights Controversy: The Essential Contradictions of Normative Constitutional Scholarship," p. 1096, see also 1096–1103.

53. Brest, "Fundamental Rights," pp. 1096–1103.
54. Paul Brest, "Interpretation and Interest," p. 773.
55. See, e.g., Thomas S. Grey, "Do We Have an Unwritten Constitution?"
56. His honesty is impressive because only one year earlier he had defended such theories. See Brest, "Misconceived Quest."
57. Brest, "Fundamental Rights," pp. 1105–8.
58. Brest, "Misconceived Quest," pp. 222–23.
59. Brest, "Misconceived Quest," p. 224.
60. Brest, "Misconceived Quest," pp. 228–29 and 237.
61. Brest, "Misconceived Quest," pp. 231–32.
62. Brest, "Misconceived Quest," pp. 231–32. Emphasis added.
63. Brest, "Interpretation," p. 769. Mark Tushnet makes the same point in "A Note on the Revival of Textualism in Constitutional Theory," and in the app. to ch. 1 of *Red, White, and Blue*.
64. Brest, "Fundamental Rights," pp. 1096–1103.
65. Like Tushnet and the legal realists before him, Brest gives great emphasis to the level-of-generality difficulty. This difficulty is elaborated in the text section above devoted to a discussion of Tushnet. Brest discusses this difficulty in all three of his articles treating the problem of constitutional interpretation: Brest, "Misconceived Quest," pp. 209–11, 220–24, and "Fundamental Rights," pp. 1091–93, and "Interpretation," p. 769.
66. Brest, "Fundamental Rights," p. 1065.
67. Brest, "Interpretation," pp. 770–73.
68. Brest, "Misconceived Quest," p. 235.
69. Mark Tushnet, "Legal Realism, Structural Review, and Prophecy."
70. E.g., Frederick Schauer, "Easy Cases"; Stephen L. Carter, "Constitutional Adjudication and the Indeterminate Text: A Preliminary Defense of an Imperfect Muddle."
71. Tushnet, "Revival," pp. 686–91, and app. to ch. 1 of *Red, White, and Blue*.
72. Elsewhere he does acknowledge this force. Mark Tushnet, "Post-realist Legal Scholarship," p. 1401.

Madison referred to this power of the Constitution to mold beliefs in his remarks introducing the Bill of Rights to Congress:

> [Such statements of rights] have a tendency to impress some degree of respect for them, to establish the public opinion in their favor, and rouse the attention of the whole community [and thus] may be one means to control the majority from those acts to which they might be otherwise inclined.
> *Annals*, vol. 1, p. 455 (June 8, 1789).

73. *Lochner v. New York*, 198 U.S. 45 (1905).
74. *Roe v. Wade*, 410 U.S. 113 (1973).
75. Brest, "Misconceived Quest," pp. 224, 231–34.

76. The usage of "invites" in this context was first suggested to me by the late Herbert Storing.

77. See Chapter 3.

78. *Marbury v. Madison*, 5 U.S. (1 Cranch) 137 (1803).

79. Incidentally it is virtually never obvious that legislators or administrators are acting in this purely private, corrupt way; consequently, a truly minimal-rationality due process doctrine would virtually never invalidate a law.

80. Additional protections of citizen rights appear in Art. I, Secs. 9 and 10; Art. III, Sec. 2, cl. 3, and Sec. 3; and Art. IV, Secs. 2 and 4.

81. *The Slaughterhouse Cases*, 83 U.S. (16 Wallace) 36 (1873).

82. For a powerful defense of the claim that this is not only a sound textualist reading but also the reading demanded by even the strictest of intentionalist standards, see Curtis, *No State*.

83. *Adamson v. California*, 332 U.S. 46 (1947), Black dissenting, at 68–123. In fact, Justice Black insisted that not just the privileges or immunities clause, but also the due process and equal protection clauses—"the provisions of the Amendment's first section, separately, and as a whole," at 71—accomplished this incorporation. At a number of points in his opinion, however, he referred to the privileges or immunities clause specifically—e.g., at 78, 85–86. See also *Duncan v. Louisiana*, 391 U.S. 145 (1968), Black concurring, at 162, where—at 163–64—he relies on his dissent in *Adamson* but emphasizes more forthrightly, at 166–67, the privileges or immunities clause as his textual basis for Bill of Rights incorporation.

84. *Bolling v. Sharpe*, 347 U.S. 497 (1954).

85. Brest, "Misconceived Quest," pp. 232–33.

86. *Korematsu v. United States*, 323 U.S. 214 (1944).

87. *Bolling*, at 499–500, including n. 3.

88. They were Justices Black, Douglas, Frankfurter, Reed, and Jackson.

89. *Korematsu*, at 216–20, 223–24. See also *McLaughlin v. Florida*, 379 U.S. 184 (1964), at 191–92, citing both *Bolling*, at 499, and *Korematsu*, at 216, for the rule that racial classifications are "constitutionally suspect" under the Fourteenth Amendment equal protection clause.

90. *Korematsu* upheld a conviction under part of a statutory scheme that resulted in the wartime incarceration (without trial or charges) in detention camps of 112,000 persons of Japanese descent, more than 70,000 of whom were U.S. citizens. Alfred H. Kelly, et al., *The American Constitution: Its Origins and Development*, pp. 562–65.

91. *Griswold v. Connecticut*, 381 U.S. 479 (1965), Black dissenting, at 507, quote at 517 n. 10. Black's views on this point are treated at much greater length in Chapter 2.

92. For examples of race-based legislation in the founding period, see Chapter 2, note 30.

93. The list of doctrines here pointedly has omitted the doctrine of funda-

mental unwritten rights, which, as Brest recognizes, is a doctrine at odds with textualist concerns. For attempts—in my view unsuccessful—to defend on both textualist and intentionalist grounds this doctrine, see David A. J. Richards, "Constitutional Legitimacy and Constitutional Privacy"; and Douglas Laycock, "Taking Constitutions Seriously: A Theory of Judicial Review."
94. For elaboration of this point, see Chapter 4.
95. Brest, "Interpretation," p. 773.
96. Radical not in the political sense, but in the sense of cutting more deeply at the roots of what we experience.
97. Felix Cohen, "Field Theory and Judicial Logic," pp. 240–41, cited in Michael S. Moore, "A Natural Law Theory of Interpretation," at p. 304 n. 50. Law review articles of late often cite literary theorist Jacques Derrida or his followers, but the core point for those citations shows up here—squarely within the American legal realist tradition. This core point, then, seems to be that the reading of a text is infinitely variable and is shaped by the structures of understanding the reader brings to bear on the text. Those structures in turn derive from the reader's lived experience as a situated member of a particular society (i.e., situated within a class, gender, national group, etc.). The critical analysis of these structures of understanding is more or less what is meant by "deconstruction." For a relatively brief introduction to the Derridean approach, one can recommend Jacques Derrida, "Différances"; Joseph Margolies, "Deconstruction; or the Mystery of the Mystery of the Text"; and Jonathan Culler's discussion of the Derridean maxim, "Every reading is a misreading," in *On Deconstruction: Theory and Criticism after Structuralism*, pp. 175–79.
98. Robert Gordon, "New Developments in Legal Theory," pp. 287–88.
99. Representative selections appear in David Kairys, ed., *The Politics of Law*; in vol. 36, nos. 1 and 2 of *Stanford Law Review* (1984); and in vol. 6, no. 4 of *Cardozo Law Review* (1986).
100. See citations in Carter, CCL.
101. Contrast Lief Carter's description of the Gadamer presented by Richard Bernstein—CCL, pp. 144–46—with the explication of Gadamer given by David Couzens Hoy, "Interpreting the Law: Hermeneutical and Poststructuralist Perspectives."
102. See citations in note 97 above.
103. Stanley Fish, "Interpretation and the Pluralist Vision," and "Working on the Chain Gang: Interpretation in Law and Literature"; and Walter Benn Michaels, "Response to Perry and Simon."
104. Richard Rorty, *Philosophy and the Mirror of Nature*.
105. It may be more than sheer coincidence that economic substantive due process as judicial doctrine immediately preceded the heyday of Legal Realism and sexual-privacy substantive due process immediately preceded the current jurisprudential infatuation with indeterminacy. Proof of anything appropriately to be considered a causal relationship between these sorts of events, however, is far beyond human capacity.

106. This theme of the indeterminacy of all interpretation is again elaborated in Sanford Levinson, *Constitutional Faith*, ch. 5.

107. Carter, CCL.

108. Both authors also both have Ph.D.s in political science as well as law degrees. This probably *is* sheer coincidence.

109. Levinson, "Law as Literature," pp. 373–74.

110. Carter, CCL, p. xiv.

111. Carter, CCL, p. xiii.

112. For additional elucidation of Levinson's views on these divisions, see Sanford Levinson, " 'The Constitution' in American Civil Religion."

113. Carter, CCL, p. 59.

114. Carter, CCL, p. 9.

115. Levinson, "Law as Literature," pp. 386, 403.

116. Levinson elaborates this concession in "Law as Literature," p. 382, and in Sanford Levinson, "What Do Lawyers Know (and What Do They Do with Their Knowledge)? Comments on Schauer and Moore," pp. 442–44.

117. Levinson, "Law as Literature," p. 385.

118. Levinson, "Law as Literature," p. 385; Carter, CCL, p. 55.

119. Levinson, "Law as Literature," p. 391.

120. Carter, CCL, passim.

121. Levinson, "Law as Literature," pp. 382–83.

122. Carter, CCL, pp. 172–78.

123. Carter, CCL, p. 177. Levinson, in ch. 5 of *Constitutional Faith*, concedes that there is at least enough consensus in the law school professoriate to keep a course like "Law and Astrology" outside the curriculum.

124. Levinson suggests in ch. 5 of *Constitutional Faith* that the twentieth century may be experiencing the "death of law" as the nineteenth century experienced the "death of God."

125. In particular, Levinson's book contains rich and thought-provoking explorations and warrants more scholarly attention than is permitted by the confines of this discussion.

126. An additional argument could be made here—viz., that there is a more determinate content to literary, artistic, musical, and even religious texts than either Carter or Levinson seem to believe. However, that argument is tangential to the argument here and will thus be left to the literary theorists, art and music critics, and theologians. The central point here is that legal texts differ from these others. Whereas artistic texts often aim for and can be enriched by ambiguity, legal texts generally strive to avoid it and are diminished in quality to the extent that they fail to do so.

127. Russell L. Caplan, "The Paradoxes of Judicial Review in a Constitutional Democracy."

128. Fiss, "Objectivity and Interpretation" and "Conventionalism"; also, Owen Fiss, "Death of the Law?"; James Boyd White, "Law as Language."

129. Schauer, "Easy Cases."

130. Those CLS tracts that outline a program are replete with goals that characterized the New Left of the 1960s: economic equality, participatory democracy, close-knit and face-to-face communities. See, e.g., Roberto Unger, *The Critical Legal Studies Movement*.

131. Paul de Man, a Belgian-born literary critic who taught at Yale for years, was an eminent practitioner of the deconstructionist style associated with Jacques Derrida. (See discussion of deconstruction in note 97 above.) In November 1987, he was posthumously revealed to have had an active Nazi past during his twenties. Martin Heidegger's Nazi past has always been public knowledge.

132. Brest, "Fundamental Rights," p. 1109.

133. Paul Brest, "Who Decides?"

134. Brest, "State Action and Liberal Theory."

7

Conclusions

The first two chapters of this book elaborated a constitutional theory of moderate textualism. The adjective "moderate" here connotes that it is not literalist; that it looks to the text for implicit or explicit expression of broad principle, not just explicit commands; and that it considers the text-contained principles to be adaptable to changing societal circumstances. Chapters 1 and 2 explained that this textualism characterized the jurisprudence of, among others, Chief Justice John Marshall and Justice Hugo Black. The parameters of a textualist jurisprudence were set forth by distinguishing it from a number of alternative constitutional approaches popular in the 1970s and 1980s— approaches that in fact had rather close analogues in the 1770s–1820s period of the nation's founding. These competing approaches included extratextualism (which is defended by, e.g., Thomas Grey and Suzanna Sherry, and which appears to have been the clear favorite in law review scholarship of the 1970s and 1980s) and two distant cousins of textualism: constitutional symbolism (which is defended by, e.g., Michael Perry and Ronald Dworkin) and a narrow, positivistic intentionalism (the most well-known proponent of which is Raoul Berger). Both John Marshall and Hugo Black insisted that a judge who is examining a case that arises under the Constitution must look to the text of the document for ultimate guidance. The proper question for the judge to pose is this: "What general principle of law is suggested in the language of the text, and does this case fall under that general principle?" In discerning the principle, the judge must take into account the historic circumstances that gave rise to this particular text and the overall structure both of the text and of the government set forth therein.

The textualism of John Marshall did not reject the concept of natural law, or natural justice; Marshall and his contemporaries believed that the Constitution contained many natural law principles, but not *all* of them. Although John Marshall and many other judges of his time openly acknowledged that slavery violated natural justice, they none-theless upheld the unjust positive laws of the slave system. They did so because of their belief that the constitutional text did not forbid slavery and, to the contrary, intended (as it were) to accommodate it. This book has not defended their reading of the Constitution, and Chapter 1 included a brief critique of that reading. What this book has defended is the view that, *if* the constitutional text does not contain a principle conflicting with a given statute, the judge's proper job within the American system of government does not include the power to throw out such statute simply on the grounds that the judge considers it to be a bad law. Justice Black similarly emphasized that a judge under the American system of government must uphold even an unjust law if there is no principle in the constitutional text that forbids such a law.

This is not to say that a judge's understanding of justice is irrelevant to the project of constitutional interpretation. On the contrary, a jurisprudence of textualism typically leaves the judge a *range* of defensible choice either among competing principles or even as to outcome under agreed-on principles, especially in cases where the question is so close as to be appealed all the way to the U.S. Supreme Court. Two judges both implementing a textualist jurisprudence may well disagree as to which should be the dominant principle for a given case or even which is the correct outcome under a given principle. Such disagreements are normal among nonomniscient human beings; they are the reason we need judges to settle disputes; and they delimit the arena where groups of textualist judges might well differ among themselves under the guidance of alternative understandings of justice.

One might wonder what the point is in defending a constitutional theory that is supposed to constrain judicial power if two judges abiding by this theory might reach opposite results in a given case. The answer would go something like this: Given human limits, there will always be the possibility of the hard case in which thoughtful, conscientious, and wise judges—even those who share the same conception of the judicial role, including the same constitutional theory—will differ as to the proper outcome of the case. What the proper constitutional theory can accomplish is that it can delimit the proper bounds of the range of legitimate choice; it gives citizens and scholars a ground on which to stand when they conclude that—despite ingenious lawyers' arguments to the contrary that can be constructed—decisions like *Dred Scott v. Sandford*, *Plessy v. Ferguson*, and *Lochner v. New York* were illegitimate decisions. They were illegitimate because, despite the majority justices' (and even some scholars') protestations to the contrary, they did not take seriously the words and structure of the Constitution. By contrast, good textualist arguments can be constructed on *both* sides of the question whether the Fourth and Fifth Amendments permit compulsory blood tests for catching drunk drivers. Sound textualist arguments on both sides of *Plessy* or *Lochner* simply cannot be constructed.

Chapters 3 through 5—although they continued to discuss and elaborate the constitutional theory of textualism—were more frankly political in the sense that they draw out some of the interconnection between American political theory and constitutional theory. Chapter 3 returns to the origins of judicial review in the United States, and argues that the evident move among American jurists (led by John Marshall) away from extratextualist jurisprudence was not simply (as it is sometimes explained) a product of the increased popularity of positivism among legal philosophers. Rather, it was closely tied to political changes within the American polity in that rambunctious final quarter of the eighteenth century. These political changes both resulted from, and demanded, new understandings of the nature of the American polity—a polity within which judges went from being the appointees of a hereditary monarch or of his deputies to being either elected themselves or appointed by elected officials. Moreover, within the American states between 1776 and 1801 the understanding of the interrelations among a people, their legislature, and their constitution altered profoundly. That alteration accompanied a change of political practice. Whereas the early state constitutions were simply adopted by legislatures speaking as the voice of the people, after a decade or so both the theory and the practice changed. By the late 1780s the theory was espoused that the people—separate and apart from their governing bodies—reigned as the ultimate sovereign, and that the people (via specially elected conventions) adopted constitutions that laid down the rules that governed the government. Judges were to be the enforcing authority for these rules. Commensurate with this change in the structure and the understanding of the American polity came changes in the practice of judicial review. Judges shifted away from extratextualist exercises of judicial review and toward a text-based practice that justified itself by a constitutionalism founded on the principle of popular sovereignty. Simultaneous with this shift came a much wider and deeper political acceptance of judges' authority to declare statutes void.

Chapter 4 uncovers the politics of constitutional theory at an even deeper level; it argues that even *within* textualist, or "interpretivist," jurisprudence there exists such a wide range of choice that one could plausibly argue (as John Ely has done) that textualism (via such passages as the privileges or immunities clause of the Fourteenth Amendment) requires the judge to be an extratextualist, who looks outside the text for some of the fundamental values that restrict the choices of American legislatures. There is a sense in which the text by itself cannot answer the question whether *only* those values expressed, either implicitly or explicitly, in the text are to be the foundation of judges' power to declare laws void, or whether the text authorizes the judge to look elsewhere also for those values—say, to societal tradition. To the degree that this is true, political judgments must enter into the choice of one's constitutional theory, even for choices from among the range of textualist theories. Since the text of the Constitution is a regime-founding document, it should not be surprising that political understanding shapes how one reads it.

Chapter 4 argued, for instance, that both Justice Frankfurter and Justice Black were textualists but that Justice Black—consciously guided by a particular political theory—chose a version of textualism more constraining of judicial discretion than the version Justice Frankfurter chose. As Black understood it, the power to strike down laws that was left in the hands of nonelected, lifetime-appointed judges was a power that needed to be constrained such that its exercise could be based only on principles fairly inferable from the constitutional text. The rules expressed in the text had been chosen by the people; legislatures had been chosen by the people; judges had not been chosen by the people. Thus, Justice Black's preference for a textualism that, to a moderate degree, restricted judicial discretion expressed—at base—a preference for popular sovereignty.

On the other hand, one can argue (as Justice Black often did argue) that the rule that judicial review may be exercised solely on the basis of some legal principle inferable from the constitutional text is not merely the product of raw political preference. There is a sense in which this rule that constrains judicial discretion is itself indicated in the constitutional text. The Constitution sets forth a tripartite division of power: legislative, executive, and judicial. Black's argument (which argument Chapter 4 endorses) is that it is in the nature of specifically judicial power (at least judicial power as contemplated in the 1787 U.S. regime) to be limited to the interpreting of some expression of the sovereign will. Black believed that the structure of government set forth in the constitutional text was the ultimate grounding for the principle guiding judges to look for a textual basis for all rules of constitutional law, and to look for clues within the text (as well as in the structure of, and secondarily in the historic context of, the text) for guidance as to the meaning of more opaque phrases of the Constitution.

The norm that, when confronted with such an opaque phrase, a judge ought to look for clues as to its meaning within the rest of the text (including its structure) might be thought of as a rule for a "textualist textualism." The argument in favor of this rule on the grounds of the structure of government power set forth within the Constitution is one of the central arguments of this book. The tripartite division of government set out by the Constitution implies the rule that it is the job of judges to interpret and apply *legal* texts, as distinguished from the "texts" of societal tradition, contemporary morality, or what have you. Although the book does not pretend that all justices at all times (even in the 1770s and 1780s) had this view of their role, the argument is that this is how the U.S. Constitution structures—or attempts to structure—the judicial role.

Chapter 5 pursues in greater detail the import of competing theoretical conceptions of the tripartite division of power in the Constitution—in particular the political theories implied, respectively, by textualist jurisprudence and by its primary competitor: extratextualism. This chapter outlines the political system implied by each jurisprudence and provides a theoretical defense of each system, as those defenses would be articulated from the moral-political vantage point of the respective schools of thought. The chapter then argues for the superiority of the political theory of textualist jurisprudence on two separate grounds.

First, a textualist rather than an extratextualist role for federal judges appears—both from what we know about the Constitutional Convention and from the text itself—to have been the expectation of both the authors and ratifiers of the original Constitution and of its various amendments (although the case for this claim is less than airtight regarding the Fourteenth Amendment). The Constitution as a whole thus contains this expectation for judicial behavior. For this reason, a political theory preferring that government power, including judicial power, be limited by a written constitution would favor a textualist role for judges. While it is true that the "judicial power" was understood in 1787 to include the common law power to make rules for cases not covered by statutes, the latter was a power with roots in the epoch when queens or kings ruled England and judges served as their deputies. By the late 1780s, leading Americans had read their Montesquieu and had become committed to an understanding of separation of powers in which judicial power was subordinate to the power of popularly elected legislatures, while the latter was in turn subordinated to the sovereign will of the people as expressed through written constitutions. While there were some exercises of natural-law-based judicial review and some support expressed for it in the first couple of decades of the new nation, both the wording of the Constitution and the action of the Constitutional Convention in twice rejecting Council of Revision powers for the Supreme Court express a preference for a text-based role for judges.

Second, Chapter 5 argued that the norm of equal respect and concern for all people—which is endorsed as *the* fundamental moral-political principle by a number of the advocates of extratextualist, fundamental-rights jurisprudence—is probably more honored in the political theory of their opponents, the textualists, than in their own. The fundamental rights jurists would have judges uphold this norm as a matter of elite-guarded policy outcomes. However, in a nation where the general public is committed to the principle of popular sovereignty, it is highly improbable that judges would be long permitted to throw out electorally adopted statutes on the basis of personal judgments of good morality if they tried to do so openly and expressly. Thus, when they engage in extratextualism they pretend they are being textualists and are throwing out laws on the basis of rules the people themselves adopted. But a jurisprudence premised on deceit obviously fails to honor the norm of equal respect for all people.

The textualists, by contrast, build the principle of equal respect for other persons into the base of their political theory by a commitment to popular sovereignty. The weakest link in textualist political theory is the difficulty in defending the proposition that the American people, as a matter of lived reality, have actually in any meaningful sense adopted the rules of their Constitution. Chapter 5 explores a variety of political processes in the United States that it denominates the "subsystem" of constitutional politics. When this subsystem for garnering mass consent to the rules of the Constitution is taken into account, one can plausibly conclude that there exists much more "consent of the governed" to the Constitution than is generally realized. In this light, a textualist jurisprudence—because of its grounding in a democratic system of popular sovereignty—turns out to be the better expression of the norm of equal respect and concern for all people than its competitor, extratextualism.

Finally, Chapter 6 confronts the radical, postmodernist challenge to this entire discussion—which challenge has become increasingly prevalent in both the law review and political science literature. This challenge, to put it simply, asserts that the distinction between textualism and extratextualism is imaginary or fraudulent because all texts—legal or otherwise—are constantly invented by their readers. That is, texts have no fixed content. In construing a text the reader actually puts meaning there. Thus, the next reader is equally free to put a new meaning there. What we think of as textualism is, in this light, a self-deception. One's reading of a text is always, the argument goes, a product of extratextual factors. According to this challenge, the whole textualism/extratextualism debate is premised on a nonexistent dichotomy. Since all legal interpretation involves discretionary choices, the goal of modern liberal political theory—that arbitrary human power be checked by the rule of law—is unattainable; judges rule over us by raw power cloaked in the ideology of neutral, liberal legalism.

Chapter 6 takes up the specific arguments of influential scholars who put forth one or another version of this indeterminacy thesis. The chapter argues that typical to such postmodernist attacks on the rule of law is a mischaracterization of liberal theory, whether classical Lockean theory or Madisonian-Federalist liberal theory. Neither Locke, nor Madison, nor Hamilton ever expected or demanded to eliminate human discretion from the judging process. Thus, a successful proof that discretion enters into most judging does not amount to a disproof that the rule of law still restrains human behavior. Laws in fact do succeed in regulating much human behavior, including that of judges, And judges, as well as others, subjectively perceive themselves as being restrained by law.

Many of the postmodernist critics admit that there are wide areas of consensus among both jurists and citizens as to the meaning of a good deal of American law, but these critics argue that the consensus comes not from the legal texts or the political tradition providing contextual meaning to those texts. They say that the consensus comes rather from the intellectual hegemony of an elite class that includes judges. Chapter 6 pointed out a flaw of circularity in this argument. The critics say that not legal texts but the norms of the social group "jurists" are what constrain judges in fact. The flaw here is that if the norm says that legal texts should constrain judges, and the norm *does* constrain judges, then the norm would be causing the legal text to succeed in constraining judges. Thus, we are not victims of raw judicial power after all.

In the process of answering Paul Brest, one of the critics who argue that textualism cannot—to a meaningful degree, at least—constrain judicial power, Chapter 6 provides a number of textualist defenses for prevailing doctrines of constitutional law that Brest says are impossible to defend textually. For instance, there is a long-standing doctrine that the command "No person shall be deprived of life, liberty, or property without due process of law" requires that laws limiting liberty must bear a rational relation to furthering some aspect of the public good—such as safety, morality, prosperity, and so forth. (That is, it must be reasonably believable that the law in question would in some way further the public good.) At first glance it is not obvious how such a substantive requirement might stem from the textual mandate for "due process of law." But a bit of reflection reveals the connection between the text and the rule. As long as legislators and administrative rule-makers are acting in their *public* capacity—that is, in a sincere effort to further the public good—they are acting in accordance with the "process of law" that is "due" to Americans. On the other hand, if they are perverting the power of government for corrupt private ends such as revenge or greed (i.e., the only imaginable kinds of ends for which there would be *no* rationally believable connection to *any* aspect of the public good), then they have no legitimate authority for depriving other citizens of liberty and would thus violate due process of law. Other such doctrinal analyses appear in Chapter 6 and elsewhere in the book, but they are presented essentially for illustrative purposes. It has not been the central point of this book to defend one or another reading of this or that particular clause.

Rather, it has been the point of this book to defend a certain mode of judging and of legal analysis. The essence of that mode is taking the text seriously, and in particular taking seriously the potential of the text as a constraint on judicial behavior. It happened in the 1970s and 1980s that teenagers and hipsters took the word "bad" and made it mean "good." Similarly, it is a conceivable possibility that, if the legal community—aided and abetted by the rest of society (or, perhaps more imaginably, by academia)—became collectively determined to do so, they could gut laws of their meaning as linguistic restraints on human behavior. But this would be blatant folly.

It is clear that judges have some discretion and also clear that they (currently at least) subjectively experience a good deal of constraint under the laws. These constraints come from constitutions, statutes, precedents, and from professional norms about how to deal with all of these. The point of this book has been to argue that in the realm of constitutional law the best precedents and the wisest juristic norms are those that take the text seriously as a guide to judicial discretion. What is "best" about them is that they enable us to live up to the democratic principles animating the American regime.

References

Abraham, Henry. *Justices and Presidents: A Political History of Appointments to the Supreme Court*. New York: Oxford University Press, 1985.

Adams, John. *The Works of John Adams*. C. F. Adams, ed. Boston: Little, Brown, 1856.

Adams, Willi Paul. *The First American Constitutions*. Rita and Robert Kimler, trans. Chapel Hill: University of North Carolina Press, 1980.

Agresto, John. *The Supreme Court and Constitutional Democracy*. Ithaca, N.Y.: Cornell University Press, 1984.

Alfange, Dean, Jr. "On Judicial Policymaking and Constitutional Change: Another Look at the (Original Intent) Theory of Constitutional Interpretation." *Hastings Constitutional Law Quarterly* 5(1978):603–38.

Altman, Andrew. *Critical Legal Studies: A Liberal Critique*. Princeton, N.J.: Princeton University Press, 1990.

Bailyn, Bernard. *Ideological Origins of the American Revolution*. Cambridge, Mass.: Harvard University Press, 1967.

Barber, Sotirios A. *On What the Constitution Means*. Baltimore: Johns Hopkins University Press, 1984.

Basler, Roy, ed. *The Collected Works of Abraham Lincoln*. New Brunswick, N.J.: Rutgers University Press, 1943.

Berger, Raoul. *Federalism: The Founders' Design*. Norman: University of Oklahoma Press, 1987.

———. *Government by Judiciary*. Cambridge, Mass.: Harvard University Press, 1977.

Berns, Walter. "Judicial Review and the Rights and the Laws of Nature." *Supreme Court Review* 1982(1982):49–83.

Bickel, Alexander. *The Least Dangerous Branch*. Indianapolis, Ind.: Bobbs-Merrill, 1962.

———. *The Morality of Consent*. New Haven, Conn.: Yale University Press, 1975.

———. "The Original Understanding and the Segregation Decision." *Harvard Law Review* 69(November 1955): 1–65.

———. *The Supreme Court and the Idea of Progress*. New York: Harper and Row, 1970.

Black, Charles. *The People and the Court*. New York: Macmillan, 1960.

———. *Structure and Relationship in Constitutional Law*. Baton Rouge: Louisiana State University Press, 1969.

Blume, William, ed. *Transactions of the Supreme Court of Michigan. Volume 1: 1805–1814*. Ann Arbor: University of Michigan Press, 1935.

Bobbitt, Philip. *Constitutional Fate: Theory of the Constitution*. New York: Oxford University Press, 1982.

Bolingbroke, Henry St. John Viscount. *A Dissertation upon Parties*. 3rd Edition. London: H. Haines, 1735.

Bork, Robert. "Neutral Principle and Some First Amendment Problems." *Indiana Law Journal* 47(1971):1–35.

Boyle, James. "The Politics of Reason: Critical Legal Theory and Local Social Thought." *University of Pennsylvania Law Review* 133(1985):685–780.

Brest, Paul. "The Fundamental Rights Controversy: The Essential Contradictions of Normative Constitutional Scholarship." *Yale Law Journal* 90(1981):1063–1109.

———. "Interpretation and Interest." *Stanford Law Review* 34(1982):765–73.

———. "The Misconceived Quest for the Original Understanding." *Boston University Law Review* 60(1980):204–38.

———. "State Action and Liberal Theory: A Casenote on *Flagg Brothers v. Brooks*." *University of Pennsylvania Law Review* 130(1982):1296–1330.

———. "Who Decides?" *Southern California Law Review* 58(1985):661–71.

Cahn, Edmund. "Mr. Justice Black and the First Amendment 'Absolutes': A Public Interview." *New York University Law Review* 37(1962):549–63.

Caplan, Russell L. "History and Meaning of the Ninth Amendment." *Virginia Law Review* 69(1983):223–68.

———. "The Paradoxes of Judicial Review in a Constitutional Democracy." *Buffalo Law Review* 30(1982):451–98.

Carter, Lief H. *Contemporary Constitutional Lawmaking: The Supreme Court and the Art of Politics*. New York: Pergamon, 1985.

Carter, Stephen L. "Constitutional Adjudication and the Indeterminate Text:

A Preliminary Defense of an Imperfect Muddle." *Yale Law Journal* 94(1985):821–72.

Casper, Jonathan D. "The Supreme Court and National Policy-making." *American Political Science Review* 70(1976):50–68.

Choper, Jesse. *Judicial Review and the National Political Process.* Chicago: University of Chicago Press, 1980.

Cohen, Felix. "Field Theory and Judicial Logic." *Yale Law Journal* 59(1950):238–72.

Corwin, Edward S. "A Basic Doctrine of American Law." *Michigan Law Review* 12(1914):247–76.

———. *Court over Constitution.* Gloucester, Mass.: Peter Smith, 1957. (Reprint of 1938 edition.)

———. *The Doctrine of Judicial Review.* Gloucester, Mass.: Peter Smith, 1963. (Reprint of 1914 edition.)

———. "The Establishment of Judicial Review." *Michigan Law Review* 9(1911):102–25.

———. "The Higher Law Background of American Constitutional Law." *Harvard Law Review* 42(1928/29):149–85, 365–409.

———. "The Progress of Constitutional Theory between the Declaration of Independence and the Meeting of the Philadelphia Convention." *American Historical Review* 30(1925):511–36.

Cover, Robert. *Justice Accused.* New Haven, Conn.: Yale University Press, 1975.

Cox, Archibald. "The New Dimensions of Constitutional Adjudication." *Washington Law Review* 51(1976):791–829.

Crosskey, William W. "Charles Fairman, 'Legislative History,' and the Constitutional Limits on State Authority." *University of Chicago Law Review* 22(1954):1–143.

———. *Politics and the Constitution in the History of the United States.* Chicago: University of Chicago Press, 1953.

Culler, Jonathan. *On Deconstruction: Theory and Criticism after Structuralism.* Ithaca, N.Y.: Cornell University Press, 1982.

Curtis, Michael Kent. *No State Shall Abridge: The Fourteenth Amendment and the Bill of Rights.* Durham, N.C.: Duke University Press, 1986.

Debates and Proceedings in the Congress of the United States. Washington, D.C.: Gales and Seaton, 1834 .

Dellinger, Walter. "The Process of Constitutional Amendment." *News for Teachers of Political Science* 49(Summer 1986): 16–19.

Derrida, Jacques. "Différances." In Jacques Derrida, *Speech and Phenomena.* Evanston, Ill.: Northwestern University Press, 1973.

Douglass, Elisha. *Rebels and Democrats*. Chapel Hill: University of North Carolina Press, 1935.

Douglass, Frederick. *The Life and Writings of Frederick Douglass*. 4 Volumes. Philip Foner, ed. New York: International Publishers, 1950.

Dworkin, Ronald S. "The Forum of Principle." *New York University Law Review* 56(1981):469–518.

———. "Law as Interpretation." *Texas Law Review* 60(1982):527–50.

———. *Law's Empire*. Cambridge, Mass.: Belknap Press of Harvard University Press, 1986.

———. *Taking Rights Seriously*. Cambridge, Mass.: Harvard University Press, 1977.

Elliot, Jonathan. *The Debates in the Several State Conventions on the Adoption of the Federal Constitution*. 2d Edition. Philadelphia: J. B. Lippincott, 1836.

Ely, John. *Democracy and Distrust*. Cambridge, Mass.: Harvard University Press, 1980.

———. "The Wages of Crying Wolf: A Comment on *Roe v. Wade*." *Yale Law Journal* 82(1973):920–49.

Fairman, Charles. "Does the Fourteenth Amendment Incorporate the Bill of Rights? The Original Understanding." *Stanford Law Review* 2(1949):5–139.

Farrand, Max, ed. *The Records of the Federal Convention of 1787*. 3 Volumes. New Haven, Conn.: Yale University Press, 1911.

Federalist Papers. Clinton Rossiter, ed. New York: New American Library, 1961.

Fish, Stanley. "Interpretation and the Pluralist Vision." *Texas Law Review* 60(1982):495–505.

———. "Working on the Chain Gang: Interpretation in Law and Literature." *Texas Law Review* 60(1982):551–67.

Fiss, Owen. "Conventionalism." *Southern California Law Review* 58(1985):177–97.

———. "Death of the Law?" *Cornell Law Review* 72(1986):1–16.

———. "Objectivity and Interpretation." *Stanford Law Review* 34(1982):739–63.

Foner, Eric. *Free Soil, Free Labor, Free Men*. New York: Oxford University Press, 1970.

Gabel, Peter, and Duncan Kennedy. "Roll Over, Beethoven." *Stanford Law Review* 36(1984):1–55.

Glazer, Nathan. "Towards an Imperial Judiciary." *Public Interest* (Fall 1975): 104–23.

Goebel, Julius. *History of the Supreme Court of the U.S.: Antecedents and Beginnings to 1801*. Volume 1 of the Oliver Wendell Holmes Devise. New York: Macmillan, 1971.

———, ed. *The Law Practice of Alexander Hamilton*. New York: Columbia University Press, 1964.

Goldstein, Leslie Friedman. "Death and Transfiguration of the State Action Doctrine." *Hastings Constitutional Law Quarterly* 4(1977):1–34.

———. "The ERA and the U.S. Supreme Court." *Research in Law and Policy Studies* 1(1987):145–61.

Gordon, Robert. "New Developments in Legal Theory." In David Kairys, ed., *The Politics of Law: A Progressive Critique*. New York: Pantheon Books, 1982.

Graff, Gerald. " 'Keep Off the Grass,' 'Drop Dead,' and Other Indeterminacies." *Texas Law Review* 60(1982):405–13.

Graglia, Lino. "In Defense of Judicial Restraint." In Stephen C. Halpern and Charles M. Lamb, eds., *Supreme Court Activism and Restraint*. Lexington, Mass.: Lexington Books, 1982.

Grey, Thomas S. "The Constitution as Scripture." *Stanford Law Review* 37(1985):1–25.

———. "Do We Have an Unwritten Constitution?" *Stanford Law Review* 27(1974):703–18.

———. "The Original Understanding and the Unwritten Constitution." In Neil L. York, ed., *Toward a More Perfect Union: Six Essays on the Constitution*. Provo, Utah: Brigham Young University Press, 1988.

———. "Origins of the Unwritten Constitution: Fundamental Law in American Revolutionary Thought." *Stanford Law Review* 30(1978):843–93.

———. "The Uses of an Unwritten Constitution." *Chicago-Kent Law Review* 64(1988):211–38.

Gunther, Gerald. *Cases and Materials in Constitutional Law*. 10th Edition. Mineola, N.Y.: Foundation, 1980.

———. "The Subtle Vices of the 'Passive Virtues'—A Comment on Principle and Expediency in Constitutional Law." *Columbia Law Review* 64(1964):1–25.

Haines, Charles H. *The American Doctrine of Judicial Supremacy*. Berkeley: University of California Press, 1932.

Halpern, Stephen C. "On the Imperial Judiciary and Comparative Institutional Development and Power in America." In Stephen C. Halpern and Charles M. Lamb, eds., *Supreme Court Activism and Restraint*. Lexington, Mass.: Lexington Books, 1982.

Halpern, Stephen C., and Charles M. Lamb, eds. *Supreme Court Activism and Restraint*. Lexington, Mass.: Lexington Books, 1982.

Hand, Learned. *The Bill of Rights*. Cambridge, Mass.: Harvard University Press, 1958.

Harris, William. "Bonding Word and Polity." *American Political Science Review* 76(1982):34–45.

Hart, Henry M. "The Supreme Court—Foreword: Time Chart of the Justices." *Harvard Law Review* 73(1959):84–125.

Haskins, George Lee. *History of the Supreme Court of the U.S.: Foundations of Power—John Marshall, 1801–1815*. Part One of Volume 2 of Oliver Wendell Holmes Devise. New York: Macmillan, 1981.

Heller, Thomas C. "Structuralism and Critique." *Stanford Law Review* 36(1984):127–98.

Horowitz, Donald L. *The Courts and Social Policy*. Washington, D.C.: Brookings Institution, 1977.

Hoy, David Couzens. "Interpreting the Law: Hermeneutical and Poststructuralist Perspectives." *Southern California Law Review* 58(1985):136–76.

Hurst, Willard. "The Role of History." In Edmund Cahn, ed. *The Supreme Court and Supreme Law*. New York: Simon and Schuster, 1954.

Hyneman, Charles S. "Republican Government in America: The Idea and Its Realization." In George and Scarlett Graham, eds., *Founding Principles of American Government: Two Hundred Years of Democracy on Trial*. Bloomington: Indiana University Press, 1977.

Jacobsohn, Gary. "E.T.: The Extra-textual in Constitutional Interpretation." *Constitutional Commentary* 1(1984):21–42.

———. "Hamilton, Positivism, and the Constitution." *Polity* 14(1981):70–88.

———. "Modern Jurisprudence and the Transvaluation of Liberal Constitutionalism." *Journal of Politics* 47(1985):405–26.

———. *The Supreme Court and the Decline of Constitutional Aspiration*. Totowa, N.J.: Rowman and Littlefield, 1986.

Jefferson, Thomas. *The Writings of Thomas Jefferson*. H. A. Washington, ed. Washington, D.C.: Taylor and Maury, 1854.

Kairys, David, ed. *The Politics of Law: A Progressive Critique*. New York: Pantheon Books, 1982.

Karst, Kenneth. "Foreword: Equal Citizenship." *Harvard Law Review* 91(1977):1–68.

Kelly, Alfred H., et al. *The American Constitution: Its Origins and Development*. 6th Edition. New York: W. W. Norton, 1983.

Kelman, Mark. *A Guide to Critical Legal Studies*. Cambridge, Mass.: Harvard University Press, 1987.

Laycock, Douglas. "Taking Constitutions Seriously: A Theory of Judicial Review." *Texas Law Review* 59(1981):343–94.

Levinson, Sanford. "Book Review—Escaping Liberalism: Easier Said than Done." (Review of David Kairys' *Politics of Law*.) *Harvard Law Review* 96(1983):1466–88.

———. " 'The Constitution' in American Civil Religion." *Supreme Court Review* 1979:123–51.

———. *Constitutional Faith*. Princeton, N.J.: Princeton University Press, 1988.

———. "Law as Literature." *Texas Law Review* 60(1982):373–403.

———. "What Do Lawyers Know (and What Do They Do with Their Knowledge)? Comments on Schauer and Moore." *Southern California Law Review* 58(1985):441–58.

Levy, Leonard. *The Emergence of a Free Press*. New York: Oxford University Press, 1985.

———. "Judicial Review, History, and Democracy: An Introduction." In Leonard Levy, ed., *Judicial Review and the Supreme Court*. New York: Harper and Row, 1967.

Lewis, Anthony. *Gideon's Trumpet*. New York: Vintage Books, 1989.

Lincoln, Abraham. *Collected Works*. Roy P. Basler, ed. New Brunswick, N.J.: Rutgers University Press, 1953.

Litwack, Leon. *North of Slavery*. Chicago: University of Chicago Press, 1961.

Locke, John. *Second Treatise of Government*. Richard Cox, ed. Arlington Heights, Ill.: Harlan Davidson, 1982.

Lutz, Donald. *Popular Consent and Popular Control*. Baton Rouge: Louisiana State University Press, 1980.

McLaughlin, Andrew. *The Court, the Constitution, and Parties*. Chicago: University of Chicago Press, 1912.

McRee, Griffith, ed. *Life and Correspondence of James Iredell*. New York: Peter Smith, 1949. (Reprint of 1858 edition.)

Madison, James. *Notes of Debates in the Federal Convention of 1787*. New York: Norton, 1969.

———. *The Writings of James Madison*. Gaillard Hunt, ed. New York: G. P. Putnam's Sons, 1901.

Main, Jackson T. "Government by the People: The American Revolution and the Democratization of the Legislature." *William and Mary Quarterly*, 3rd Series, 23(1966):391–407.

———. *The Upper House in Revolutionary America*. Madison: University of Wisconsin Press, 1967.

Margolies, Joseph. "Deconstruction; or the Mystery of the Mystery of the Text." In Hugh Silverman and Don Ihde, eds., *Hermeneutics and Deconstruction*. Albany: State University of New York Press, 1985.

Mendelson, Wallace. "Was Chief Justice Marshall an Activist?" In Stephen C. Halpern and Charles M. Lamb, eds., *Supreme Court Activism and Restraint*. Lexington, Mass.: Lexington Books, 1982.

Michaels, Walter Benn. "Response to Perry and Simon." *Southern California Law Review* 58(1985):673–81.

Miller, Arthur S. *Toward Increased Judicial Activism: The Political Role of the Supreme Court*. Chicago: Greenwood, 1982.

Moore, Michael S. "A Natural Law Theory of Interpretation." *Southern California Law Review* 58(1985):277–398.

Murphy, Walter. "The Art of Constitutional Interpretation." In M. Judd Harmon, ed., *Essays on the Constitution of the United States*. Port Washington, N.Y.: Kennikat Press, 1978.

———. "Book Review, Constitutional Interpretation: The Art of the Historian, Magician, or Statesman." *Yale Law Journal* 87(1978):1752–71.

———. "An Ordering of Constitutional Values." *Southern California Law Review* 53(1980):703–60.

Noonan, John. *The Antelope*. Berkeley: University of California Press, 1977.

Patterson, Bennett. *The Forgotten Ninth Amendment*. Indianapolis, Ind.: Bobbs-Merrill, 1955.

Perry, Michael. "The Authority of Text, Tradition, and Reason: A Theory of Constitutional 'Interpretation.' " *Southern California Law Review* 58(1985):551–602.

———. *The Constitution, the Courts, and Human Rights*. New Haven, Conn.: Yale University Press, 1982.

———. "Interpretivism, Freedom of Expression, and Equal Protection." *Ohio State Law Journal* 42(1981):261–317.

———. *Morality, Politics, and Law: A Bicentennial Essay*. New York: Oxford University Press, 1988.

Peters, Ronald M. "The Written Constitution." In George and Scarlett Graham, eds., *Founding Principles of American Government*. Bloomington: Indiana University Press, 1977.

Pole, J. R. *Political Representation*. New York: St. Martin's, 1966.

Powell, H. Jefferson. "The Modern Misunderstanding of Original Intent." *University of Chicago Law Review* 54(1987):1513–44.

———. "The Original Understanding of Original Intent." *Harvard Law Review* 98(1985):885–948.

Rawls, John. *A Theory of Justice*. Cambridge, Mass.: Belknap Press of Harvard University, 1971.

Rehnquist, William. "The Nature of Judicial Interpretation." In *Politics and the Constitution: The Nature and Extent of Interpretation.* Washington D.C.: National Legal Center for the Public Interest and American Studies Center, 1990.

Richards, David A. J. "Constitutional Legitimacy and Constitutional Privacy." *New York University Law Review* 61(1986):800–62.

————. "Sexual Autonomy and the Constitutional Right of Privacy." *Hastings Law Journal* 30(1979):957–1018.

Rorty, Richard. *Philosophy and the Mirror of Nature.* Princeton, N.J.: Princeton University Press, 1979.

Rossiter, Clinton. *Seedtime of the Republic.* New York: Harcourt Brace, 1953.

Schauer, Frederick. "Easy Cases." *Southern California Law Review* 58(1985):399–440.

Sherry, Suzanna. "The Early Virginia Tradition of Extra-textual Interpretation." *Albany Law Review* 53(1989):297–326.

————. "The Founders' Unwritten Constitution." *University of Chicago Law Review* 54(1987):1127–77.

Snowiss, Sylvia. "From Fundamental Law to Supreme Law of the Land: A Reinterpretation of the Origin of Judicial Review." *Studies in Americal Political Development* 2(1987):1–67.

————. "From Fundamental Law to Supreme Law of the Land: A Reinterpretation of the Origin of Judicial Review in the U.S." Paper presented at annual meeting of American Political Science Association, New York, 1981.

————. *Judicial Review and the Law of the Constitution.* New Haven, Conn.: Yale University Press, 1990.

Storing, Herbert. "The Constitution and the Bill of Rights." In Ralph Rossum and Gary McDowell, eds., *The American Founding.* Port Washington, N.Y.: Kennikat, 1981.

Stourzh, Gerald. "The American Revolution, Modern Constitutionalism, and the Protection of Human Rights." In Kenneth Thompson and Robert Myers, eds., *Truth and Tragedy: A Tribute to Hans Morgenthau.* New Brunswick, N.J.: Transaction Books, 1984.

"Symposium." *Hastings Constitutional Law Quarterly* 6(1979):403–635.

Tarcov, Nathan. *Locke's Education for Liberty.* Chicago: University of Chicago Press, 1984.

Thorpe, F. N. *The Federal and State Constitutions, Colonial Charters, and Other Organic Laws of the States, Territories, and Colonies.* Washington, D.C.: Government Printing Office, 1909.

Tribe, Laurence. *The Constitutional Protection of Individual Rights.* Mineola, N.Y.: Foundation Press, 1978.

―――. *The Constitutional Structure of American Government*. Mineola, N.Y.: Foundation Press, 1978.

―――. *God Save This Honorable Court*. New York: Random House, 1985.

Tucker, St. George, ed. *Blackstone's Commentaries with Notes of Reference to the Constitution and Laws of the U.S. and of the Commonwealth of Virginia*. 5 Volumes. South Hackensack, N.J.: Rothman Reprint, 1969.

Tucker, Thomas Tudor. *Conciliatory Hints Attempting . . . to Remove Party Prejudice*. Pamphlet reprinted in Charles S. Hyneman and Donald S. Lutz, eds., *American Political Writing during the Founding Era 1760–1805*. Indianapolis, Ind.: Liberty Press, 1983. (Reprint of 1784 edition.)

Tushnet, Mark. "Anti-formalism in Recent Constitutional Theory." *Michigan Law Review* 83(1985):1502–44.

―――. "Following the Rules Laid Down: A Critique of Interpretivism and Neutral Principles." *Harvard Law Review* 96(1983):781–827.

―――. "Legal Realism, Structural Review, and Prophecy." *Dayton Law Review* 8(1983):809–39.

―――. "A Note on the Revival of Textualism in Constitutional Theory." *Southern California Law Review* 58(1985):683–700.

―――. "Post-realist Legal Scholarship." *Wisconsin Law Review* 1980(1980):1383–1401.

―――. *Red, White, and Blue*. Cambridge, Mass.: Harvard University Press, 1988.

Unger, Roberto. *The Critical Legal Studies Movement*. Cambridge, Mass.: Harvard University Press, 1986.

Varnum, James. *The Case Trevett against Weeden*. Providence, R.I.: John Carter, 1787.

Vose, Clement. *Constitutional Change*. Lexington, Mass.: Lexington Books, 1972.

Ward, Harry M. *Statism in Plymouth Colony*. Port Washington, N.Y.: Kennikat, 1973.

Warren, Charles. *Congress, the Constitution, and the Supreme Court*. Boston: Little, Brown, 1925.

―――. *The Supreme Court in U.S. History*. Boston: Little, Brown, 1923.

Wechsler, Herbert. "Toward Neutral Principles of Constitutional Law." *Harvard Law Review* 73(1959):1–35.

Weisberg, Richard H. "Text into Theory: A Literary Approach to the Constitution." *Georgia Law Review* 20(1986):939–94.

White, G. Edward. *History of the Supreme Court of the United States: The Marshall Court and Cultural Change, 1815–1835*. Volumes 3 and 4 of the Oliver Wendell Holmes Devise. New York: Macmillan, 1988.

White, James Boyd. "Law as Language: Reading Law and Reading Literature." *Texas Law Review* 60(1982):415–45.

Wiecek, William M. *The Guarantee Clause of the U.S. Constitution.* Ithaca, N.Y.: Cornell University Press, 1972.

———. *The Sources of Antislavery Constitutionalism in America 1760–1848.* Ithaca, N.Y.: Cornell University Press, 1977.

Williamson, Chilton. *American Suffrage from Property to Democracy.* Princeton, N.J.: Princeton University Press, 1960.

Wilson, James. *The Works of James Wilson.* Robert McCloskey, ed. Cambridge, Mass.: Harvard University Press, 1967.

Winter, Ralph K. "The Growth of Judicial Power." In Leonard Theberge, ed., *The Judiciary in a Democratic Society.* Lexington, Mass.: Lexington Books, 1979.

Wolfe, Christopher. *The Rise of Modern Judicial Review.* New York: Basic Books, 1986.

Wood, Gordon. *The Creation of the American Republic 1776–1787.* Chapel Hill: University of North Carolina Press, 1969.

———. *Representation in the American Revolution.* Charlottesville: University of Virginia Press, 1969.

Wright, Benjamin F. *American Interpretations of Natural Law.* Cambridge, Mass.: Harvard University Press, 1931.

Zuckert, Michael. "The Recent Literature on Locke's Political Philosophy." *Political Science Reviewer* 5(1975):270–304.

Index

abolitionists, 32, 38n81, 115n6, 129; *see also* Garrisonian abolitionists
abortion, 100, 118n43, 128, 139, 147n52
Abraham, Henry, 6n1
Adams, John, 70, 86n19, 90n76
Adams, Willi Paul, 69, 86n17, 87n22, 89n56
Adams Manufacturing v. Storen, 64n51
Adamson v. California, 43, 62–63, 120n62, 172, 187n83
Adkins v. Children's Hospital, 115n11, 130, 133, 146n43
aesthetics, 179–89
age for voting, 59–61
Agresto, John, 107–10, 116n18, 118, 121, 150n87
Alexander v. TVA, 145n38
Alfange, Dean, 33n4
Altman, Andrew, 182n1
amendment, constitutional, 18, 87n39, 99, 107–19, 122n82, 135, 137, 138–41, 150–51, 159; politics of, 138–41, 151
American Communications Association v. Doudy, 64n45
American Revolution, 69–72, 79, 183n19

Antelope case, 28–29, 38n90, 143n18
anti-miscegenation statutes, 96
Aquinas, 85n2
Aristotle, 85n2, 185n46
Article V, 19

Bailey v. Drexel Furniture, 151n92
Bailyn, Bernard, 69, 85–88
Baker v. Carr, 128
balancing, judicial, 175
Baldwin, Henry, 94, 114n4
Barber, Sotirios, 116n18, 150n85
Barron v. Baltimore, 53, 64n43, 146n46
Batson v. Kentucky, 34n16
Bayard v. Singleton, 78, 80
Beauharnais v. Illinois, 62n18
Berger, Raoul, 4, 33n1, 34n12, 44, 100, 103, 106, 111, 116n16, 119, 133, 147n51, 149n71, 162, 191; jurisprudence of, contrasted with John Marshall's, 8–11
Berger v. New York, 62n15
Berns, Walter, 85n2, 89n60, 91n101
Bernstein, Richard, 188n101
Bible, 5, 178
Bickel, Alexander, 95–97, 115–18, 151n101, 180, 184n38

213

judicial activism, 1, 14, 98, 105, 115n13, 117

judicial discretion, 45–48, 61, 93, 106, 110–11, 115n9, 118n41, 141, 163–65, 167, 175, 181, 192, 194, 198

judicial history, and extratextualism, 130–31; *see also* extratextualism, in eighteenth-century jurisprudence

judicial power, 83, 94–96, 98–100, 104–14, 115n9, 118n43, 120n65, 128, 134, 153–54, 161, 164–65, 170–71, 175, 185n45, 192, 195–96, 198

judicial restraint, 1, 98, 105, 109, 110–12, 115n13, 117n30, 118n69, 121n69

judicial review, 5–6, 11, 15, 29, 31, 35n35, 94–95, 100, 122–23, 135–36, 141, 145n36, 158–59, 162, 170–71, 193–94; as tool of popular sovereignty, 79–83, 95; at Constitutional Convention, 68; in eighteenth century, 77–84; peaceful substitute for revolution, 79; transformed by John Marshall, 83; *see also* democracy, tension with judicial review

judicial role, 55–56, 61, 94–96, 98–100, 104, 106–7, 111, 113–14, 123n96, 125, 135–36, 141, 171–72, 175, 192, 194–95

judicial socialization, 169

judicial supremacy, 116n21

Judiciary Act of 1789, 21

jurisprudence. *See* constitutional theory

jury service, 12, 96

justice, 132, 141–43, 149n74, 156, 174, 192; *see also* natural justice

Kairys, David, 188n99

Kamper v. Hawkings, 82, 88n46

Karst, Kenneth, 132, 147

Katz v. United States, 62n5

Katzenbach v. McClung, 121n73

Kelly, Alfred H., 90

Kelman, Mark, 182n1

Kennedy, Duncan, 144n30

Knox v. Lee, 146n45

Korematsu v. United States, 49, 63n27, 65n51, 173, 187

Kovacs v. Cooper, 62n7

LaBelle Iron Works v. United States, 63n28

La Jeune Eugénie case, 28–30, 38n84

Lamb, Charles M., 117n30

Langdellian jurisprudence, 177

law and economics, 6n4

law of nations, 15, 27, 77

Law's Empire, 13, 34n18

Laycock, Douglas, 188n93

Legal Realism, 115n9, 159, 162, 176, 180, 186n65, 188n97

Legal Tender Cases, 128, 130

level of generality, 163, 168, 175–76, 186n65

Levinson, Sanford, 154, 177–79, 181–82, 184n27, 189n106

Levy, Leonard, 33n2, 62n19, 85n4, 121n77

Lewis, Anthony, 63n24

liberal legal theory. *See* liberalism

liberal political theory, 154; *see also* liberalism

liberalism, 154–63, 166; of Federalists, 157–68, 176, 197; of John Locke, 155–57, 159–61, 164–65, 197

literary theory, 177

Lincoln, Abraham, 107, 121n73, 139, 151n97

Lindsay v. Commissioners, 82, 91n98

literalism, 191; of Hugo Black. *See* Black, Hugo

literary theory, 154, 178, 188–89

Litwack, Leon, 63n30

socialization of judges, 135, 164
South Pacific v. Arizona, 64n51
Spaight, Richard, 80, 91n86
spirit of Constitution, 16, 22, 31,
   35n35, 101, 128, 148n69
Spooner, Lysander, 38n81
Springsteen, Bruce, 179
state constitutions, 71, 74, 76, 83,
   88n39, 91n89, 193
state legislatures, 71–72, 74, 78, 82,
   141, 159
State v. Hall, 151n89
State v. Michel, 145n38
Stewart, Alvan, 38n81
Stewart, Potter, 98, 117
Stone, Harlan, 63n28, 120n67,
   148n70
Storing, Herbert, 88n41, 187n76
Story, Joseph, 11, 16, 21–22, 29,
   39n94, 127, 143n17, 146n46
Stourzh, Gerald, 88–90
strict scrutiny test, 49, 173
structuralism, 159, 176–77, 184n29,
   188n97
structure of Constitution, 4, 14, 41,
   50, 53, 104, 108, 125, 128, 171, 191,
   193, 195; in Hugo Black's jurisprudence, 58–61
structure of government, 2, 3–5, 8,
   53, 93, 97, 104–5, 108–11, 120n61,
   125, 130–31, 134, 145n38, 154, 172,
   180, 191, 193–95, 199; in Hugo
   Black's jurisprudence, 54–61
substantive due process, 68, 84, 95,
   98–100, 103, 115n11, 118n43, 128,
   130, 146n46, 148–49, 170–72,
   188n105
substantive equal protection, 130–31
suffrage, 70–72, 96, 146n48; *see also*
   vote
supplementers. *See* extratextualism
supremacy clause, 6n8, 20, 36n46,
   59, 108, 121n67, 136

*Takahashi v. Fish and Game Com-
   mission,* 49, 63n32
Taking Rights Seriously, 13, 34n14,
   143n13
Taney, Roger, 114n2, 127
Tarcov, Nathan, 183n16
Taylor v. Louisiana, 151n90
*Tennessee Electric Power Co. v.
   TVA,* 145n38
Tenth Amendment, 102, 113, 122n95
Terrett v. Taylor, 16, 21–22, 35–36,
   143n17
textualism, 2–5, 7, 11, 93–94, 107,
   110, 126, 128, 131, 135–38, 141–43,
   153, 162–64, 167, 194–99; and judicial role, 56–58; as supported by
   wording of Constitution, 136, 171;
   as constraint on judicial power,
   105–7, 111–12, 114; compatible
   with anti-slavery view, 32–33, 38;
   considers structure, 53; contrasted
   with Dworkinism, 46; defined, 3;
   implied by separation of powers,
   111; not a denial of judicial discretion, 46, 61; not incompatible with
   natural rights, 11–12; of Hugo
   Black, 41–61; of John Marshall,
   14–23, 31–33; of 1787–1803, 14–23;
   see also moderate textualism
textualist textualism, 105, 195
Thirteenth Amendment, 146n46, 174
Thompson, William, 39n94
Thorpe, F., 88n49
title of nobility clause, 32
Todd, Thomas, 39n94
treason, 51
Trevett v. Weeden, 75, 78
trial by jury, 75–76, 122n94, 145n38
Tribe, Laurence, 6n1, 101, 118–19
Tucker, St. George, 25–27, 37n64,
   137, 150n84
Tucker, Thomas Tudor, 77, 79–80,
   89–90

About the Author

LESLIE FRIEDMAN GOLDSTEIN was born in 1945 in Cleveland, Ohio. She attended the University of Chicago, where she earned an A.B. (1965) and A.M. (1967) in Political Science. She then attended Cornell, where she earned a Ph.D. in Government (1974). Since 1973 she has been employed at the University of Delaware, where she currently serves as Professor of Political Science.

Professor Goldstein is the author of *The Constitutional Rights of Women* (University of Wisconsin Press, 2d ed., 1988) and a co-author of *Women in the Judicial Process* (by Cook, Goldstein, O'Connor, and Talarico; published by the American Political Science Association, 1988). She has also authored numerous articles on a variety of subjects in political philosophy and in constitutional law